COSMOPOLITAN
CIVILITY

COSMOPOLITAN CIVILITY

GLOBAL-LOCAL REFLECTIONS WITH FRED DALLMAYR

EDITED BY
RUTH ABBEY

Cover art: Klee, Paul (1879–1940) © ARS, NY. *Fire at Full Moon*, 1933. Canvas, 44.1 × 57 cm. Folkwang Museum. Photo Credit: Erich Lessing / Art Resource, NY.

Photo of Fred Dallmayr (back cover) courtesy of Matt Cashore.

Published by State University of New York Press, Albany

© 2020 State University of New York

All rights reserved

Printed in the United States of America

No part of this book may be used or reproduced in any manner whatsoever without written permission. No part of this book may be stored in a retrieval system or transmitted in any form or by any means including electronic, electrostatic, magnetic tape, mechanical, photocopying, recording, or otherwise without the prior permission in writing of the publisher.

For information, contact State University of New York Press, Albany, NY
www.sunypress.edu

Library of Congress Cataloging-in-Publication Data

Names: Abbey, Ruth, 1961– editor.
Title: Cosmopolitan civility : global-local reflections with Fred Dallmayr / edited by Ruth Abbey.
Description: Albany : State University of New York Press, [2020] | Includes bibliographical references and index.
Identifiers: LCCN 2019011269 | ISBN 9781438477374 (hardcover : alk. paper) | ISBN 9781438477367 (pbk. : alk. paper) | ISBN 9781438477381 (ebook)
Subjects: LCSH: Cosmopolitanism. | Internationalism. | Humanism. | Dallmayr, Fred R. (Fred Reinhard), 1928–
Classification: LCC JZ1308 .C666 2020 | DDC 306.2—dc23
LC record available at https://lccn.loc.gov/2019011269

10 9 8 7 6 5 4 3 2 1

Contents

Editor's Introduction   1
   Ruth Abbey

Chapter 1
Philosophy of Hope   11
   Edward Demenchonok

Chapter 2
Fred Dallmayr's Spiritual Cosmopolitanism   29
   Richard Falk

Chapter 3
Anticipating Ethical Democracy in East Asia: Engaging with
Fred Dallmayr   41
   Sungmoon Kim

Chapter 4
Toward a Mega-Humanism: Confucian Triadic Harmony for
the Anthropocene   57
   Chenyang Li

Chapter 5
The Problem of Secularism: Rawls, Taylor, and Dallmayr   69
   Ronald Beiner

Chapter 6
Between Berlin and Königsberg: Toward a Global Community of
Well-Disposed Human Beings   83
   Herta Nagl-Docekal

Chapter 7
Learning and Scholarship: Unearthing the Roots of Humanism
and Cosmopolitanism in the Islamic Milieu   97
   Asma Afsaruddin

Chapter 8
Where to Explore the Political in Islamic Political Thought   111
   Ahmet Okumuş

Chapter 9
"*Docta Ignorantia*" and "*Hishiryō*": "The Inexpressible" in
Cusanus, Dōgen, and Nishida   127
   Michiko Yusa

Chapter 10
Paradigms of the Perfect Human and the Possibility of a
Global Ethos   143
   Marietta Stepanyants

Chapter 11
Upholding Our World and Regenerating Our Earth:
Calling for a Planetary *Lokasamgraha*   161
   Ananta Kumar Giri

Chapter 12
Philosophy and the Colonial Difference Revisited   173
   Walter D. Mignolo

Chapter 13
Dallmayr's Reply to Contributors   187
   Fred Dallmayr

Contributors   199

Index   207

Editor's Introduction

Ruth Abbey

This collection was convened to mark, via scholarly engagement with some of its key concerns, the incredible career of the prolific, pioneering, and wide-ranging scholar Fred Dallmayr. It was spurred by the milestone of Dallmayr's ninetieth birthday on October 18, 2018. Dallmayr has been an active scholar for more than fifty years. During that half-century, he has published about thirty books. He has edited or coedited another seventeen. He has published more than 130 book chapters and about 190 journal articles. Just as, if not more, remarkable than this profuse output is the range of topics he masters. Dallmayr's research interests range across modern and contemporary political theory and include some of the most formidable and theoretically demanding figures and movements within that: Heidegger, Hegel, hermeneutics, phenomenology, Frankfurt School writers (Adorno and Habermas), continental political thought (Derrida, Foucault, Ricoeur), democratic theory, multiculturalism, environmentalism, cosmopolitanism, comparative political thought, and non-Western political thought. His work on non-Western political thought encompasses Chinese political thought, Islamic political thought, Indian political thought, Latin American political thought, and Buddhist political thought. In fitting tribute to and reflection of the interdisciplinary and international character of Dallmayr's scholarship, the twelve contributors come from an array of disciplines and countries.

In "Philosophy of Hope," Edward Demenchonok observes, as do so many of Dallmayr's commentators, how deeply and sensitively his philosophical work engages with manifold pressing contemporary social, ethical, and political problems across the globe. But Demenchonok's chapter also highlights Dallmayr's efforts to change the ways in which philosophy is done in order to grapple with those challenges. He characterizes Dallmayr's work as "dialogic, intercultural and cosmopolitan . . . invok[ing] religious, spiritual, and ethical resources for positive global transformations" (12). His chapter draws out Martin Heidegger's influences on Dallmayr's distinctive philosophical approach, accentuating the deep respect for the individual and her agency that lie at the core of the Heideggerian approach. (Which is not, of course, to suggest that Heidegger is the only source for the regard for the individual and her agency that marks Dallmayr's thought.) This focus on agency in turn opens up new vistas for positive and innovative action, inspired by care, to address urgent contemporary problems. In unfolding Heidegger's legacy for Dallmayr, Demenchonok also highlights Dallmayr's distinctive reading of Heidegger. He then goes on to underscore the central and multifaceted role that dialogue plays in Dallmayr's philosophical work. Dallmayr's dialogical engagement with many different cultural and religious traditions has, in turn, enabled him to elicit a convergent concern with the Heideggerian notion of care for the world from many of them. Demenchonok's chapter culminates in a discussion of Dallmayr's signature brand of cosmopolitanism, which convenes such concepts as care, being in the world, world maintenance, relationality, democracy as relational praxis, and spirituality.

Exploring "Fred Dallmayr's Spiritual Cosmopolitanism," Richard Falk effectively echoes Demenchonok's appreciation of the wide and deep reach of Dallmayr's philosophy and its continuous engagement with such practical issues as nuclear war, climate degradation, and growing socioeconomic inequalities within and across nations. And like Demenchonok, Falk provides a synoptic overview of Dallmayr's work. Although he believes it to be powerfully motivated by emancipatory intent, Falk also poses some questions about how realistic or realizable Dallmayr's elevated vision of the future is. He concludes that light and dark, optimism and pessimism, are equal but dueling dynamics in Dallmayr's assessment of the global situation. And Dallmayr readily acknowledges that the quest for a better future is bound to take place within an ambience of uncertainty. But to nourish the hopeful side of Dallmayr's outlook we find his writings peppered with positive examples of action for change from such historical figures as Gandhi, Martin Luther King, Desmond Tutu, the Dalai Lama, and Pope Francis. Whereas Demenchonok imputes to Dallmayr a "philosophy of hope," Falk effectively calls attention to a complementary praxis of hope. Falk also points to the ways in which Dallmayr's cosmopolitanism, with its emphasis on humanity's wholeness and solidarity, stands against the regressive nationalism and xenophobia currently in evidence in too many countries. A globalization that has liberated capital flows across national borders, either to the neglect or the detriment of the well-being of many, must be kept in mind when explaining this regression to a defensive and nasty nationalism. Falk imputes to Dallmayr a spiritual cosmopolitanism but, as much as Demenchonok, he insists on the dialogical nature of Dallmayr's cosmopolitanism. And while Falk also agrees with Demenchonok about Heidegger's seminal role in shaping Dallmayr's perspective, he also shines a light on the influence of American philosopher John Dewey and in particular his insistence that democracy is an ethical, as much as it is a political, conception. Dallmayr claims that he came late to Dewey's work, but when he got there found "a rich source of political reflection."[1]

This Dewey-inspired ethical approach to democracy is taken up by Sungmoon Kim's chapter, "Anticipating Ethical Democracy in East Asia." As Kim insightfully points out, Dallmayr adduces a view of democracy that is not structured by the binary oppositions that dominate contemporary political theory. Dallmayr's approach is therefore neither individualist nor communitarian, elitist nor populist, secular nor religious. Kim briefly surveys these reigning approaches, eliciting the problems in each from Dallmayr's perspective. Kim also provides a succinct but compelling account of the attractions of the Deweyan alternative. Dallmayr's understanding of democracy is, moreover, informed by non-Western as much as by Western theories and practices. And just as his work has been significantly shaped by non-Western sources, so Kim puts Dallmayr's thought to work in evaluating some recent attempts to develop a Confucian form of democracy for East Asia. Surveying briefly some of the political appropriations of Confucianism currently on offer, Kim concludes that none satisfies Dallmayr's definition of democracy because in addition to being, or perhaps because they are, too elite-focused, they neglect Confucianism's capacity for self-transformation through openness to non-Confucian traditions. Whatever progress has been made so far in these directions, an ethical Confucian democracy remains a democracy to come.

The ethical resources contained within the Confucian tradition are also the subject of Chenyang Li's reflections. In "Toward a Mega-Humanism: Confucian Triadic Harmony for the Anthropocene," Li insists that when it comes to the environment, we live in a brand-new epoch. This new epoch calls, in turn, for a new form of humanism. The Anthropocene thus provides a generative context for rethinking the possibility of a new humanism, for which Li borrows the term "mega-humanism." In this new variant, humanity is accorded substantial value and status, as is the case with all humanisms, but humanity's unrivaled capacity to do both harm and good is also acknowledged. This recognition brings in its wake a deep sense of responsibility rather than of entitlement. This new humanism must promote well-being, prosperity, and harmony for all while synthesizing two key themes. First, it must reflect a productive and effective response to environmental challenges. Second, it must have cultural roots. Even a humanism with a universal character needs to connect with particular cultural traditions. Li proposes that the Confucian philosophy of the triadic harmony of Heaven-Earth-Humanity provides a departure point for a humanist philosophy suitable for the Anthropocene. It accords a significant creative role to humanity while recognizing human entwinement with both heaven and earth. However, Li is clear that this new humanism could not be exclusively Confucian: its proponents do not have to accept an entire Confucian metaphysic. Indeed, this new humanism will be more viable if those proponents can find its philosophical foundations in their respective cultural traditions.

In his reflections on the problems of secularism, Ronald Beiner brings Dallmayr's ideas about the appropriate relationship between religion and politics into conversation with those of John Rawls and Charles Taylor. Beiner stimulates this conversation by outlining the Rawlsian compromise, which places limits on the ways in which any comprehensive doctrine—religious or not—can be brought into the public sphere. The aim here is, of course, state neutrality, so that no citizens are discriminated against because of their reasonable comprehensive doctrines. But as Beiner insists, the liberal state cannot be neutral about certain fundamental liberal values such as citizen equality, liberty, reciprocity, and so on. Conceptions of the good might be buried within, but they are never thoroughly banished by, political norms. So although Beiner agrees with Rawls that no citizen should be able to impose his or her religious beliefs on any other, he does not accept that Rawls has found the most effective way to convey this commitment to citizen liberty and equality. Underscoring the moral commitments that underlie and inform liberal citizenship in this way is for Beiner in part a legacy of the liberal-communitarian debate of the 1980s, and in particular the contributions to that debate by Taylor. For this reason, Beiner is surprised by Taylor's Rawlsian turn when it comes to thinking about the right relationship between religion and politics. Beiner is also dismayed by this turn because of the inadequacies he perceives in Rawls's treatment of the question. Yet the unexpected, and for Beiner unwelcome, convergences between Rawls and Taylor on this question serve to highlight the distinctiveness of Dallmayr's contribution to this conversation. Dallmayr joins Rawls and Taylor in their commitments to religious liberty, citizen equality, and repudiation of any form of theocentrism. But Dallmayr does not expel comprehensive doctrines from the domain of the political. Inspired by the work of Raimon Panikkar, Dallmayr eschews binaries of the spiritual and the political, the sacred and the secular, the immanent and the transcendent, the human and the divine in this domain. No matter how admirable Dallmayr's more inclusive and synthetic vision might be, Beiner articulates the secularist fear of an unintended theocratic potential of such collapsed dichotomies. Such fear of religious domination has, after all, been the bête noire of the liberal tradition since its inception in the seventeenth century.

Herta Nagl-Docekal's engagement with Dallmayr's work also takes place on the terrain of Western political theory. "Between Berlin and Königsberg: Toward a Global Community of Well-Disposed Human Beings" takes up one of the problems Dallmayr has long wrestled with, which she characterizes as "the inner tension of the modern world" (83). This refers to the erosion of community and social ties in the pursuit of individualism—either in terms of rights protection or economic interests. She reminds us that in Hegel, Dallmayr (like Charles Taylor) found a fecund resource for addressing these questions and for the possibility of mediating between the individual and her community in a way that respects the individual and her liberty while also countering atomism without taking recourse to premodern nostalgia. Picking up on a positive but passing remark from Dallmayr, Nagl-Docekal sets out to show that Kant is also a highly valuable resource for imagining a truly human, cosmopolitan, ethical community. She maintains that authors within the orbit of the Frankfurt School, such as Habermas, Axel Honneth, and Rainer Forst, remain wedded to a concept of morality that is tied to contractualist logic, whether they realize this or not. The underlying vision seems to be one of individuals in conflict who resolve their differences via contractual means. Yet this dominant image of colliding individuals contracting their social relations is untrue to our experience. Nagl-Docekal advocates a return to Kant for clearer guidance on these questions, with particular attention to the concepts surrounding his idea of a universal ethical community. As Kant points out, a contractualist approach to morality can gain little traction on the all-important internal perspective of the agent. In this vein, he also reminds us of the power of conscience in guiding or constraining action. Cultivating an awareness of how our actions might affect others is also key, and it is especially important to ascertain when those others need help and support. In this context, the duty to assist might fall unequally. But for Kant, reciprocity is a long-term social goal, not a short-term calculation determining whether I should help others. In short, Nagl-Docekal strives to demonstrate that solidarity is very much a Kantian good, and that his manner of theorizing this, while also entrenching a commitment to moral individualism, remains valuable today. She thus offers a friendly corrective to Dallmayr's view of Kant, which although respectful and admiring of the accent on duty, remains frustrated by "Kant's division between inner and outer domains and the insufficient attention . . . to the cultivation of dispositions needed for the performance of duty."[2]

The quest for a humanist, cosmopolitan ethos also lies at the heart of Asma Afsaruddin's chapter, but she traces its lineaments in the Islamic tradition, with particular emphasis on the value accorded to knowledge and education therein. Afsaruddin briefly maps the social and institutional history of some key educational institutions in the first five centuries of Islam—viz. from the seventh to the eleventh centuries of the Common Era. She outlines a typical Madrasa curriculum, with the caveat that the personal proclivities of the instructors also shaped the learning students received. As this intimates, Afsaruddin's survey of Islamic education remains cognizant of more than just the formal public institutions and practices and stated programs of learning, striving, where possible, to acknowledge its more informal and unstructured sources. She also recognizes the role of female educators and students in this tradition. Quite early in this period we witness Islamic interest in Greek, Persian, and Indian learning, with some of the seminal texts from these traditions being translated into Arabic so as to foster their wider dissemination. Just as the Christian tradition did, so Muslim scholars had to struggle to assimilate so-called pagan Greek learning into their own monotheistic outlook. As a consequence of such exposure to non-Islamic cultures and traditions, a more cosmopolitan multicultural, multiethnic, and multireligious Islamic identity became available. Afsaruddin also discerns the evolution of a specifically Islamic humanism based on the concept of *adab*, defined as "the total educational system of a cultured Muslim who took the whole world for his object of curiosity and knowledge" (105). This period gave birth to a diversity of humanistic strands—philosophical, intellectual, literary, religious, legalistic—within Islam. Afsaruddin concludes that "[a]t its best and most confident, medieval Islamic civilization came the closest to the modern conception of a vibrantly diverse, multicultural, and tolerant society as was possible in the premodern period" (107).

Ahmet Okumuş's chapter also focuses on the Islamic tradition, taking the idea of the political regime from Plato and Aristotle and seeing if it has any traction within the Islamic tradition. The regime refers to the entire form of the shared life of a people, and so includes but goes beyond its political structure. As Okumuş explains it, "A regime serves as an ethical framework, facilitates ethical formation, and is thus a context of habituation into a form of life guiding and guided by its characteristic set of excellences" (116). The breadth and significance of the idea of the regime has, according to Leo Strauss, been eclipsed by the modern Western social sciences, and so turning to the Islamic tradition, which has been untouched by those developments, seems fruitful. Dallmayr himself draws attention to the value of the classical idea of the regime and laments that it has been somewhat forgotten in modern Western scholarship about democracy. He discerns, however, a sub-tradition within this scholarship that has kept the importance of the idea of the regime alive.[3] At first blush it appears that there is no equivalent to the idea of the regime in the Islamic tradition of political thought. The prominent role that sharia, or revealed law, has played in Muslim thinking about politics could perhaps explain this because it is believed that sharia would give rise to, and sustain, authentic justice. The candidate for Islamic political thinker most likely to harbor some conception of the regime is Al Farabi, writing in tenth-century Baghdad, who coined the term for political philosophy in Arabic. Okumuş does indeed detect some evidence for a version of the idea of the regime in his work, particularly with regard to his attention to "mores, customs, and the ethical dispositions prevailing in different cities" (115). He concludes his inquiry into "Where to Explore the Political in Islamic Political Thought" with some reflections on how past thinking can invigorate the present.

Just as Afsaruddin writes of the exposure that Islamic scholars had to non-Muslim traditions, so Michiko Yusa recounts a later encounter by the Christian thinker Nicholas of Cusa with a Latin translation of the Koran in the fifteenth century. She contends that this opening to a world of new, diverse, and vibrant ideas informed the development of his concept of learned ignorance, which encapsulates a humble and respectful awareness of the limits of human knowledge. Coming to accept this important concept allows humans to "intuit the reality of the living universe" (129). Yusa goes on to compare this idea with Dōgen's belief that some things remain beyond knowledge. Dogen was a thirteenth-century Japanese Zen master whose dialogue between a monk and a Zen master about the relationship between thinking, non-thinking, and beyond thinking has been interpreted in a number of different ways by scholars. Yusa further compares these ideas with Nishida Kitarō's insistence that there is always something that remains beyond the reach of the knowable. Nishida wrote in the late nineteenth and early twentieth centuries. Yusa's chapter demonstrates from these three cases a cross-cultural convergence on the tension between the ineffable and that which can be said (or the apophatic and the kataphatic) that transcends particular historical and cultural conditioning. Her speculation that Dallmayr should find kindred spirits in these three thinkers is supported by his own remarks about "an insight gleaned from personal experience . . . that one can cherish and even love a person without fully knowing or being able to define that person in every way. Religiously, it is acknowledged that one can love God or the divine without epistemic cognition or comprehension."[4] Shortly after, he describes Cusanas as an exemplary voice[5] and had already expressed his excitement at being introduced to the thought of Nishida.[6]

Like Yusa, Marietta Stepanyants looks across three cultural traditions to see in each what it means to be human. All three of her resources are non-Western, however, for she looks to Indian, Chinese, and Muslim reflections on this topic. In the ancient Hindu tradition, for example, she finds that the word for human is often synonymous with the verb to think. What distinguishes humans from animals there is the former's ability to follow the moral law. The belief in reincarnation has given rise to an imperative not to injure other humans or animals. Like Chenyang Li, she considers that status afforded to the human being in the Confucian tradition. She also points to that tradition's emphasis on the individual in relation with others and to the quest for harmony between individual and society. Like Afsaruddin, she accords some attention to gender, asking to what extent these traditional paradigms of the perfect human apply equally to women as to men. Yet in full recognition that sources this large and complex could not be univocal, Stepanyants discerns within each what she calls a "normative social" strand (including cosmocentrism and theocentrism) and a more individualistic strand. The latter manifests itself in Buddhism rather than Hinduism in India, in Taoism rather than Confucianism in China, and within Sufism in Islam. Stepanyants closes her chapter with some considerations about the benefits and challenges of adducing a global ethos from both religious and nonreligious viewpoints. She ends up effectively agreeing with Li that even if there are universal values, they must get their "fillings" from particular cultures.

Whereas Stepanyants draws from some of the ethical traditions available within Indian civilization, Ananta Kumar Giri zeroes in one of these classical Indian sources to explore what it means to uphold the world in our contemporary context. In a similar vein to Stepanyants, this ethos provides an exemplary, but also accessible and attainable, way for humans to live within themselves, with one another, and with their natural environment. Giri maintains that these wider implications of the *Purusartha* pathway have rarely been explored, yet they provide invaluable guidelines for ethical living. Dallmayr himself writes about how in later life the central issue for him has become "how to live one's life and how to live it peacefully and properly with other human beings in a community."[7] Giri even portrays Dallmayr as the embodiment of such an ethos, which seeks to improve the world for all its inhabitants—human, animal, the natural environment—without subscribing to a dogmatic progressivism or linear, European notions of development. Giri explains that upholding the world within this non-anthropocentric framework requires right living and conduct at the individual and social levels, the ethical generation and distribution of wealth, and the nonviolent expression of desire. With these resources, Giri opens up the possibility of a multifaceted yet integral concept of development that eschews strict binary oppositions and is especially needed in the current era, which has witnessed such massive environmental degradation. His chapter concludes by gesturing toward some of the ways in which this classical Indian ethos could intersect with comparable concepts in other cultures.

Walter Mignolo's contribution exhibits the interest in comparative philosophizing that marks the chapters by Li, Kim, Afsaruddin, Okumuş, Yusa, Stepanyants, and Giri, although his chapter at the same time problematizes what we mean and what we are doing when we call something philosophy. The organizing principle of his discussion is the colonial difference, viz. the way in which systems and practices of thought in non-Western contexts have been deemed inferior to the Western tradition of philosophy. Indeed, in some cases these systems and practices of thought have not even been recognized as philosophy at all. In addition to asserting a hierarchy among ways of life and civilizations, the colonial difference makes such differences appear as ontological and thus conceals their true source in the operations of power. Against this, Mignolo advocates and tries to enact a type of decolonial thinking. His project of decolonizing philosophy (which can also be extended to other intellectual disciplines) requires seeing philosophy in the narrow sense as a discipline that is modern, Western, and colonial. The sort of meaning-making activity it embodies is, however, a human universal that can be identified, albeit in different shapes and forms, over time and across cultures. Not all such activities have, moreover, sought abstract and universal truths; in some cases they have aimed for more pragmatic principles for living. Mignolo goes on to connect the project of decoloniality with that of border thinking, which avoids abstractions and rejects any either/or dichotomies. His chapter, "Philosophy and the Colonial Difference Revisited," draws, as is only appropriate for its theme, from a diversity of contexts and cultures around the globe to illustrate both the existence of the colonial difference in these different contexts as well as lines of resistance to it. I am hopeful that Mignolo would see in all the comparative chapters of this volume, influenced and inspired as they are by Dallmayr's example, scholarly work that is not defined by, but instead actively defies, the colonial difference.

Any volume inspired by Dallmayr must comment on the remarkable life he has lived, a life that both reflects and consolidates his intellectual and ethical convictions. In 2017 Dallmayr published *On the Boundary: A Life Remembered*, which records the fusion of academic research and global travel that have marked his long, rich life. It provides great insight into the thinkers and events that have shaped his outlook. This short but thoroughly engaging text adds another layer to those who seek to understand Dallmayr's thought. The current collection closes with Dallmayr's thoughtful response to each of these chapters. He finds his own way of ordering the contents and, as he responds to each author, draws connections between his life and thought.

Notes

1. *On the Boundary: A Life Remembered* (Lanham, MD: Hamilton Books, 2017), 75.
2. Ibid., 74.
3. Ibid., 75.
4. Ibid., 73.
5. Ibid., 74.
6. Ibid., 67.
7. Ibid., 72.

Chapter 1

Philosophy of Hope

EDWARD DEMENCHONOK

"War and Peace" III (5.10.51. II), Pablo Picasso's surreal war scene, depicts a warrior with a dove, fighting with only a sword against a tank, with an innocent human face superimposed on the scene. That stark image confronts us on the cover of Fred Dallmayr's aptly titled *Against Apocalypse: Restoring Humanity's Wholeness* (2016). The image symbolically expresses the main theme of the book and its key message, which warns about the risk to innocent humanity in our "nuclear age": the threat of war pushing the world to the precipice of apocalypse, opposed to the hope for peace that yet remains inherent in the human spirit.

Dallmayr's deeply humanist position, with its opposition to violence and war and its commitment to human dignity secured by justice and peace, is the leitmotif of his numerous books and articles. His arguments reflect not only the intellectual reasoning of a philosopher, but also the traumas of a wounded human being (he was barely ten years old when World War II started). He tries to regain mindfulness and social consciousness and to warn of the problems plaguing our world. He implores us to seek solutions before it is too late. He confronts not only the external problems of injustices and violence, but also the internal problems that keep us mired in the status quo—stereotypic thinking, dogmatic mind-sets, and the internalized dependence of conformist "slave mentality." From his ethical position, Dallmayr undertakes an uncompromising critical assessment of the current global situation, characterized by global disorder. He shows the groundlessness of neoconservative and neoliberal theories that preserve the status quo. He critiques the economic-political system that results in violence and human suffering and is pushing humanity toward the precipice of nuclear or ecological catastrophe.

To realize its transformative potential in a conflicted world and to respond constructively to internal theoretical and external social-cultural challenges, philosophy itself needs to undergo a self-transformation. The emerging philosophy introduces a new perspective on our understanding of what philosophy is, of its history, methods, and forms of articulation. In dialogue with other philosophers, Dallmayr actively contributes to this transformative endeavor. He presents a philosophy that is dialogic, intercultural, and cosmopolitan, and one which invokes religious, spiritual, and ethical resources for positive global transformations.

In this chapter, I analyze Dallmayr's creative elaboration on Martin Heidegger's philosophy of history and on the conception of "event of Being," articulating the view of human existence (*Dasein*) as potentially transformative, a being moved by care (*Sorge*) in an ongoing search for meaning and truth. Dallmayr's contributions to the intercultural philosophical dialogue between Western and Eastern thought traditions are surveyed. I examine how Dallmayr's intercultural analysis has led him to conclude that the concept of world care is shared by virtually all cultural and religious traditions around the globe. Finally, I briefly describe Dallmayr's conception of the cosmopolis to come.

In Dialogue with Heidegger's Legacy

Among influential philosophers such as Hans-Georg Gadamer, Karl-Otto Apel, Maurice Merleau-Ponty, Jacques Derrida, Michel Foucault, and Raimon Panikkar, Dallmayr holds a special regard for Martin Heidegger. He first published on Heidegger as early as in 1986 and was among the first in the English-speaking world to realize that Heidegger's philosophical work "was much broader than the particular Nazi episode."[1] In 1993 Dallmayr published *The Other Heidegger*. He uncovered fruitful contributions of Heidegger's work to contemporary social and political thought and delineated the contours of an alternative political perspective therein.

Heidegger lamented Western "mass society," mass culture, and the depersonalized "they" (*das Man*), and criticized the instrumental reason and abuse of technology that inaugurated the "nuclear age." He saw this as a crisis of Western civilization that threatens the future of humanity. He was concerned about the freedom and welfare of individuals as well as the whole of humanity and tried to identify alternatives for their rescue. As Dallmayr tells us, Heidegger "seemed to address precisely the questions that troubled me," such as the question of "being." In opposition to traditional formulations, Heidegger noted that "being could no longer be grasped as a substance or fixed concept but needed to be seen as a temporal process or happening, an ongoing 'disclosure' (and sheltering) of meaning in which all beings participate."[2] Dallmayr explicates Heidegger's concept of *Dasein*, defining human existence as "being-in-the-world," as well as his other key concepts, such as care (*Sorge*), solicitude (*Fürsorge*), letting-be (*Seinlassen*), event (*das Ereignis*), and dwelling (*Wohnen*), to move his political philosophy beyond the traditional paradigm, rooted in individual subjectivity, toward a view of human beings and society that emphasizes connectedness and "relationality."

Heidegger's writing powerfully expresses the fragility of human existence and acknowledges not only the possibility of the end of the human race, but also the fact that *das Man* has effectively created the means of its own self-destruction. Dallmayr embraces Heidegger's personalistic defense of individual persons, seeking to liberate them from depersonalizing influences exerted by the social system. In Heidegger Dallmayr finds a thinker able to realize the dramatic situation of Western civilization and to see the root causes of its problems, which had burgeoned during the World Wars and the Cold War and have continued to escalate ever since. He creatively continues Heidegger's line of thought. The qualitatively new perspective he highlights is that contradictions and perilous tendencies in Western society are now escalating to the level of being global problems, which brings us to the precipice of self-destruction—nuclear or ecological.

While recognizing the importance of Heidegger's admonishments, Dallmayr, in a more hopeful vein, emphasizes the positive alternatives to the possibility of self-destruction. He brings together insights and ideas found scattered or latently present in Heidegger's works, creatively developing them in the light of our contemporary situation. He relates what he gleans to some concepts of political philosophy and tries to find answers to such questions as "What is the status of individualism and of traditional Western humanism?" and "How should one construe the relations between self and other human beings bypassing the options of contractual agreement and simple rational convergence?"[3] Dallmayr highlights Heidegger's contributions to studies of the status of the "subject" as a political agent; the character of political community; the issue of cultural and political development; his notion of a "homecoming through otherness," and the perspectives of emerging cosmopolis.[4]

Another connection between Dallmayr and Heidegger is the philosophy of history. In studies about Heidegger, scant attention has been paid to this topic, yet his critical revision of traditional conceptions and attempt to ground a radically new approach underlie his fundamental ontology. It is latently present in *Being and Time* (1927/1996), which analyzes the modern concept of time underlying the teleological representations of society and history. The book was a reaction against "temporal fetishism" and G. W. F. Hegel's historicism, where history is viewed as a teleologically determined rational system. Within this framework, an individual's role is limited by conformity to existing social trends and power structures. One can see the main features of historicism lurking behind contemporary theories of industrial-postindustrial society, of the "invisible hand" of neoliberal market economy, of the postmodern concept of the "end of history," as well as of the neoconservative doctrine with its "imperial designs" and the messianic role of a "chosen nation."

Being and Time is polemically directed against the concepts of historicism that Heidegger saw as the main error of European philosophy. He argues that "Da-sein *and only* Da-sein is primordially historical."[5] Only the human being as an individual really has history: "Temporality reveals itself as the *historicity* of Da-sein. The statement that Da-sein is historical is confirmed as an existential and ontological fundamental proposition. It is far removed from merely ontically ascertaining the fact that Da-sein occurs in a 'world history.' "[6] Heidegger believes that philosophy should liberate itself from this historicist aberration and open people's eyes to the value of individual agency: "The existential and ontological constitution of historicity must be mastered in *opposition to* the vulgar interpretation of the history of Da-sein that covers over."[7] He continues, "*the analysis of the historicity of Da-sein attempted to show that this being is not 'temporal,' because it 'is in history,' but because, on the contrary, it exists and can exist historically only because it is temporal in the ground of its being.*"[8] Individuals exist in time, but are not manipulated by it: by the very mode of their being, individuals themselves are time. Society "has" history, but human persons have the ontological privilege of "being history." *Dasein* means that the individual is included in world history but not reduced by its temporary movement, is not predetermined by it, and has internal independence from it. From *Dasein* emanates the historicity of any other processes that result from human activity. *Dasein* is opposed not only to the vulgar view of history, but also to the sociocentric, sociological "being-from-society"; that is, the socially predetermined being. This approach aims to be a radical change in the philosophy of history.

Heidegger aims to dispel any notion of "historical necessity" to free individuals from their subjection to statist and hegemonic projects. An important concept is that of possibility (*die Möglichkeit*), which is related to other categories of fundamental ontology, such as understanding, project, destiny, existence, and Being. According to Heidegger, the category of possibility acquires its own adequate meaning only in relation to individuals or *Dasein*. Accordingly, "possibility as an existential is the most primordial and the ultimate positive ontological determination of Da-sein."[9] Being-possible is related to "to know" and to "to be able to." Being-possible allows us to move from the sense of being powerless individuals subordinated to an inexorably predetermined future to one that embraces individual agency. Because it has a character of project and "because it *is* what it becomes or does not become, can it say understandingly to itself: 'become what you are!' "[10] In other words, "realize your own possibilities!"

In an ontological interpretation of possibility, one can see a human being who has certain vocations or callings, who feels destined for a certain form of existence and the achievement of a unique life. The existential "possibility" implies that personal possibilities are the living forces of our being, its energy or potency. Possibility-vocation can be interpreted in the way that an individual may view him- or herself as being sent into the world with a unique, subconsciously perceived mission, the understanding and fulfillment of which should be the overarching goal of life. Self-realization is considered as a process of self-transformation, which results in a radical anthropological change in an individual's self-perception and views of people, of the world, and of time. In fundamental ontology, the personalistic idea of an individual's striving for authentic personality obtains a new impetus for self-transformation and subsequently as the way toward a more humane alternative to the existing world. Dallmayr follows Heidegger beyond any self-centered type of "existentialism." According to him, in *Being and Time* human existence (*Dasein*) is presented not as self-constituted or a fixed substance, but as open-ended and potentially transformative, a being moved by care (*Sorge*) in an ongoing search for meaning and truth.[11]

Event of Being

Heidegger characterized the decline of the Western world, quoting Nietzsche, who said that "the wasteland grows."[12] Dallmayr invokes this characterization, noting that with globalization, the wasteland is growing. Behind this desert-world there is, according to Heidegger, a deeper devastation, namely the abandonment and oblivion of Being. This leads to the possibility of global destruction:

> The unconditional establishment of machination and the aligning of mankind to this establishment constitute the installation of the abandonment of beings by being. . . . The machinational basic form of the devastation is the new world order, which can be fully carried out only in a struggle over the supremacy of ordering and of claims of order. . . . This blowing up of the globe by the *animal rationale* will be the last act of the new order.[13]

One of the most important challenges of our time for Dallmayr is to find antidotes or radical counterpulls to the global devastation and destruction. This requires "a radical change of paradigm or change of register, away from the hegemonic world view—not into mere negation or antithesis, but into 'another thinking' beyond dialectics."[14] The first step is to depart from oppressive power (*Macht*) and manipulative domination or machination (*Machenschaft*). For the most part, people are involved in everydayness and servile entanglements; they succumb to the lure of wealth, power, and self-satisfaction. To exit from this mode of existence requires renouncing the triumphalism of human beings and changing hearts and minds. The relation of human *Dasein* to Being as "care" cannot just be a cognitive or neutral-analytical one. It requires a transformation of the entire human way of life.

The search for viable antidotes to our current perilous trajectory can fruitfully start with concepts put forth in *Being and Time*. However, as Dallmayr points out, in that work Heidegger did not yet clearly show "how *Dasein's* care related to Being and how, more generally, the 'difference' between Being and beings was to be conceived."[15] To elucidate these issues, Dallmayr turns to the later works, such as "Building, Dwelling, Thinking" (1971) and *Das Ereignis* (*The Event*) (2013). In *The Event*, Heidegger sharpens his criticism of Western metaphysics as the course of thinking from Plato to

Nietzsche.[16] He stresses the opposition between a historicist, or teleological, view of history and human individuals. As Heidegger writes:

> Humans are "present" to themselves by maintaining their inaugural essence instead of proceeding to a self-made task whose pursuit confirms them only in an unappropriated self-absorption. . . . In the current historical moment, the self-absorption of metaphysical mankind declares the ready-made historical task to be "the mission" "of" history. Historical mankind inceptually knows no mission, since it has no need of one, having been consigned enough in the arrogation of the truth of beyng [Being].[17]

Dallmayr examines Heidegger's use of the term "event" (*Ereignis*) and offers his own interpretation. He pays special attention to the term "*Zueignung*" (arrogation), which he translates as "dedication" or "handing over a gift," which is a central feature of the event. Being hands itself over to the care of human beings, constituting the humanity of *Dasein*. In Heidegger's words, "In arrogating and adopting the essence of the human being out of the beginning and for the beginning, the event first allows humans to come to themselves, i.e. to their essence as that essence in appropriated in the appropriating event."[18] Dallmayr further elucidates how such arrogation or handing over occurs and how the event (*Ereignis*) can reach human beings. The event does not approach human beings with categorical imperatives. Rather, Being in *Ereignis* can try to reach human beings through a voiceless voice, a word sheltered in silence. As Heidegger continues, "The voice disposes in that it adopts the essence of the human being to the truth of beyng [Being] and thus attunes that essence to the disposition in all the attitudes and comportment which are thereby first awakening . . . The word, in its event-related [*Ereignis*-related] essence, is soundless."[19]

Heidegger writes about "the responsibility (*Verantwortung*) of the response (*Antwort*), which prepares the word (*Wort*) of language for the claim of the event. 'Responsibility' is meant here not in a 'moral' sense but, rather, with respect to the event and as related to the response." The response is the human counter-word of language to the voice of being, "to the disposition, in which guise the soundless arrogation and adoption claim the essence of the human being for the preservation of the truth of the inceptuality."[20] As Dallmayr explains, the voice of Being extends not a command but a graceful greeting. He tells us that event discloses in

Being an uncanny potency—beyond power—to nurture and sustain beings without force, through an appeal or "greeting." It is through sounding that a certain "tuning" is established, which, given human responsiveness, may lead to "attunement." In handing itself over to *Dasein*, Being comprises the very core of human beings. According to Dallmayr, "its voice comes not so much from the outside or beyond, but dwells in the innermost heart of humans."[21] Nevertheless, Dallmayr concludes, it is still up to us to listen to this voice and decide a proper response.

Intercultural Philosophical Dialogue: Theory and Practice

Dallmayr once told me that since Plato, philosophy is always questioning, it is a question and answer—a dialogue. Such a dialogical approach permeates both his philosophy and his life. In his work on other philosophers, he tries to elucidate their underlying dialogical motifs, which helps to better understand their meaning. The dialogism of Heidegger's works is more clearly shown against the background of his contemporary Mikhail Bakhtin, who is well known for his dialogic philosophy. In one of his innovative early works, *Toward a Philosophy of the Act*, which was written around 1920 (but could not be published until more than six decades later), Bakhtin expressed some ideas similar to those of Heidegger's *Being and Time* (1927). Without knowing each other, both were working in the same philosophical area and defended human personality from a depersonalizing domination. Bakhtin viewed dialogue as a universal phenomenon, permeating all human relationships. For him, dialogical relationships between I and the other (and ultimately between I and the Absolute "Other") constitute the structure of Being understood as "the unitary and once-occurrent event of Being."[22] "Being as event" also means "co-being" or an event that is shared simultaneously—coexistence. Bakhtin held that dialogism is a constitutive characteristic of language and expanded the meaning of dialogue to include intercultural relations. One can see in Heidegger's conceptions of Being and of event (*Ereignis*), interpreted as a radical ontological relationality, their dialogical underpinning. He stressed the crucial role of language in human knowledge and understanding and laid the groundwork for a dialogical interaction.

Dallmayr has also elucidated the dialogism of Hans-Georg Gadamer, Emmanuel Levinas, and Maurice Merleau-Ponty. He stresses the importance of an "authentic dialogue" and elaborates on Raimon Panikkar's conception of "dialogical dialogue" and interreligious dialogue.[23] Dallmayr emphasizes Gadamer's ideas that every interpersonal encounter and every interpretation of texts (hermeneutics) involves dialogue in search for the meaning, and that the ethical precondition to genuine dialogue is goodwill and the recognition of the other as equal. Dallmayr sees the problems of Western modernity in the monologic mind-set, which was rooted in Cartesian cogito and became an instrumental rationality coupled with egocentric "will to power" and domination. He passionately promotes dialogue as theory and practice as a means for overcoming the monologic unilateralism and for establishing relationships of mutual understanding and collaboration, aiming for peaceful coexistence and justice.

In his words, dialogue means to approach alien meanings of life-forms in a questioning mode conducive to a possible learning experience. He tells us, "pursued in a genuinely dialogical mode, some questioning is liable to call one's own perspective in question, triggering a modification or correction of initial assumptions."[24] With this dialogical disposition, openness to the other, appreciation of cultural diversity, and studies of non-Western cultures, Dallmayr was well prepared to be engaged in dialogue with the philosophical traditions of India, China, and the Islamic world. This was not a mere cerebral awareness of similarities and differences of traditions of thought as separate entities, but a dialogical personal engagement with different culturally embedded intellectual-spiritual universes. His encounter with Eastern philosophical cultures resulted in a transformative "turn," like *Kehre*, in Dallmayr's philosophical path. This strengthened his critical views of Eurocentric self-enclosure, anthropocentrism, and cognitive self-sufficiency. At the same time, his appreciation of the best in Europe's philosophical traditions served as "possible springboards to broader, cross-cultural or transcultural explorations."[25]

Dallmayr saw the end of the Cold War as opening up "new possibilities of human and social life, that encouraged and required creative social imagination."[26] This involved new interpenetrations of universality and particularity, of identity and differences, which were inspired by the emerging field of intercultural studies. One of Dallmayr's theoretical contributions to the intercultural movement in political philosophy was what he called "comparative political theory" from a global cross-cultural perspective. To that end, he edited and contributed to a special issue of *The Review of Politics* titled "Non-Western Political Thought" (1997), which was followed by his *Alternative Visions: Path in the Global Village* (1998), *Border Crossing: Toward a Comparative Political Theory* (1999), *Achieving Our World: Toward a Global and Plural Democracy* (2001), and *Post-Liberalism: Recovering a Shared World* (2019).

One way Dallmayr applies the idea of dialogue in his political philosophy is in the conception of democratic politics as "relational praxis." This lays the groundwork for a new understanding of democracy, challenging its equation with the pursuit of individual or collective self-interest and insisting that more ethical conceptions are possible and that different societies should nurture democracy with their own cultural resources.[27] Ideas of dialogue operate at all levels—from intersubjective and social to intercultural and intercivilizational—as means for peace and humane transformation of the world. Dialogic philosophy also stands for dialogue among civilizations and provides a theoretical basis for a new, dialogical civilization.[28]

Recovering Humanity's Wholeness

Dallmayr approaches issues from an eagle-eyed civilizational perspective in dialogue with both Western and Eastern philosophical traditions. Studies of these philosophies have led him to see some common trends in the variety of culturally diverse ways of philosophizing. Both are generally characterized by two contrasting perspectives. One is the sober assessment of the realities of the world and of the situation of human beings, expressing a grave concern about humanity's future. The other, the "idealistic," is more focused on the search for possible solutions to the problems and a hopeful alternative. Humanity has reached a historical "turning point" and is at the crossroads. One endeavor tends toward preserving the status quo, with the escalation of social and global problems, heading toward a nuclear or ecological apocalypse. The other leads toward alternatives—through the awakening of the global consciousness and mobilization of the intellectual-spiritual resources for necessary changes, for transformation of minds and hearts of individuals and of societies.

Similar themes can be found in the *Bhagavad Gita*, which speaks to two human "natures" in the world: the one aims for bliss and goodwill, the other for destruction, striving "by unjust means to amass unlimited wealth."[29] Dallmayr evinces courage to face these problems and confront hegemonic ideologies and politics in order to try to wake people up. It also takes an even greater courage to hope—not to escape into an illusory dream of powerlessness as suggested by historicism but to assert belief in real possibilities for averting such tragedy.

This mind-set is expressed in Dallmayr's conceptions of "world maintenance" and "cosmopolis." He embraces Heidegger's definition of human existence as "being-in-the-world," where existence and world are intimately connected and world includes fellow-beings, nature, and the (divine) cosmos. Dallmayr elaborates on the Heideggerian notion of "care," which means concern about Being or what it means to be. Because, in the case of human beings, *Dasein* as being-in-the-world is part and parcel of being human, then care for Being also means care for world and care about humanity or humaneness. This can lead to well-being-in-the-world, which in the end coincides with the quest for peace and justice.

Such caring attention to world maintenance can be found in Western and Eastern religious and philosophical traditions. As religious examples, Dallmayr mentions the Jewish mystical traditions (*Sohar*), Sufi mystical poetry in Islam, and Christian mystical writings about a promised land, with peace and justice. The philosophical example is Kantian universalism, especially Kant's *Perpetual Peace*. To this, one can add examples from Russian religious-philosophical thought, such as Vladimir Solovyov's ideas of "Godmanhood," "positive wholeness," and "unity-of-all," which mean that in the divine order, all individual elements of the universe complement each other and form a harmonious organism.

The *Bhagavad Gita* emphasizes the basic ethical and ontological obligation, namely, the caring attention to world maintenance or "welfare of the world" (*loka-samgraha*) as the highest perfection of righteous human conduct. Such conduct should be in conformity with the classical teaching about universal connectedness and harmony. This conformity can only be achieved through a distinction between selfish and unselfish conduct. Only in this way is it also possible to maintain a synergy or harmony between the paths of knowledge, behavior, and action. As Dallmayr demonstrates, these ideas continue in contemporary India. Mahatma Gandhi used the *Gita* as his source of inspiration, and in his political philosophy, world maintenance was closely linked with the ideas of *ahimsa* (nonviolence) and *swaraj* (self-rule). Today, this tradition continues in the so-called *Sarvodaya* Movement (movement for "universal uplift" or "progress of all"), as networks of popular self-organization, exemplifying the idea of world maintenance "from the bottom up."

Parallels can be found in many other traditions. In China, for example, these ideas can be seen in the concept of "All-Under-Heaven" (*Tian-Xia*). At the heart of Confucian teaching is mutual care and fidelity, a care that ultimately extends to the relational fabric of the entire world. Most important in relationships is "*jen*"—goodness, benevolence, humaneness, a compassionate love for humanity or for the world as a whole. It remains as a "living metaphor" for an ethical and properly humanized way of life.

Dallmayr's intercultural analysis has led him to conclude that the concept of world care is shared by virtually all cultural and religious traditions around the globe. In collaboration with philosophers from India, China, Japan, Malaysia, Turkey, Iran, Egypt, Russia, and other countries, through conferences and publications, he promotes the idea that we need to work to restore and safeguard our world, thus preventing an apocalypse. Indeed, it is important to regain the vital heritage of mankind, what Paul Ricoeur called "memory of humanity" (*mémoire d'humanité*), that always speaks to us again in an ethical sense and connects us with the best of human values and dignity.[30] It is also important to revitalize intellectual and spiritual resources of humanity through intercultural and interreligious dialogue.

Dallmayr shows the pertinence of the conception of world care as articulated in Heidegger's "Letter on Humanism," where he characterized a human being as the caretaker or guardian of Being: "Humankind is not the master of reality, but rather the shepherd of Being."[31] Hence human existence shoulders a responsibility and is called into caring service. In a way, Heidegger's notion of the "fourfold" (*Geviert*)—a convergence of relationships bringing together the earth, the heaven, mortals, and divinities—can be seen as a deepening of the relational character of human being. Dallmayr elaborates on this relationality and on human-ness as open-ended, pointing beyond itself, from actuality to potentiality or possibility: "This constitutive openness brings into view humanity's transformative quality: that is, its possible transformation into a more genuine or deeper humanity (*Menschwerdung*) or a being at the boundary of the divine (sometimes called '*theosis*')."[32] These ideas resonate with some of the insights of a new philosophical anthropology, such as "synergic anthropology."[33]

In the discussions about "postsecularity," Dallmayr rejects any dichotomy of immanence and transcendence, which leaves one choice only between "materialism" and religious fundamentalism. He sees in Raimon Panikkar's holism a third possibility, pointing to the potential overcoming of the "transcendence-immanence" conundrum. Panikkar is critical of both an agnostic immanentism lacking spirituality and a radical transcendentalism indifferent to social-ethical problems. Inspired in part by the idea of the Indian *Advaita Vedanta* that we all belong to the cosmic unity, he holds the possibility of recovering a proper balance of life, which requires an acknowledgement that our belongness to a cosmic "rhythm of being" happens in a relational or "cosmotheandric" mode, connecting the divine, the human, and nature. This view of holism is open to cultural pluralism, as promoted in his works on interreligious-intercultural philosophy. This is congenial to Dallmayr's own nondualistic views.[34] He interprets the term "postsecularity" in the sense of an ethically and spiritually nurtured cosmopolitan commitment.

Dallmayr goes beyond traditional humanism, arguing for the need of "humanizing humanity" and developing a new, post-secular humanism with an emphasis on spirituality and religious dimensions. This "new" or "apophatic" humanism should embrace the humanistic ideas from the various world cultures. He highlights the spiritual dimensions of religious-philosophical and theological thought as an intellectual-spiritual source for the search for a more humane alternative to the global disorder.[35]

Cosmopolis and New Horizons

Dallmayr's philosophical and ethical-political ideas culminate in his conceptualization of cosmopolis, an "emerging global city" or community. He expresses dissatisfaction with some of the interpretations of cosmopolitanism: empirical, focused on economic and technological globalization, while hiding ethical deficits; and normative, which refers to international law and a legal world order but ignores local and regional contexts. He favors an approach that gives primacy to practice, "pointing to the need for concrete engagements across national, cultural, and religious boundaries" for "the building of a pluralistic and dialogical cosmopolis."[36] He thus views cosmopolitanism not just in legal and institutional terms but in a broader cultural and philosophical sense. He again finds useful insights in Heidegger's conception of temporality, meaning that human being-in-the-world is constantly "temporalized" in the direction of future possibilities. He also refers to Deweyan pragmatism, Alfred North Whitehead's process philosophy, hermeneutics, and other sources. Based on these, he develops his conception of "a 'becoming cosmopolis' beckoning from the future as a possibility and a promise."[37]

Dallmayr embraces the fresh dimensions of a "new cosmopolitanism" as reflexive, critical, democratic, rooted, dialogical, intercultural, and transformative. He develops his conception of cosmopolis in dialogue with the ideas of such theorists of cosmopolitanism as Karl-Otto Apel, Daniele Archibugi, Seyla Benhabib, Richard Falk, Raul Fornet-Betancourt, Jürgen Habermas, David Held, James Ingram, Martha Nussbaum, and Walter

Mignolo, among others. At the same time, his conception of cosmopolis has some distinctive characteristics that are related to his interpretation of being-in-the-world, care, relationality, democratic politics as relational praxis, world maintenance, and spirituality.

Dallmayr's thought—beyond both a conflict-ridden state-centric system and hegemon-centric dystopia—strives for an ideal of a domination-free, cross-cultural, dialogical world order of peace and justice. He examines the conditions for progress in the direction of such a cosmopolitan order. Gross material disparities, hegemonic domination, and violence are problems that must be solved on the way to this goal. Equally important is regaining social ethics and cultivating co-responsibility and shared well-being. To homogenizing globalization he opposes the importance of the diversity of cultural traditions[38] and education. It is necessary to go beyond instrumental rationality and be open to dialogue and listening, cross-cultural and inter-religious interaction, ethics, and spiritual insight. In contrast to the idea of a uniform global imperial super-state dominating the world, cosmopolis means a shared aspiration negotiated among local or national differences.

Cosmopolitan reflections are futile if the only reality to be taken into account is the present, ignoring future horizons. According to Dallmayr, the opening of such horizons requires not just a change of individual attitudes but also "a change of the entire modern paradigm or frame of significance, that is, of our mode of 'being-in-the-world.'"[39] One of the problems of the metaphysically encrusted categories of Western modernity is the concept of freedom, anchored in a fixed subject and dogmatically asserted privilege, which is the opposite of social solidarity. This requires a rigorous rethinking of the polar categories used in political thought. Dallmayr views freedom not as an exclusionary property but rather as "an openness to the unfolding horizons of truth challenging us to find our way in the world." Seen in this light, "solidarity is not the opposite, but rather the intimate corollary of our living freely in the world."[40]

A challenge we face is to reconnect freedom and solidarity. But this is extremely difficult in the prevailing political conditions of the super-Leviathan surveillance state, which seeks to subject the population to near-total control, of the atomization of social life, and of eroded ethics. Dallmayr explores the possibility of a transition from the modern paradigm toward a new beginning in which freedom and solidarity can be reconnected. This intimates a basic paradigm shift.[41] It is a hope predicated on the progressive maturation and transformation of humanity.

Much inspiration for resisting disorder and for positive transformations can be derived from the great world religions and also from prominent philosophical and wisdom traditions around the world. Dallamyr's works invoke religious, spiritual, and ethical resources for global renewal. He also addresses the question of religion in public life. Religion and spiritual traditions, alongside moral ones, provide resources for encouraging a disposition toward the common good. He views the possibility of future horizons as a "promise," "to come." Cosmopolis cannot just be humanly manufactured by calculative rationality and social engineering, but also requires "spiritual guidance by pathfinders in the present desert."[42]

On a personal note, he has humbly remarked, "perhaps my life's journey and all my endeavors were nothing but a gloss on a single word in the Lord's prayer: *adveniat*, 'may it come.' "[43] That is prayerfully soliciting to come "your reign." Such a reign "cannot be purely clerical nor purely secular; it cannot be purely 'transcendental' nor 'immanent.' " It must be for the whole, embracing all cultures and traditions, and allowing for "a multitude of differences and even for absences and the 'unknown.' " He adds that in scripture, "we are exhorted to 'seek your face' (*faciem tuam requiram*)—which is nothing but the radiant face of (transcognitive) truth, goodness, and justice."[44] Dallmayr's work shines brightly against the grim background of recent hegemonic and neototalitarian degeneration. This confirms his prophetic warnings against the global disorder that threatens humanity's future. At the same time, this makes even more pertinent his vision of a positive alternative, predicated on mindfulness, relationships of dialogue and solidarity for the common good, spirituality, and the possibility of human transformation or "*metanoia*," aspiring to the cosmopolis to come.

Notes

1. Fred Dallmayr, *On the Boundary: A Life Remembered* (Lanham, MD: Hamilton Books, 2017), 43.
2. Ibid., 43–44.
3. Ibid., 45.
4. Fred Dallmayr, *The Other Heidegger* (Ithaca, NY: Cornell University Press, 1993), 63.
5. Martin Heidegger, *Being and Time: A Translation of Sein und Zeit*, trans. Joan Stambaugh (Albany: State University of New York Press, 1996), 359.
6. Ibid., 305.

7. Ibid., 344.

8. Ibid., 345. Here and in all other quotations, emphases in original.

9. Ibid., 135.

10. Ibid., 136.

11. Fred Dallmayr, *Against Apocalypse: Recovering Humanity's Wholeness* (Lanham, MD: Lexington Books, 2016), 83.

12. Martin Heidegger, *What Is Called Thinking?*, translated by J. Glenn Gray (New York: Harper & Row, 1968), 38, 46. The reference is from Nietzsche's *Thus Spoke Zarathustra*, 417. See *The Portable Nietzsche*, ed. Walter Kaufmann (New York: Viking Press, 1968).

13. Martin Heidegger, *The Event (Studies in Continental Thought)*, trans. Richard Rojcewicz (Bloomington: Indiana University Press, 2013), 85–66.

14. Dallmayr, *Against Apocalypse*, 88.

15. Ibid., 88.

16. Heidegger, *The Event*, 148.

17. Ibid., 132.

18. Ibid.

19. Ibid., 145.

20. Ibid., 134.

21. Dallmayr, *Against Apocalypse*, 96.

22. Mikhail Bakhtin, *Toward a Philosophy of the Act*, ed. Michael Holquist and Vadim Liapunov, trans. Vadim Liapunov (Austin: University of Texas Press, 1993), 12.

23. Fred Dallmayr, *Spiritual Guides: Pathfinders in the Desert* (Notre Dame, IN: University of Notre Dame Press, 2017), chapter 2.

24. Dallmayr, *On the Boundary*, op. cit., 64.

25. Ibid., 65.

26. Ibid.

27. Fred Dallmayr, *Democracy to Come: Politics as Relational Praxis* (New York: Oxford University Press, 2017); *Post-Liberalism: Recovering a Shared World* (Oxford: Oxford University Press, 2019).

28. He was influential in his decade-long service as co-chair of the international World Public Forum "Dialogue of Civilizations" and continues his important role as a member of the Supervisory Board of the Dialogue of Civilizations Research Institute.

29. Dallmayr, *Against Apocalypse*, op. cit., 2.

30. Paul Ricoeur, *Political and Social Essays*, ed. David Stewart and Joseph Bien (Athens: Ohio University Press, 1975), 70.

31. Martin Heidegger, "Letter on Humanism," in *Martin Heidegger: Basic Writings*, ed. David F. Krell (New York: Harper & Row, 1993), 221–31.

32. Dallmayr, *Against Apocalypse*, op. cit., 84.

33. Sergey S. Horujy, *Practices of the Self and Spiritual Practices: Michel Foucault and the Eastern Christian Discourse*, ed. Kristina Stoeckl, trans. Boris Jakim (Grand Rapids, MI: William R. Eerdmans, 2015).

34. Fred Dallmayr, *Being in the World: Dialogue and Cosmopolis* (Lexington: University Press of Kentucky, 2013), chapter 8.

35. Dallmayr, *Spiritual Guides,* op. cit.

36. Dallmayr, *On the Boundary,* op. cit., 83.

37. Ibid., 82.

38. Fred Dallmayr, "After Babel: Journey Toward Cosmopolis," in *Intercultural Dialogue: In Search of Harmony in Diversity*, ed. Edward Demenchonok (Newcastle upon Tyne: Cambridge Scholars Publishing, 2016), 365–78.

39. Dallmayr, *On the Boundary,* op. cit., 84.

40. Ibid., 85.

41. Fred Dallmayr, *Freedom and Solidarity: Toward New Beginnings* (Lexington: University Press of Kentucky, 2015). See also Fred Dallmayr and Edward Demenchonok, eds., *A World Beyond Global Disorder: The Courage to Hope* (Newcastle upon Tyne: Cambridge Scholars Publishing, 2017).

42. Dallmayr, *On the Boundary,* op. cit., 88; See also *Spiritual Guides*, op. cit.

43. Dallmayr, *On the Boundary,* op. cit., 86.

44. Ibid., 87.

Chapter 2

Fred Dallmayr's Spiritual Cosmopolitanism

RICHARD FALK

Preliminary Considerations

In Fred Dallmayr's arresting words, "What is radically new in our time—often called the 'nuclear age'—is that for the first time life itself is under attack, that life as such on the planet can be annihilated without remainder, leaving only 'desert' behind."[1] He makes clear that he has in mind not only climate change as well as nuclear warfare, but the atomization of selfhood being caused by a capitalist world order that is responsible for grotesque degrees of inequality while subjugating humanity to a nihilistic technology and wealth-driven materialism that results in a devastating despiritualization of the human condition.

Dallmayr is philosophically erudite and astonishingly eclectic, as well as politically attuned to the discordant rhythms of our age and ethically responsive to desperate calls for empathy and ecological sensitivity on a global scale. He is such an extraordinary expositor that unsuspecting readers may be inclined to overlook the originality and relevance of Dallmayr's own creative and synthetic journey of ideas, which illuminates a progressive way of thinking, acting, and feeling that richly deserves to be widely disseminated, carefully reflected on, and, hopefully, embraced. Because Dallmayr's work encompasses so much, evolves over time, is historically contextualized, and is expository, critical, and visionary, it is impossible to categorize or do justice to even a single aspect or fragment of the immense corpus of his scholarly achievement spread by now over more than six productive decades.

Dallmayr's outlook can be sampled in numerous books that often address similar themes, yet, quite remarkably, each of his academic writings yields an illuminating and fresh encounter between author and reader. Although his concerns abide, reading Dallmayr book after book leaves impressions of valuably new thinking rather than a repetitive rendering of well-ploughed fields. This appreciation of Dallmayr's unflinching dedication to continuous exploration is the greatest praise that one scholar can give to another!

My effort here is to depict and respond to Dallmayr's recent work that addresses vital issues of human identity, including the acute tensions between attachments by humanity to its component parts versus the affirmation of its encompassing whole, as well as the scientific versus the secular, the religious versus the spiritual, and the present and past versus the future. I want to consider Dallmayr's contributions to our understanding of these matters by briefly reviewing the distinct elements of his approach, which when considered together achieve a high degree of coherence and persuasiveness. Overall, Dallmayr produces a compelling approach to the challenges of this historical moment, which if acted upon on a large enough scale could have a major emancipatory impact on the human condition.

Having praised his work, I end this chapter by raising questions about whether Dallmayr's high standards of expectation with respect to ethical, spiritual, and ecological intelligence are capable or can be made capable of generating the collective societal dynamics needed to transform such elevated aspirations into a viable political project. Dallmayr's goals can also be regarded as imperatives, given the severity and urgency of the present global challenges facing humanity. The required responses depend on species- and habitat-sustaining transformations of values, structures, and behavior of immense magnitude. Dallmayr sets forth his version of what I have described elsewhere as "a necessary utopia" without overlooking the formidable obstacles blocking the path to its realization.[2]

In this spirit, Dallmayr conveys throughout his work a sense of foreboding about the negativity he associates with the materialism and militarism of late capitalist modernity, perhaps epitomized by choosing *Against Apocalypse* as the ominous title of a recent book. Yet Dallmayr is never content to settle for a gloom and doom view of the human condition. This positive dimension of his political sensibility is expressed by this same book's hopeful subtitle, *Recovering Humanity's Wholeness*. Without a careful understanding of this pattern of light and dark that colors Dallmayr's rendering of the world situation, it is easy to read his work as either overly optimistic or excessively pessimistic. It is neither.

Dallmayr is impressively aware of the global problematique in all its aspects, and fashions his radical remedial program in response, not venturing an opinion as to the outcome, yet insisting on engagement in the struggle. This is crucial. Part of the human condition is to be enmeshed in a web of uncertainties, which explain two features of Dallmayr's praxis: first, there is no reason to accept as a fait accompli the future as determined by the darkness of the present; and secondly, the appropriate ethical and political response is to struggle amid uncertainty for the future we need and desire.

Sources of Inspiration

Several characteristics of Dallmayr's thought pervade his writing: a wide-ranging reliance on twentieth-century European philosophical thought, enriched by a recognition of the relevance of non-Western, especially Asian, worldviews. Dallmayr is particularly appreciative of the thought and practice of Gandhi. He also expresses his admiration for exemplary moral authority figures who have had inspirational impacts because of their courageous refusal to submit to oppressive structures and unjust practices. Among those mentioned in various places are Nelson Mandela, the Dalai Lama, Martin Luther King Jr., Archbishop Desmond Tutu, Mahatma Gandhi, Saint Francis of Assisi, and Pope Francis. The list discloses Dallmayr's orientation.[3] His moral and political affinities are a deeply considered response to several influential thinkers whom he acknowledges as his "mentors," above all, Martin Heidegger, but also Montesquieu, Confucius, Aristotle, Plato, Raimon Panikkar, Erasmus, John Dewey, Whitehead, Hegel, Hobbes, and Kant; and a bit less centrally, Jonathan Schell, author of *The Unconquerable People*. and John Cobb and Herman Daly, authors of *The Common Good*.[4] Schell offers a compelling account of the primacy of people in achieving change for the better and offering resistance to evil. Cobb and Daly offer an ecological ethics that would enable humanity to live in dynamic harmony with its natural surroundings, rather than as now, in a relationship of dominion that is causing disruptions, devastating backlashes, and trending toward catastrophe.

Heidegger seems crucial in framing Dallmayr's basic quest: diagnosing what is fundamentally wrong about the way the world is organized, giving rise to exploitative and destructive patterns of behavior exhibited in recurrent warfare as abetted by a technologically dominant mentality and with a stultifying materialism taking the contemporary form of neoliberal capitalism. In stark opposition to this diagnosis, Dallmayr affirms the potential of democratic forms of governance by reference to a crucial transformative commitment to what he calls "democracy to come." Dallmayr attributes the substance of this futurist and normative view of democracy to Montesquieu's insistence that the essential trait of embodied democratic values is "the spirit of equality."[5]

This is a timely, seemingly counterintuitive assessment, given recent trends toward ever greater inequality within and between sovereign states, which in turn is principally responsible for producing social responses of rage, alienation, and a terrifying susceptibility to demagogic leaders. In other words, democracy can go terribly wrong in practice and effects, without altering democratic rhetoric if the modalities of economic, social, and political development exhibit pronounced tendencies toward greater inequality. In this crucial respect, Dallmayr displays his attunement to what has become the most accepted explanation of disequilibrium dominating the political horizons of the early twenty-first century.

Although his publications so far stop short of the Trump presidency and the related global phenomenon of Trumpism, this turn to the populist right in America is not an unexpected development given the effects that growing inequality is having in the United States, making the very rich even richer while the rest of society treads water or sinks into poverty. Rather than constructively address the problem, Trump provides a demagogic alternative that puts a hostile spin on immigrants as menacing strangers in our midst, as well on "the shithole countries" of Africa and elsewhere who are exporting their most depraved residents to engage in terrorism, disseminate drugs, and steal jobs from "real" Americans. Trump also blames the dismal economic situation of the American underclass on the bad trade deals made by his immediate predecessors in the White House, particularly Obama, and vows to end or radically revise economic arrangements that have allowed other countries, especially China, to flourish at the expense of the United States.

As Dallmayr so well understands, ultra-nationalist responses are regressive and inherently dysfunctional. They also contribute to massive distress within countries, which facilitates a potentially fatal distraction from the overriding historical challenge of achieving viable political and ecological habitats, which for Dallmayr presuppose operationalizing "humanity's wholeness." To so move means strengthening greatly the sense of human identity in relation to national and other fragmentary identities, which is the direct opposite of this currently prevalent global pattern of revitalizing the nationalist agenda at the expense of regional and global priorities.

In some respects, because his published work preceded this turn away from democracy and globalisms, Dallmayr may strike readers as unresponsive to the scary salience of these recent political trends. To write of "democracy to come," which resembles Derrida's focus on what it might mean "to live together, well," does not seem sensitive to the realities of what might be described as the global phenomenon of "de-democratization," or, as some have put it, the rise of "illiberal democracies." This regressive set of developments involves the rebalancing of society/state relations by tilting toward autocratic rulership linking security to exaggerated fears of the other and thereby providing rationalizations for harsher police controls over the citizenry. Such a political pattern reinforces nationalism with policies that punish immigrants and construct walls symbolically and substantively designed to keep unwanted strangers out, widening the gaps among the peoples of the world and thereby ripping apart the holistic fabric of humanity that is central to Dallmayr's prescription for a benevolent future.

Although Trump and Trumpism are the most blatant instances of de-democratization, the same and related dynamics are evident in many other contexts, including Brexit, and the success of right-wing populists, autocrats, and demagogues in such countries as China, Russia, Turkey, Japan, India, Israel, East Europe, the Philippines, as well as the disturbing rise of neofascist political parties in almost all of the world's leading "democracies." Such commonalities across regions and stages of development imply a structural explanation taking the form of a series of backlashes against the polarizing effects of neoliberal capitalism dominating the global marketplace, privileging capital flows over the well-being of people.

In Dallmayr's view, the rationality and instrumentalism of the Enlightenment, privileging the rise of science, excessive reliance on instrumental rationalism, and false connections between technology, progress, and human happiness lend credence to a radically critical stance for which Heidegger provides the most helpful framing. It also makes it understandable why Dallmayr should be drawn to the approaches taken by Raimon Panikkar, the deceased Berkeley professor of comparative religion, for both his emphasis on religion as a means of grasping the universality and true nature of the human condition and the related need to be receptive to the wisdom and insights of non-Western civilizational perspectives.

I find it helpful to formulate this holistic quest as follows: we now live in a world where the parts are much greater than the whole, especially the larger parts, whether the particular part is a state, religion, ideology, or private sector constituted by corporate/financial entities. By contrast, to achieve sustainability and well-being, the overriding goal is the transformation of this fragmented reality called "world order" into a more coherent whole that is greater than the sum of its parts. As a result, the idea of humanity is no longer a vague abstraction with little political traction, and rather becomes the foundation of what Dallmayr calls "relational praxis," which situates the primary orientation for individual and group identity, thereby shaping the unfolding of individual and collective life.[6]

John Dewey's influence in diagnosing the ills of American democracy seems of great relevance to the construction of Dallmayr's ideas about a "democracy to come." Dallmayr agrees with Dewey's explanation of the decline of American democracy as attributable to the triumph of "a money culture" producing a citizenry of "atomized individualism." Mainstream procedural conceptions of democracy miss the indispensable realization that democratic legitimacy is about far more than the free elections. For Dewey, as for Dallmayr, democracy fails the citizen if it loses its essential character as "an ethical conception." Dewey bemoans the loss of the wildness of the early American experience so well depicted by the lyric intensity of Walt Whitman's celebratory poetry, an outlook unabashedly endorsed by Dallmayr.[7]

Choosing the Road of Spiritual Cosmopolitanism

Although Dallmayr's views of the future of existing societies are preoccupied with fulfilling the potential of democracy—ethically, ecologically, and economically—his broader vision is shaped by hopes and fears surrounding the apolitical destiny of the human species as a totality. It is this broader vision that I would describe as one of "spiritual cosmopolitanism," a sense of humanity as a whole achieving transcendence by a spiritualized interpretation of the meaning of life. This understanding should not be confused with a theological metaphysics projecting a hierarchy of divine being(s) shaping human experience from above, much less a readiness to entrust human destiny to the guidance of institutionalized religion. It may be difficult to articulate the various cultural embodiments of spirituality. What can be clearly grasped is Dallmayr's recognition that human destiny is not well served by subscribing to the various secular fundamentalisms that flow from the post-Enlightenment rise of scientific rationalism and its boundless confidence in technological empowerment.

Here also Heidegger's profound interpretations of being-in-the-world exert a strong influence on Dallmayr's outlook, or this may be better considered as a matter of congeniality of these two thinkers, disguised by Dallmayr's overt deference to one of the towering, if controversial, philosophical figures of the prior century. Rather than thinking abstractly about the human condition, being-in-the-world is the proper ontological starting point, suggesting that every human experience is embedded in the concreteness of time, place, and consciousness. Beyond this circumstance of "being" is the complementary reality of "becoming," the all-pervasive reality of process and change. In conceiving of the becoming aspects of being-in-the-world, Dallmayr acknowledges Alfred North Whitehead as an inspirational guide, and notes the affinities of his thought with that of "process theology" as developed by John Cobb and David Ray Griffin.

Dallmayr adds to this beingness of humanity, the degree to which our best lens to perceive reality is by way of hermeneutics, that is, our inescapable dependence on interpretation. Such a dependence makes our interpretation of reality contingent on the particularities of observation and gives plural civilizational perspectives an equal purchase on reality, although some may have more or less relevance to the prime imperative of recovering and constituting the wholeness of humanity.

This relational engagement, as combined with time/place/social location/civilizational differences, creates a natural disposition toward dialogue as vital for mutual respect and an affirming appreciation of difference in ways that do not undermine the specifics of identity. In other words, dialogue is not a race to the bottom, via the downgrading of difference, but its upgrading through building a brighter future by taking advantage of individual and collective diverse civilizational strengths. Such an understanding creates the basis for a normative view of dialogue as more than conversations with others, but rather as an approach well articulated by Michael Sandel, which recommends "reasoning together" toward a respectful acceptance of transnational and transcivilizational diversities, an acceptance of which is posited as an integral dimension of citizenship in a globalizing world.[8]

Heidegger also provides the parameters of critique that guides Dallmayr. He emphasizes the contemporary loss of spiritual grounding creating disruptions that are severely aggravated by obsessive technological enchantment and its tendency to produce a materialist societal temperament that contrasts unfavorably with the premodern organic connectedness to nature and the cosmos. For Dallmayr, as well, these fatal shortcomings of modernity point to a postmodern preferred reconfiguration of being-in-the-world that far exceeds in its imaginative and normative sweep the deconstructionist turn of European postmodernism. Dallmayr also derives from Heidegger the relational essence of being-in-the world, which informs his sense of social and political engagement. By accepting the Gandhian embrace of pacifism as a crucial part of the transformational agenda, Dallmayr engages liberal critics, such as Richard Beardsworth, who urge the more modest goal of "the possibility of a less violent politics."[9] Dallmayr's diagnosis of the troubles of the world rests on the utter necessity of a more radical and prescriptive political therapy. Making feasible responses to present challenges, however sensible, will not get the job done. Many would dismiss Dallmayr's call as "utopian," but for him it is a matter of doing what is right as reinforced by what is necessary.

Against this background, Dallmayr constructs a vision of an ideal polity whose citizens assume responsibility for acting ethically and prudently with regard to human destiny, including going beyond dialogue toward "loving the other," which reflects the historical circumstance of establishing a human community that incorporates all the fragmented national communities that remain defining characteristics of a state-centric world order. Given the affirmations of spirituality and democratic values, it seems quite natural that Dallmayr would affirm an ecumenical version of cosmopolitanism that departs from the Stoic legacy that fits more easily with modernist secularism.[10]

Dallmayr posits this hoped-for future as a decontextualized preference, offering no insight as to transitions from here to there. Consistent with being-in-the-world, he acknowledges the difficulties of any transition from the troubled present to a desired future: "The obstacles standing in the way of an ecumenical cosmopolitanism, nurtured by democratic equality, are surely staggering and nearly overwhelming. But if we are serious about democracy, they have to be confronted. In a word, democracy means continuous striving and struggle. As the saying goes: la lotta contua."[11]

It would not be misleading to characterize this overview of Dallmayr's approach to human identity as that of "a new realism" attentive to the actualities of the historical situation. Such an attentiveness leads to a blending of aspiration and self-doubt, the affirmation of spiritual cosmopolitanism with a lively realization that the transition from here to there now seems nearly impossible. Dallmayr champions a utopian adventure that is rescued from a sense of futility by the recognition that struggle amid uncertainty can produce unexpected emancipatory changes that inform our historical experience. Notable among such changes is the collapse of European colonialism, the transformation of apartheid South Africa, and the ending of the Cold War. To some extent, this is similar to the faith that guides the citizen-pilgrim to embark on the long journey to a better future.[12]

A Concluding Comment

The post-9/11 battlefield exhibits the deterritorialization of war, with political extremists striking violently anywhere on the planet, while the United States and its allies in the Global War of Terror ignore sovereign rights of foreign countries by sending drone missiles wherever an adversary can be found. As suggested, the contradictory phenomenon occurs when walls and security are tightened along borders to keep refugees and migrants out, and protectionist forms of economic nationalism resurrect the tariffs mindless of the lessons the Great Depression brought about in the 1930s by trade wars. These spatially divergent developments lure our policy gaze away from the urgencies associated with global warming, and its secondary effects, and the precarious maneuvers of geopolitical nuclearism, creating unacceptably high risks of catastrophic warfare. In effect, our surveillance technology allows our leaders to look everywhere, but it remains surprising how little they see! This is the discouraging irony of a potent technology of destruction interacting with an obsolescent politics of militarized security.

Despite Dallmayr's impressive scholarly achievements and global reputation, he remains in my judgment "the greatest unknown political philosopher of our time." It may be partly Dallmayr's fault, or maybe not a fault, but an expression of his humility and the selfless integrity of carrying out his lifelong frantic search for usable knowledge in a precarious time in ways that could enhance the human experience in all of its dimensions. This includes the current formidable challenge, which he so well articulates, of multiple threats to the survival and well-being of the human species and its diverse habitats. It should be stressed that Dallmayr is not content to confine his inquiries to the domain of thought. He is always intent on exploring how to make ideas vehicles for political change, what he calls "moral praxis."

With the dedication of a lifetime, Dallmayr has bestowed on us a cartography of emancipation and empowerment, with a navigational compass guided by the values and visions associated with the theory and practice of ecumenical cosmopolitanism. This gift of engaged wisdom provides the needed guidance, but as the subtitle of one of Dallmayr's books wryly asks, "Who will listen?" Dallmayr's remarkably rich palate of eclecticism, based on the widest exposure to the best thought past and present, makes him the most accomplished academic listener I have ever encountered.[13] He has not only constructed his distinct worldview and proposed lines of engagement on the basis of this deep exposure to some of the most demanding texts in the Western canon, but he also has taken steps to meet and interact with several of these influential European thinkers. The stunning result is what I label "cosmopolitan spiritualism," which is strikingly similar to what Dallmayr calls "ecumenical cosmopolitanism." I have done my best to listen to these wide outpourings, but we still need to pose and heed a variant on Dallmayr's hauntingly ironic question: "will there be enough listeners to make a difference?"

Notes

1. Asserted with urgency in his *Against Apocalypse*, op. cit., 1. I have made similar assessments with slightly different phrasing, emphasizing the fundamental shift from *civilizational* jeopardy as discussed in Jared Diamond's *Collapse* to a situation of *species* jeopardy that encompasses non-human as well as human forms of life. See Richard Falk, *Power Shift: On the New Global Order* (London: Zed, 2016), especially 253–62.

2. See Richard Falk, "Toward a Necessary Utopianism: Democratic Global Governance," in *The Writings of Richard Falk* (Delhi, India: Orient BlackSwan, 2012), 430–47.

3. All of these individuals acted with courage in the world, but with a motivation rooted in religious faith and conviction. Only Mandela can be regarded as principally secular, although his politics of reconciliation seemed spiritually grounded. I reached this conclusion after a meeting and conversation, struck by Mandela's moral radiance, which seemed to be a manifestation of an inner spirituality.

4. Jonathan Schell, *Unconquerable World: Power, Nonviolence, and the Will of the People* (New York: Metropolitan Books, 2003).

5. Fred Dallmayr, *Democracy to Come: Politics as Relational Praxis* (Oxford, UK: Oxford University Press, 2017), 5–6; Alexis de Tocqueville is also invoked along similar lines, suggesting that challenges to monarchy as premised on hierarchy based on the establishment of democracy rested their legitimacy on the opposite principle of equality. That French commentators should choose such an emphasis is not surprising in view of the hierarchical character of the French monarchy in its most absolute forms as well as its providing the national backdrop for the most revolutionary challenge from a mobilized citizenry giving a modern rebirth to the earlier Greek embrace of democracy.

6. The central political metaphysic of *Democracy to Come*, n. 5.

7. For Dewey's views, see *The Public and Its Problems* (1927, 1954), as interpreted by Dallmayr in *Freedom and Solidarity*, especially the chapter on "Reimagining Social Democracy," the source of my references.

8. Michael Sandel, *Justice: What's the Right Thing to Do* (New York: Farrar, Strauss, and Giroux, 2009), 19–20, 260–61; see also Sandel, *What Money Can't Buy* (New York: Farrar, Strauss, and Giroux, 2012), on which Dallmayr also comments favorably.

9. See Dallmayr, *Being in the World: Dialogue and Cosmopolis* (Lexington, KY: University Press of Kentucky, 2013), 84 passim.

10. See *Peace Talks—Who Will Listen* (Notre Dame, IN: Notre Dame University Press, 2004), 64–110.

11. These are the apt final words of *Democracy to Come*, 151.

12. For presentation of the citizen pilgrim as the engaged global citizen embarked on a journey to a desired and necessary future, that is, insisting that time as well as space be integral to the ideals of twenty-first-century citizenship, see Richard Falk, *The Writings of Richard Falk: Towards Humane Global Governance* (Delhi, India: Orient Black Swan, 2012), 480–87.

13. For elaboration, see the autobiography of Fred Dallmayr, *On the Boundary: A Life Remembered* (New York: Hamilton Books, 2017).

Chapter 3

Anticipating Ethical Democracy in East Asia

Engaging with Fred Dallmayr

SUNGMOON KIM

Fred Dallmayr is one of the most insightful, prolific, and engaged political theorists of our time. Over the past fifty years he has produced numerous path-breaking studies in areas as diverse as hermeneutics, phenomenology, German critical theory, French postmodernism, human rights, cosmopolitanism, and non-Western and comparative political theory, to name only the most salient few. Many of his works in these areas have been vigorously engaged by both his critics and, more often, those inspired by his ideas and philosophical insights with special attention to the way he brings his earlier immersions in continental philosophy to developing multicultural cosmopolitanism from a cross-cultural/comparative perspective.[1] Little attention, however, has been paid to his contribution to democratic theory, despite his sustained interest in a mode of democratic theory that is neither liberal individualist nor communitarian; neither elitist nor populist; neither secular nor (overtly) religious. In fact, in a series of recent publications, Dallmayr has forcefully revealed his passion for democracy of the kind that navigates the creative middle ground—the "ethical" ground, as he, following Dewey, calls it—with which such entrenched binaries in social and political theory of late can hardly come to grips.[2]

This work was supported by the National Research Foundation of Korea Grant funded by the Korean government (NRF-2017S1A3A2065772).

In advancing his vision of democracy, Dallmayr draws philosophical inspiration not only from Western thinkers such as Montesquieu, de Tocqueville, Dewey, and Derrida, among others, but also from non-Western thinkers including Gandhi, Tzvetan Todorov, Abed al-Jabri, Tu Weiming, and many others. It is a curious question how Dallmayr generates his own theory of democracy by dialectically integrating the insights gained from his admirable cross-cultural engagement with Western and non-Western philosophical and political thought into a coherent and practicable normative system. Equally curious in developing an alternative theory of democracy is how much and what kind of impact his engagement with non-Western political theories has made. Although a thorough investigation of these questions seems to be necessary for understanding (as well as evaluating) the multicultural and truly cosmopolitan nature of Dallmayr's democratic theory, I put them aside in this short chapter and instead focus on a different, though related, question: what we can learn from Dallmayr's vision of democracy in developing a non-Western political theory, Confucian political theory, in particular? After articulating Dallmayr's "ethical" conception of democracy, I critically evaluate various proposals of Confucian meritocracy that are fashionable in recent Confucian political theory. I conclude by suggesting that the Confucian democracy of an ethical understanding is a democracy *to come* in East Asia.

Beyond Dualism

One of the biggest problems that Dallmayr has with the contemporary development (or rather "impoverishment") of democratic theory is the Manichean dualism that it succumbs to—between liberal individualist and communitarian, between elitist and populist, and/or between secular and religious. The result has been not only the infelicitous separation of the political science of democracy from the social and political theory of democracy but also, more crucially, an utter inability to come to terms with the fundamentally "ethical" nature of democracy that defies such entrenched dualisms.

First of all, in Dallmayr's view, liberal democracy that is premised on the assumption of rights-bearing and interest-seeking individualism only makes democracy an approximation of the market, rendering citizens as consumers (*homo economicus*) and subordinating democratic will formation to market imperatives. What gets stressed and thus encouraged in liberal democracy is instrumental rationality, one's ability to maximize his or her material interest and one's untrammeled claim to his or her individual right to, among other things, private property.³ While liberal democracy is preoccupied with protecting and espousing individual agency (autonomy, choices, rights, and interests) as maximally as possible, communitarianism, when sought as its corrective, tends to go to an opposite extreme, emphasizing the common good and social harmony at the expense of public freedom and democratic equality. In its extreme form, communitarianism succumbs to what can be called "political messianism," in which the qualitative relationship among citizens who are equal to each other is completely sidelined, often suppressed, by the monolithic understanding of the common good and the frantic zeal to maximally realize it by means of social engineering.⁴ As such, neither liberal nor communitarian democracy allows for the possibility that individual agency can be properly balanced with the common good or that the common good is in a symbiotic relationship with the (social) individual's personal flourishing. In either extreme form of democracy, neither individual agency, properly understood, nor the common good, in its most authentic sense, can be achieved.

Second, Dallmayr finds the dichotomy between elitist and popular democracy equally problematic, as both misrepresent the true "spirit" of democracy. By "elitist democracy," Dallmayr means a conception proposed by political scientists such as Joseph Schumpeter and Giovanni Sartori, who understand the gist of democracy in terms of an institutional "method"—most notably, voting and elections—by which to select political leaders or to resolve political conflict.⁵ For Dallmayr, it appears, the problem of elitist democracy is threefold. First, by understanding democracy in this minimal sense, elitist democracy fails to capture the "wellspring or animating soul" of democracy—namely an *equal relationship* among citizens, which presents democracy not so much as a mere institutional mechanism but as a way of life, the point forcefully made by de Tocqueville and Dewey.⁶ Second, whereas political scientists prefer the elitist or minimalist conception of democracy because of the scientific rigor that it promises in measuring "democracy" cross-culturally, Dallmayr sees here a dogma of Western-style liberal democracy posited as the final destination of a linear development of the political regime "across temporal and spatial contexts," allowing for "little or no qualitative change regarding [the] meaning [of democracy]."⁷ Finally, divorced from its animating soul and singularly equated with *liberal* democracy, elitist democracy tacitly authorizes an external intervention for regime change, which on Dallmayr's account is another face of political messianism.⁸

Often emerging as a reaction to elitist democracy, populist democracy has its own problem in its strong emphasis on the sovereign will of the people because it no less dismisses qualitative relationality among citizens than its elitist counterpart does. The kernel of the problem with populist democracy lies in the very notion of "the people," understood as the fixed embodiment of ultimate political power. Taking political power to be a "thing" to be possessed and the people to be a substantive entity with immutable self-identity and unified agency ("People-as-One"), populist democracy, again when decoupled from its relational ethical quality, has an inner tendency to depend on a vanguard political organ or a charismatic leader who presents it- , him- , or herself as the sole and authentic instrument of the popular will, only to destroy the civic foundation of democracy characterized by social pluralism, thereby leading to totalitarianism.[9]

Third, and finally, Dallmayr finds it deeply misleading that modern democracy is commonly thought—because of the influence of the principle of the Wall of Separation or *laïcité*—to be secular, having nothing to do with religion. In arguing for a certain important connection between religion and democracy, however, Dallmayr has no desire to politicize faith or reestablish religion as public power.[10] Rather, the points he is trying to make are, first, that the prevailing conception of modernity (of which modern democracy is an important part) is hopelessly limited in fulfilling the telos of politics, which is nothing other than to *care for the well-being of the people without domination and the use of violence*,[11] and, second, that this profound goal of politics can be made intelligent and rendered practicable only if "a longing for goodness or the good life" has its proper place in politics, which in Dallmayr's judgment constitutes the essence of religion.[12] Here religion denotes not so much a uniform totality or a monism but a productive "holism" that recognizes "a certain transcendence in its immanence," thereby bridging the mundane and the sacred in "a differentiated and constantly unfolding relationship."[13] Seen in this way, for Dallmayr, the heart of religion lies in qualitative relationality (that is neither secular nor otherworldly religious), and the place that houses its true spirit is civil society, not the state. The public life animated by "this-worldly transcendental" religion is, in a nutshell, a politics of civil society whose nature is "ethical," as powerfully argued and/or demonstrated by Hegel, Weber, and, most tellingly in relation to a democratic way of life, Dewey.[14]

Democracy to Come

In Dallmayr's view, the ethical holism that defies misguided and misleading dichotomies between liberalism and communitarianism, between elitism and populism, and between religion and (democratic) politics is best presented in Dewey's "holistic pragmatism." Objecting to a lingering tendency among Dewey scholars to understand the gist of Dewey's antifoundational pragmatism in terms of "scientism" or sheer "instrumentalism" focused on problem solving, Dallmayr draws attention to Dewey's holistic (à la Hegel) understanding of "experience," which goes beyond yet another set of dichotomies between idealism and empiricism and between subject and object.[15] Of special interest to Dallmayr here is experience in the concrete sense in which one engages as a *social being*, situated in or encumbered by his or her concrete social conditions. Dewey famously called such a mode of (both philosophical and, more importantly, social) engagement "inquiry," which renders experience as "an ongoing learning process in which both the target of inquiry and the inquirer undergo a formative, and possibly transformative, experience." Put differently, the inquiring mind is "challenged and reversed, leading to a seasoning of reflective intelligence."[16]

This Deweyan notion of (social) individual agency exercised in the self-transformative and self-enlarging process of social inquiry is of critical importance to Dallmayr's democratic theory. It is precisely this sort of human agency, which brings mind and body, subject and object, and thinking and doing into an integrated, holistic, and organic experience, that the contemporary discourse of democracy in political science and social and political theory has generally failed to capture because of its preoccupation with analytical dualism and obsession with one particular—especially rational, economic, and instrumental—dimension of human agency. It is by cultivating human agency of this holistic kind in association with others, Dewey is convinced, that citizens can form democratic will and make civil society ethical. In the ethical civil society, otherwise abstract democratic ideals of equality and freedom acquire their concrete and lived social meanings with full public significance, further vindicating the inextricable intertwinement between one's distinctive (not abstract) individuality and one's ineluctable sociality.[17] Dewey called an ethical civil society of this sort, the home of social individuality, "the Great Community," and distinguished it from the Great Society, which is nothing but a mechanical association contracted by self-interested individuals holding no common purpose, no social intelligence, and no democratic will to self-government.[18]

Dewey articulated his ethical ideal of democracy nearly a century ago, but in Dallmayr's view it remains an unfulfilled vision, a sort of prophesy. Yet while Dewey struggled for democracy in the emerging machine age when the public was being eclipsed by the administrative state equipped with technocratic bureaucracy, civic bonds were being helplessly eroded by the unconstrained pursuit of economic interests and democratic politics was being radically displaced by interest politics. The challenge for us is more complex and daunting under new "postmodern" social circumstances marked by pluralism, multiculturalism, and globalization. At this juncture, Dallmayr turns to Jacques Derrida's notion of "democracy to come" (*à venir*).

Derrida, inspired by Emmanuel Levinas, engaged in an extensive critique of modern sovereignty and democracy predicated on epistemic rationality. The problem with the modern notion of sovereignty, in Derrida's view, is that it is premised on the assumption of absolute political mastery when in fact our political life—both national and international—is defined by "unconditionality," radical indeterminacy and contingency defying any attempt to reify social reality and rejecting any kind of human control. Like what the notion of "*khora*" from Plato's *Timaeus* signifies, where the term means (or Derrida interprets it to mean) "a place before any place, a spacing before the world or cosmos or globe," democracy in our time is "the event to *come*" or *advent*.[19] In this postmodern understanding, democracy is "without [a fixed epistemic] concept, devoid of sameness and ipseity [identity]." Here the concept of democracy "remains free, like a disengaged clutch, in the free play of its indeterminacy."[20]

Dallmayr welcomes Derrida's deconstruction of modern sovereignty and celebrates his advocacy of "international juridico-political space" that can directly or unconditionally serve global human rights.[21] More germane to the current context, Dallmayr also embraces the notion (or anti-notion) of democracy whose concept is radically unconditioned, open to "what or who *comes* and comes to affect [who or what is already there],"[22] as it rejects all kinds of modern attempts to reify democracy as a fixed form without due consideration of its relational quality, its potential for perennial self-transformation. However, there remains a lingering question for Dallmayr: how can we be confident that what is expected to come is democracy rather than something vile and destructive?[23] Recall that for Dallmayr one of the greatest deficits in contemporary political science and theory is a near complete nonchalance toward the kind of human agency that Dewey valorized. Interestingly, what is critically missing in Derrida's postmodern redefinition of democracy is precisely Deweyan human agents who are capable of paving the way to the *coming* of democracy by removing various sorts of legal, social, economic, and political obstacles that are in the way of the well-being of the people, by educating active and intelligent citizenship, and by cultivating public judgment and democratic will to self-government—in other words, social individuals who co-participate in social inquiry. Thus, Dallmayr submits, "Without claiming self-mastery, and especially without pretending to master the coming event, human beings are still called upon to ready themselves through transformative praxis. Traditionally, transformative praxis is a synonym for the cultivation of virtues, a cultivation that—like piano playing—requires steady application and diligence."[24]

In the end, Dallmayr's democratic theory straddles Deweyan deliberative democracy and Derridean postmodern democracy.[25] And, quite surprisingly, Dallmayr finds the best manifestation of this theoretical amalgam in political theories advanced by such non-Western (i.e., non-European and non-North American) thinkers as Tzvetan Todorov and Enrique Dussel. What brings these two thinkers (as well as Dewey, I would add) together is the idea of a "political field" composed of mutually constitutive relationships among the people (*potentia*), political agencies in the public institutions (*potestas*), and orienting goal (well-being, *eudaimonia*).[26] None of these elements is featured as a fixed, self-same, and immutable embodiment; they are open to and co-variant with one another as each gains its distinctive social meaning and place in "the dynamic, precarious, and never static character" of the constellation that they together constitute and maintain.[27] As Dallmayr, by enlisting the insight of Dussel, puts it, "When *potestas* remains attentive to and in tune with the undergirding empowering spirit of *potentia*, we encounter the 'noble vocation of politics' a politics geared toward the well-being of the entire community."[28] Thus understood, the success of democratic politics consists of the relational quality between these key political constituents. Dallmayr's final conviction is that, as Derrida forcefully argues, this creative ethical constellation between the people, political agencies, and well-being should be not only the noble vocation of national politics but, with more increasing importance, that of global politics.[29]

Confucian Meritocracy

If relational democracy anticipates a democracy to come, Dallmayr's democratic theory is especially relevant to the political theory of Confucian democracy because in East Asia, Confucian democracy remains an ideal, something that never existed historically and that has yet to be realized. Indeed, in various writings, Dallmayr himself has advocated Confucian democracy as a specific form of ethical democracy best suited in East Asia.[30] But how should we conceive of Confucian democracy? In tackling this question, it is worth noting that an increasing number of Confucian political theorists have begun to advocate so-called "Confucian political meritocracy." Such advocates of Confucian meritocracy generally agree on three key points: that the theory (1) is perfectionist in nature, allowing the state to promote the comprehensive Confucian conception of the good life or certain Confucian virtues or values; (2) should be responsive to value pluralism; and (3) has some democratic components, elections in particular. That being said, there are different versions in the existing proposals of Confucian meritocracy, and they can be divided roughly into three distinctive normative positions: *maximalist Confucianism, meritocratic comprehensive Confucianism*, and *meritocratic political Confucianism*. I examine each of these positions briefly from the philosophical standpoint of ethical relationality and suggest that Confucian democracy of an ethical understanding offers the best way to realize a good public life in East Asia.

Maximalist Confucianism

By "maximalist Confucianism" I mean the attempt to revive Confucianism as maximally as possible, most tellingly by making it the state religion or dominant political ideology. Though scholars championing this position acknowledge some limited value of pluralism, certain human rights, and baseline moral equality, they either reject democratic values such as popular sovereignty, political equality, and the right to political participation wholesale, or they embrace democratic elections only for selecting the members of the lower house in the legislature that is constrained by the upper house(s) consisting of, among others, Confucian scholars.[31] In Dallmayr's terminology, maximalist Confucianism is chiefly focused on the *potestas* with a questionable concern with the common good as it *can* be determined singularly by Confucian political and cultural elites without citizen deliberation and participation, thereby putting a significant constraint on the civic and political *potential* of the people. Nor can the putative common good adequately accommodate the cultural, moral, and political interests of minority cultural groups given the prized political status of Confucianism as a state orthodoxy, which is likely to make the supposed common good a volatile source of political conflict and social disharmony. As Joseph Chan characterizes it, this is an extreme form of Confucian perfectionism, as it is strongly predisposed toward dangerous "political messianism" in the sense intended by Dallmayr.[32]

Meritocratic Comprehensive Confucianism

Meritocratic comprehensive Confucianism is most dominant in recent Confucian political theory. It shares the aim of political meritocracy with maximalist Confucianism, but it is not so ambitious as to elevate Confucianism to a dominant political position as a state religion or ideology. More specifically, meritocratic comprehensive Confucianism allows the state to be practically controlled by the nondemocratically selected upper house composed of the so-called "best and brightest" and authorizes it to actively promote the comprehensive Confucian conception of the good life or values that are integral to the Confucian "comprehensive doctrine" in the Rawlsian sense.[33] Though champions of this position disagree as to how best to select the most virtuous and the most intelligent (examination, recommendation, or meritocratic experiment), they generally agree that democratic authority must be significantly limited for the sake of the effective operation of political meritocracy. Although its perfectionist ambition is not as maximal or dangerous as that of maximal Confucianism, it is equally, even more explicitly, concentrated on the *potestas* of the political elites at the expense of the *potentia* of the people and pays little attention to the creative relationality between the two. Meritocratic comprehensive Confucianism does, to be fair, show a concern for the well-being of the people, but, like maximalist Confucianism, its focus is almost exclusively on the people's economic well-being and hardly on their potentiality for civic empowerment. Moreover, the putative common good that it aims for is likely to be determined unilaterally by the selective elites who are allegedly more virtuous than the ordinary people without the latter's participation or involvement. Elitist, undemocratic, and comprehensively Confucian, it is quite dubious that this position can genuinely respect the plurality of values in civil society.

Chan would judge meritocratic comprehensive Confucianism to be an equally extreme form of perfectionism, as he identifies any form of perfectionism affiliated with a comprehensive doctrine as "extreme,"[34] but it seems to me much more moderate than maximalist Confucianism. Nevertheless, even when it integrates a democratic element within its institutional structure, it still dismisses the ethical importance of relational democracy no less than does maximalist Confucianism.[35] When it does embrace democracy, this merely signifies "minimalist democracy," as Dallmayr calls it, because it is only election as a modus operandi to select political leaders (though significantly constrained by the members of the meritocratic upper house) that gets attention. Therefore, it is hardly surprising that when Confucian meritocrats attempt to go beyond liberal democracy, they tend to go beyond democracy in toto.[36]

Meritocratic Political Confucianism

By ascribing both maximalist Confucianism and meritocratic comprehensive Confucianism to extreme perfectionism, Chan distinguishes his normative Confucianism from them by calling it "moderate Confucian perfectionism." This is moderate in the sense that his theory's "Confucianism" is completely severed from any sort of comprehensive Confucianism.[37] Interestingly, though, Chan's moderate Confucian perfectionism largely agrees on all the meritocratic components, including bicameralism, proposed by meritocratic comprehensive Confucians. Like other Confucian meritocrats, Chan rejects political equality and the universal right to political participation (and many other *civic* virtues) while endorsing a meritocratic upper house. Also, distinguishing between the (institutional) *constituents* of democracy—mainly elections—and the (civic or social) *conditions* of democracy and emphasizing the former to the exclusion of the latter,[38] Chan, too, subscribes to the minimalist conception of democracy without grappling much with the ethical balance between *potentia*, *potestas*, and the well-being of the people.

The key difference between Chan and other Confucian meritocrats is that he reconstructs Confucianism in terms of a bundle of "items" encompassing some selected agency goods and prudential goods such as "valuable social relationships, practical wisdom and learning, sincerity, harmony, social and political trust and care, moral and personal autonomy, and economic sufficiency and self-responsibility" without affiliating them with the distinctive ethical and cultural way of life that Confucianism represents.[39] Deliberately separated from comprehensive (or ethical) Confucianism, Chan's Confucian perfectionism is *political* in the similar sense that Rawls calls his liberalism "political," distinguishing it from "ethical" liberalism of the kinds suggested by Joseph Raz and Ronald Dworkin.[40]

Compared with meritocratic comprehensive Confucianism, Chan's meritocratic political Confucianism seems to be more "moderate" in that the traits or goods it allows the state to promote can be compatible with a variety of comprehensive doctrines. But Chan's theory achieves its moderate character only by sacrificing the rich ethical potential for which Confucianism is best known. Focused on traditional Confucianism's monistic comprehensive nature and yet redressing it purely by a philosopher's fiat, Chan does not seem to do justice to Confucianism's inner potential to transform itself into a kind of (modern) Confucianism that extends ethical relationality, traditionally confined to five cardinal human relationships, to equal citizens,[41] as well as to a mutually empowering relationship between citizens and their political representatives. Nor does he allow the opportunity for Confucianism as a comprehensive moral ideal accompanied by relevant social practice to dialectically interact with other comprehensive doctrines in civil society, so that we can anticipate a new version of Confucianism as the product of such intercultural communication, which thereby incorporates multiplicity and becomes perennially open-ended. Contrary to Chan's strategy of persisting in a sanitized Confucianism undergirded by political meritocracy, Dallmayr would see the gist of the moderateness of Confucianism in its ethical capability for self-transformation and its openness to non-Confucian values and social practices, including democratic ones.

A Democracy to Come in East Asia

From Dallmayr's perspective, what Confucian meritocrats of all persuasions fatally gloss over is the Deweyan insight that a good public life is not so much something that can be socially engineered by a few political elites, however virtuous or able they may be, but something that grows in the course of creatively balancing the tension-ridden relationships between the people, political leaders, and the common good. Democracy is a good public life that emerges from such a complex balancing process. In its relational or ethical understanding, democracy is a complex, indeterminate, and open-ended process in which citizens engage with one another on equal and reciprocal terms; participate in self-government through various forms of authorization, public trust, and delegation; and arrive at the common good by producing common will and judgment.

Of course, there is no denying the paramount importance in politics of making sure that government works meritoriously and the common good is attained. Dallmayr's Deweyan argument, which I endorse wholeheartedly, is just that democracy is a distinctive constellation of ever-changing relationships in which political leaders work meritoriously in a way accountable to citizens, political power is exercised in a way justifiable to those citizens, and the common good is pursued in a way agreeable to citizens who subscribe to different conceptions of the good life. For Deweyans, Confucian democracy is a democracy of this sort—an ethical democracy, in other words—whose constitutive relationships make sense to citizens whose mores, civilities, social habits, and moral sentiments are still characteristically Confucian despite their subscriptions to diverse values, faiths, and beliefs as private individuals.[42] Following Dallmayr, I submit that this is a democracy *to come* in East Asia.

Notes

1. Stephen K. White, ed., *Life-World and Politics: Between Modernity and Postmodernity—Essays in Honor of Fred R. Dallmayr* (Notre Dame, IN: University of Notre Dame Press, 1990); Stephen F. Schneck, ed., *Letting Be: Fred Dallmayr's Cosmopolitan Vision* (Notre Dame, IN: University of Notre Dame Press, 2006); Farah Godrej, ed., *Fred Dallmayr: Critical Phenomenology, Cross-Cultural Theory, Cosmopolitanism* (London: Routledge, 2017).

2. See Fred R. Dallmayr, *Achieving Our World: Toward Global & Plural Democracy* (Lanham, MD: Rowman & Littlefield, 2001); *The Promise of Democracy: Political Agency and Transformation* (Albany, NY: State University of New York Press, 2010); *Democracy to Come: Politics as Relational Praxis* (New York: Oxford University Press, 2017).

3. Dallmayr, *Democracy to Come*, 26–29.

4. Ibid., 52.

5. Ibid., 3, 27–28. Also see Dallmayr, *The Promise of Democracy*, 170–72.

6. Dallmayr, *Democracy to Come*, 5.

7. Ibid., 2, 4.

8. Ibid., 53–55.

9. Ibid., 7–9, 57–59.

10. Ibid., 9.

11. In Dallmayr's view, this ideal is best illuminated in Gandhi's idea of self-rule (*swaraj*), which is predicated on related values of nonviolence (*ahimsa*) and truth-force (*satyagraha*). See Dallmayr, *Democracy to Come*, chap. 6 ("Gandhi for Today: Self-Rule, Nonviolence, and Struggle for Justice") and "Political Self-Rule: Gandhi and the Future of Democracy," in *Being in the World: Dialogue and Cosmopolis* (Lexington: University Press of Kentucky, 2013), 151–61.

12. For Dallmayr's philosophical explorations of the good life in today's multicultural and cosmopolitan context, see *In Search of the Good Life: A Pedagogy for Troubled Times* (Lexington: University Press of Kentucky, 2007).

13. Dallmayr, *Democracy to Come*, 140.

14. Notice, though, that Dallmayr does not employ "this-worldly transcendentalism" to present his holistic and ethical notion of religion. For the conceptualization of religion in terms of "this-worldly transcendentalism," see S. N. Eisenstadt, "This

Worldly Transcendentalism and the Structuring of the World: Weber's 'Religion of China' and the Format of Chinese History and Civilization," *Journal of Developing Societies* 1 (1985): 168–86. For Dallmayr's ethical interpretation of Hegel's idea of civil society, see *The Promise of Democracy*, chap. 2 ("Hegel for Our Time: Negativity and Democratic Ethos"). On the important Hegelian (and Tocquevillian) legacies in Max Weber's idea of civil society, see Sung Ho Kim, *Max Weber's Politics of Civil Society* (Cambridge: Cambridge University Press, 2004). For an insightful survey of the modern idea of civil society with a special focus on its ethical dimension, see Adam B. Seligman, *The Idea of Civil Society* (Princeton: Princeton University Press, 1992).

15. Fred Dallmayr, "Democratic Action and Experience: Dewey's "Holistic" Pragmatism," in *The Promise of Democracy*, 45–48.

16. Ibid., 48.

17. Ibid., 58.

18. See John Dewey, *The Public and Its Problems* (Athens, OH: Swallow Press, 1954).

19. Dallmayr, *Democracy to Come*, 37; "Jacques Derrida's Legacy: Democracy to Come," in *The Promise of Democracy*, 131.

20. Jacques Derrida, *Rogues: Two Essays on Reason*, trans. Pasacle-Anne Brault and Michael Naas (Stanford, CA: Stanford University Press, 2005); reprinted in Dallmayr, *Democracy to Come*, 37.

21. Dallmayr, *Democracy to Come*, 38.

22. Ibid., 37.

23. Ibid., 39.

24. Dallmayr, "Jacques Derrida's Legacy," 134.

25. Dallmayr suggests a certain compatibility between deliberative democracy and Derrida's "apophatic" democracy with two requirements that the former be open to (1) "new possibilities, new paradigms and horizons of thought" and (2) hermeneutics (*Democracy to Come*, 40). As Dallmayr seems to agree, unlike the rationalist deliberative democracy advocated by Amy Gutmann and Dennis Thompson, Deweyan deliberative democracy is largely immune to these two challenges.

26. Dallmayr, *Democracy to Come*, 16.

27. Ibid., 19.

28. Ibid., 76.

29. See Fred R. Dallmayr, "Global Governance and Cultural Diversity: Toward a Cosmopolitan Democracy," in *Achieving Our World*, 35–50.

30. For my critique of his vision of Confucian democracy, see Sungmoon Kim, "Fred Dallmayr's Postmodern Vision of Confucian Democracy: A Critical Examination," *Asian Philosophy* 28, no. 1 (2018): 35–54.

31. See Jiang Qing, *A Confucian Constitutional Order: How China's Ancient Past Can Shape Its Political Future*, ed. Daniel A. Bell and Ruiping Fan, trans. Edmund Ryden (Princeton: Princeton University Press, 2012).

32. Joseph Chan, "On Legitimacy of Confucian Constitutionalism," in *A Confucian Constitutional Order*, 99–112.

33. Ruiping Fan, *Reconstructionist Confucianism: Rethinking Morality after the West* (Dordrecht: Springer, 2010); Chenyang Li, "Equality and Inequality in Confucianism," *Dao* 11 (2012): 295–313; Tongdong Bai, "A Mencian Version of Limited Democracy," *Res Publica* 14 (2008): 19–34; Daniel A. Bell, *Beyond Liberal Democracy: Political Thinking for an East Asian Context* (Princeton: Princeton University Press, 2008). Though in his recent book Bell is no longer committed to bicameralism, all remaining components of meritocratic comprehensive Confucianism discussed in this section apply to his new theory of political meritocracy. See Daniel A. Bell, *The China Model: Political Meritocracy and the Limits of Democracy* (Princeton: Princeton University Press, 2015).

34. See Joseph Chan, "Legitimacy, Unanimity, and Perfectionism," *Philosophy and Public Affairs* 29 (2000): 5–42.

35. Therefore, while criticizing Jiang's maximal Confucianism, Dallmayr voices a certain worry toward its "moderate" critics, including Chenyang Li, Tongdong Bai, and Joseph Chan. See Dallmayr, *Democracy to Come*, chap. 5.

36. On this very ground, Dallmayr criticizes Bell's political proposal. See Fred Dallmayr, "Exiting Liberal Democracy: Bell and Confucian Thought," *Philosophy East and West* 59 (2009): 524–30.

37. Joseph Chan, *Confucian Perfectionism: A Political Philosophy for Modern Times* (Princeton: Princeton University Press, 2014).

38. On this distinction and for my critique, see Sungmoon Kim, *Confucian Democracy in East Asia: Theory and Practice* (New York: Cambridge University Press, 2014), 82–86.

39. Chan, *Confucian Perfectionism*, 203–4.

40. John Rawls, *Political Liberalism* (New York: Columbia University Press, 1993). For a critical examination of Chan's meritocratic political Confucianism, see Sungmoon Kim, *Public Reason Confucianism: Democratic Perfectionism and Constitutionalism in East Asia* (New York: Cambridge University Press, 2016), chap. 1.

41. For this suggestion, see Fred Dallmayr, "Confucianism and the Public Sphere: Five Relationships Plus One?," in *The Politics of Affective Relations: East Asia and Beyond* (Lanham, MD: Lexington Books, 2004), 41–59; and Sungmoon Kim, "Beyond Liberal Civil Society: Confucian Familism and Relational Strangership," *Philosophy East and West* 60, no. 4 (2010): 476–98.

42. Elsewhere, though, I argue that a Deweyan democrat cannot afford to gloss over the instrumental value of formal democratic institutions and procedures as well because of the critical importance of the legitimate and effective coordination of complex social interactions among citizens under the fact of pluralism. See Sungmoon Kim, "Pragmatic Confucian Democracy: Rethinking the Value of Democracy in East Asia," *Journal of Politics* 79, no. 1 (2017): 237–49. Note, however, that in drawing attention to democracy's institutional and instrumental value,

I do not suggest a minimalist understanding of democracy; rather I explore a way to integrate instrumental and intrinsic values of democracy into a single democratic political theory from a Deweyan perspective, with full attention to two inseparable dimensions of democracy as a political system *and* as a way of life.

Chapter 4

Toward a Mega-Humanism

Confucian Triadic Harmony for the Anthropocene

CHENYANG LI

> . . . nature is not just an "environment," but is part of us and penetrates into our being. What this penetration brings into view is the broader web of things, the infinitely rich and varied source of all beings—a source for which we have no definition or agreed upon name but which gratitude impels us to cherish and to venerate.
>
> —Dallmayr 2017: 89

Humanism as a philosophy takes humanity as the foundation of value configuration; it places paramount value on human beings as its point of departure. Humanism in this broad sense hardly needs to be promoted today. As Charles Taylor has famously characterized, we live in a "secular age." In today's largely disenchanted world, humanity is already placed at the center of the universe, for better or for worse. Even the vast majority of the religious population openly or tacitly subscribes to some form of humanism. We live in a "new epoch," however. A new epoch calls for a new form of humanism. In this chapter, I argue first that, as we develop a new humanism that promotes well-being, prosperity, and harmony for

---

Research for this chapter was financially supported by a SSRC grant from Singapore's Ministry of Education (MOE2016-SSRTG-0007).

all, two defining themes must be integrated. The first is that this new humanism must reflect our response to the challenge of the Anthropocene. A new humanism is already outdated if it fails to understand fully and to address effectively today's environmental challenges (and more). The epoch of the Anthropocene calls for a "mega-humanism." The second theme is that it must have cultural roots. A humanism, even though with a universal character, is without vitality if it is cut off from cultural traditions. This chapter presents a Confucian perspective on a new humanism that would integrate the two essential themes.

The Anthropocene announces that the human species is now the dominant force in shaping the Earth. As observed by Will Steffen and his colleagues, the "human imprint on the global environment now rivals some of the great forces of Nature in its impact on the Earth system."[1] They claim, in addition to the carbon cycle as manifested in climate change, that human beings now are:

(1) significantly altering several other biogeochemical, or element cycles, such as nitrogen, phosphorus and sulphur, that are fundamental to life on the Earth;

(2) strongly modifying the terrestrial water cycle by intercepting river flow from uplands to the sea and, through land-cover change, altering the water vapor flow from the land to the atmosphere; and

(3) likely driving the sixth major extinction event in Earth history.[2] Steffen and his colleagues write that, "[t]aken together, these trends are strong evidence that humankind, our own species, has become so large and active that it now rivals some of the great forces of Nature in its impact on the functioning of the Earth system."[3] We should note that the situation is not about merely an expansion of the human impact on nature. It signifies not only a quantitative but a *qualitative* shift in that impact.

Scientists have not reached an agreement on the appropriateness of the concept of a new epoch and, if appropriate, on its starting point. The disagreements, however, are about stratigraphy rather than about the fact of amplified human impact on nature.[4] There is little doubt that human beings have become a global geophysical force and are capable of fundamentally transforming the Earth. As 1995 Nobel Laureate Paul J. Crutzen and his coauthor, C. Schwägerl, put it, "It's no longer us against 'Nature.' Instead, it's we who decide what nature is and what it will be."[5] The Anthropocene reflects a fundamental fact of our time. We are in an epoch that is profoundly different from previous times. While almost all previous versions of humanism were developed for the Holocene, they are behind us now. In our epoch, any form of meaningful humanism must take into account the decisive impact of human activities on the environment and on ourselves.

The idea of the Anthropocene is not only about environmental issues; it is for a new geologic epoch. Moreover, it is *a new worldview, a new philosophy*. Morally speaking, increased human impact comes with increased responsibility. Not only are pre-humanistic views that rely exclusively on divine protection no longer viable, but extreme anthropocentric views that take all non-human existents merely in their instrumental values to serve narrowly defined human interests have also become senseless. Conversely, the central idea of the Anthropocene flies in the face of extreme biocentric or deep-ecological views that place humanity at the level of a mere thing among all other things (or a mere species among other species) in the world. A new humanism appropriate for the Anthropocene must guard itself on both fronts. Humanity is not merely an ordinary piece in the puzzle of mapping the universe, nor is it the absolute center. A new humanism needs to find its balance in view of the Anthropocene.

Furthermore, no form of humanism is viable without cultural roots. The report of UNESCO's 2011 "High Panel on Peace and Dialogue among Cultures" on "Towards a new humanism and reconciled globalization" declared that the purpose of a new humanism is to "create a climate of empathy, belonging and understanding, along with the idea that progress with respect to human rights is never definitive and requires a constant effort of adaptation to the challenges of modernity."[6] This understanding of the new humanism emphasizes a common humanity beyond particular cultural traditions, with a goal of building "a single human community." Such a goal is worthwhile and admirable. However, such a vision for a humanism has yet to take into account the new epoch of the Anthropocene. As such, it would have been outdated even before it was constructed.

A single human community at the global level cannot exist without cultural foundations, for at least three reasons. First, the full realization of the individual requires local communities as well as a global human community. We can travel around the world, but ultimately we need a home to return to. Any form of a viable new humanism must have its cultural roots. Second, a new humanism cannot be developed successfully without using various cultural resources. A viable new philosophy does not appear suddenly in a vacuum. It has to be established on previous explorations, of both success and failure. Third and finally, as we develop a new world philosophy of humanism, we cannot ignore the very fact that, even considering world secularization, the vast majority of the world's population is nevertheless religious. The "disenchanted world" of our "secular age" is not totally disenchanted. Religion is at the center of most world cultural traditions. Western humanism since early on, especially during the Renaissance, has had an intricate relationship with the Christian church. We cannot ask the world population to leave their gods or spiritualities behind to embrace a new humanism. For these and other reasons, a viable and effective new humanism must be rooted deeply in cultural traditions of the world.

Therefore, if successful, we should have a common new humanism that can be articulated and justified from various cultural perspectives. This new humanism does not depend on the hegemony of any single cultural tradition, nor does anyone have to embrace a particular cultural tradition or all cultures to come on board. Yet this new humanism does rely on a foundation provided collectively by world cultures. Perhaps John Rawls's proposal of "overlapping consensus" is relevant here. Rawls is concerned with the issue of how a multicultural society can produce public reason to serve as the foundation for justice for all. He proposes that a multicultural society where people subscribe to fundamentally different "comprehensive doctrines" may nevertheless agree on principles of justice that are justified respectively in the metaphysics of each cultural tradition. He writes, "Comprehensive doctrines of all kinds—religious, philosophical, and moral—belong to what we may call the 'background culture' of civil society. This is the culture of the social, not political."[7] Rawls is concerned with the political in society. For political arrangements, people can collaborate without sharing the same comprehensive doctrine in their background culture.

Our challenge of establishing a new humanism goes deeper than the political. In an important sense, humanism is a cultural tradition. But it is a cultural tradition that does not belong exclusively to any particular historical cultural tradition. It can be shared by people of different comprehensive doctrines. Our new humanism is not only a moral philosophy; it is also a metaphysical theory. Such a metaphysical theory can be a fundamental philosophy to be shared by people of varied cultural traditions. People of Hindu traditions, for example, can subscribe and contribute to such a humanism without having to accept the Confucian philosophy of triadic harmony; the rich Vedic cultural traditions can provide adequate resources in shaping and in support of the humanism of the Anthropocene. Therefore, in a significant way, my proposal goes one step further than Rawls in that it requires us to tap into the comprehensive doctrines of various cultural traditions.

The new humanism must resonate with various cultural traditions and gather synergy from every direction. Of course, such a new humanism is not yet available in a ready-made, completed form within any cultural tradition. It has to be generated. Its generation involves a two-way process. On the one hand, various cultural traditions provide resources for the construction of a new humanism. On the other hand, this process also provides opportunities for the self-examination of cultural traditions, for them to adjust, reform, and rearticulate their value configurations.[8] Advocates of the new humanism must engage themselves on both fronts to advance such a noble cause.

I believe, on both accounts of the Anthropocene and cultural roots, Confucian philosophy has important resources to contribute to a new humanism. At the center of Confucian philosophy is the ideal of harmony. Over a long history, this notion has been interpreted and misinterpreted in various ways. Its contemporary encounters in China have added at least as much to its misfortune as to its fortune. It is therefore worthwhile to reiterate that, philosophically, Confucian harmony is not mere agreement, conformity, or even superficial stability. It is instead a dynamic generative process in which the prospect of every party getting its due is optimized. Harmony can be achieved at various levels of existence, in an individual, a group, society, and the entire world.[9]

At its fundamental level is the Confucian holistic philosophy of the triadic harmony of heaven, earth, and humanity. Together these three elements form a unity of grand harmony. In the Confucian scheme of harmony, each of these three has its proper role and function; each promotes, and is promoted by, the others; and each contributes to the overall harmony of the universe. This ideal of the unity of heaven, earth, and humanity can be traced back to the Confucian classic *Book of Change*. The *Xici Commentary* of the text states, "There is the way of heaven; there is the way of earth; and there is the way of humanity."[10] These three ways are not separate, with each on its own path; rather, they work together and provide the framework for cosmic harmony. The idea is to integrate these elements (*jian san cai* 兼三才) without collapsing them into one single thing. This view is not anthropocentric because it does not hold that only humanity has intrinsic worth; nor does it claim that all other things in the world exist merely to serve human needs. Confucian harmony philosophy accords everything its own worth and recognizes its legitimate place in the universe. It is not antihumanistic either because it rejects the view that in the biotic community humans merely hold a status equal to nonhuman members. It gives humanity a special place in the universe. The mission of humanity is to work with heaven and earth to achieve harmony in the world. We can label this Confucian notion of harmony "triadic harmony."[11]

Within this triadic harmony of heaven, earth, and humanity, "earth" stands for Mother Earth, on which we humans depend for our lives; the earth is a living entity with a life of its own. "Humanity" is more than a mere biological species, but the humankind with moral consciousness. In this view, human beings are not just one of numerous species on earth; we are a unique kind of being, endowed not only with superior capacities but also with a special mission to contribute in a unique way toward the harmony of the cosmos. Xunzi, a key Confucian thinker during the classic period, compared human beings with other things in the world and argued for the fundamental distinction of humanity:

> Water and fire have vital energy (*qi* 氣), but not life (*sheng* 生); plants and trees have life, but no consciousness (*zhi* 知); birds and beasts have consciousness, but no sense of appropriateness/rightness (*yi* 義). Humans have vital energy, life, consciousness, and, in addition, a sense of appropriateness/rightness. This is why humans are the most valuable beings under the heaven.[12]

Because only human beings are capable of moral construction and because only through moral construction can the world become harmonious, it follows that humanity is valuable in a unique way.

The meanings of "heaven" are complex. It has both enchanted and disenchanted meanings. The Chinese philosopher Fung Yulan 冯友兰 found that the idea of heaven, "*tian* 天," has at least five meanings. They are, 1, as the sky; 2, as the personified god; 3, as unavoidable fate; 4, as the natural course of the world; 5, as moral reason.[13] In the context of heaven-earth-humanity, heaven can be taken to mean different things by Confucians of various streams. To philosophers like Tu Weiming, "heaven" means a force that is "omnipresent and omniscient," or divine, a force that holds the ultimate meaning of the world.[14] Understood in this way, heaven somewhat resembles "God" in monotheist traditions. It is the ultimate source of morality or legitimacy. The *Zhongyong* states that "what is endowed by heaven is human nature 天命之谓性." Mencius also commented that heaven is about to confer a great responsibility on him ("this man") 天将降大任于斯人也 (*Mencius* 6B). Yet even with this understanding, heaven is not a personified God as found in monotheist traditions. While heaven is a leading creative force of the universe, it is not the only creative force. In the Confucian conception of the triadic harmony, heaven is a co-creator with earth and humanity.

For secular Confucians, "heaven" can mean the universe beyond earth, though it may be laden with spirituality. The classic Confucian thinker Xunzi took "*tian*" largely to mean the natural course of things. He included the universe beyond earth as part of "*tian*." For instance, Xunzi wrote, "What is the relation of order and chaos to *tian*? I say: the revolutions of the sun and moon and the stars and celestial points that mark off the divisions of time by which the calendar is calculated were the same in the time of [the sage-king] Yu as in the time of [the despot] Jie."[15] And "[o]f the things of *tian*, none is brighter than the sun and moon; of the things of the earth, none is as bright as fire and water."[16] In the sense used above, "*tian*" stands for what is above the earth in the universe. As humans extend our capacity to exert impact into space, and colonization of the space is now a real possibility,[17] this part of the triadic structure should be taken more seriously than ever before. With this conception of triadic harmony, we can allow heaven to be open to different interpretations, accommodating both secular Confucians and Confucians with a religious orientation.

In the Confucian triadic conception of harmony, while humanity is not the center of the world, it is more than just one member of the animal kingdom. Humanity is a member of the biotic community, but it is not a member with equal status to other members because it has the capacity to transform the world. At the risk of being overly simplistic, I would say that in the Confucian view, humanity bears at least a third of the weight in this triadic cosmos. Thus, a Confucian holistic philosophy may assign humanity a status in the universe that is considerably higher than is found in the holistic sustainability philosophies developed in the West, such as Land Ethics and Deep Ecology.

The *Wenyan Commentary* of the *Book of Change* spells out that the unity of humanity, heaven, and earth implies that, when humanity acts prior to heaven, heaven does not go to the contrary.[18] The *Zhongyong* states that heaven and earth "attain" their proper order "when equilibrium and harmony are realized to the highest degree."[19] Humanity is of course an active force in realizing equilibrium and harmony. Rather than immersing humanity into heaven, both texts recognize a leading role for humanity in the Triad. In the Confucian system, all three components are required to generate and maintain harmony in the cosmos. Without the thriving earth, human beings cannot survive. Without heaven, either the world would lose its spiritual and moral roots (in an enchanted sense) or the earth could not continue, as it is part of the cosmos (in a disenchanted sense). Finally, without humanity, the world would be hollow in meaning, and there would be no conscious agency to actively engage and promote harmony in the cosmos. Confucians see the fundamental value of humanity in its constructing and promoting the Way (*dao*), which is a unique human capacity.

The notion of triadic harmony is a metaphysical view in the sense that it presents a foundational framework for the deep relationships between heaven, earth, and humanity. According to this notion, the cosmos is not monopolized by any one party. Nor is humanity the center of the cosmos. Heaven and earth are not there just to provide resources for human consumption. Each has its own purpose and worth. Humanity is not part of heaven or earth; it is their guardian and partner. Humanity as an active and powerful participant in the triadic harmony has a responsibility to do its share in promoting and maintaining such a harmony.

The Confucian philosophy of triadic harmony may be illustrated in terms of three principles. The first principle is the humanity principle, namely that humanity represents the quintessence of the myriad things between earth and heaven and that it bears an inescapable responsibility to play an active role in harmonizing the world. Second, the earth principle, according to which the earth is not merely a source of resources. Earth has its own life and its own place in the cosmos. It retains its own dignity. Third and finally is the heaven principle. In the enchanted Confucian world, heaven serves as the ultimate source of morality. In the disenchanted Confucian world, heaven represents all spheres beyond earth. It refers mainly to all in space beyond earth, and it provides the environment in which earth and humanity exist. The heaven principle in the disenchanted sense requires humanity to respect the dignity of space and not to use it for narrowly defined human or earthly purposes. In the age of the Anthropocene, the heaven principle becomes even more important, as it has implications for what we humans should and should not do with respect to space.

Tu Weiming has called the Confucian view "anthropocosmic."[20] Such a view is not theocentric ("God-centered" or "Heaven-centered") or anthropocentric, but presents an "anthropocosmic unity." The concept of the Anthropocene has provided us with a powerful idea about a significantly elevated role for humanity in the cosmos. It gives us a pressing reason to revisit and take seriously the Confucian triadic philosophy of heaven-earth-humanity. By giving a significant creative role to humanity, the threefold Confucian principle of heaven-earth-humanity has anticipated a philosophy for the Anthropocene. In the Confucian view, the Anthropocene does not amount to the replacement of an omnipotent God by humanity. In the Anthropocene, rather than monopolizing the rest of the world, humanity still dances with it (or with "heaven and earth"), even though the role of humanity has become more and more active and decisive. This is consistent with the Confucian vision. Given its magnificent status in the triad, humanity is capable of fundamentally transforming the world. We can change the world to serve our narrowly perceived interests or transform it toward the ideal of grand harmony. We want the latter. Toward that end, we need a new humanism as a guiding philosophy.

The Anthropocene has made it possible and necessary to develop an entirely new form of humanism, one that is arguably qualitatively different from all previous versions. Following Tu Weiming's use of "anthropocosmic" in characterizing Confucianism, we can call this new humanism "anthropocosmicism." As our new humanism is not meant to be confined to any single cultural tradition, Confucian or otherwise, perhaps we should avoid making too close a connection to Confucianism. After all, the rearticulated Confucian triadic harmony of heaven-earth-humanity is meant to contribute to the construction of a new humanism accessible to other cultural traditions, rather than being the new humanism itself. For this reason and because of the tremendous capacity and potency accorded to humanity in this philosophy, we can call it a "mega-humanism."[21]

The new humanism is "mega" in the sense that, in it, humanity possesses overwhelming power over nature to either destroy it or protect it. It is without any doubt a strong humanism. The "mega" is not a hyperexaggeration of the unique value of humanity; nor is it an intoxicated obsession with human narcissism. The "mega" stands for a super-vision, a powerful vantage point, from which humanity can reunderstand and reposition itself in such a way that enables it to remake the world. The mega-humanism is therefore an entirely new humanism unlike anything before it. In it, humanity is not the only intrinsic value. In comparison with traditional anthropocentric humanisms, mega-humanism places not only value but also responsibility on humanity. The role of humanity in this mega-humanism, though extremely powerful, must be properly envisioned.

In *Analects* 15.29, Confucius famously said, "it is the capacity of humanity to promote the Dao, it is not for the Dao to promote humanity 人能弘道，非道弘人。"[22] In such a Confucian view, the super-capacity of humanity places responsibility rather than entitlement on humanity. If the Confucian philosophy of the triadic harmony of heaven-earth-humanity has been a mere vision in the past two millennia, the Anthropocene has made it more real than ever. The Anthropocene brings us to a time to transform this age-old Confucian philosophy into a new humanism with true practical significance. It brings us to the real possibility of a mega-humanism. Under this new humanism, human beings are not only charged with the responsibility but also the power to harmonize with nature. Though this mega-humanism can be supported by and from the Confucian philosophy of triadic harmony, it is not exclusively Confucian. Proponents of the mega-humanism do not have to accept an entire Confucian metaphysic to embrace such a new humanism. A new humanism will be more viable if its proponents can find its philosophical foundations in their respective cultural traditions.

Over many decades, Dallmayr's philosophical inquiry has been concerned with social justice and cultural diversity. In one of his most recent books, *Return to Nature? An Ecological Counterhistory*, Dallmayr calls for a resurgence of "a chastened humanism" or "a differentiated holism." Against the dominant strand of modern Western thought in which "nature survived only as an exile or resident alien,"[23] Dallmayr advocates a view of wholeness or a holistic relationship between "humanity" and nature and a complex mode of interdependence among humans, nature, and the world in the direction of the "cosmotheandric" perspective articulated by Raimon Panikkar.[24] Characteristically for Dallmayr, developing such a view requires us to draw on different resources and cultural traditions. This chapter answers Dallmayr's call by making a contribution to developing such a new humanism from a Confucian perspective.

Notes

1. Will Steffen, Jacques Grinevald, Paul Crutzen, John McNeill, "The Anthropocene: conceptual and historical perspectives," *Philosophical Transactions of the Royal Society A: Mathematical, Physical & Engineering Sciences* 369 (2011): 842–67.

2. The Earth has endured five major extinctions. The first major extinction was probably caused by climate change approximately 440 million years ago, and

it wiped out about 25 percent of the families of marine life (there was no or little other land life-form). The second major extinction was around 370 million years ago, with 19 percent of families lost. The third major extinction took place about 245 million years ago, and 54 percent of families disappeared. The fourth extinction was approximately 210 million years ago. It wiped out 23 percent of families. The fifth major extinction was about 65 million years ago and resulted in the loss of 17 percent of families of life-forms, including the remaining terrestrial dinosaurs. For more information, see http://www.actionbioscience.org/evolution/eldredge2.html. For a discussion of the sixth extinction, see Elizabeth Kolbert, *The Sixth Extinction* (London: Bloomsbury, 2014).

    3. See their appendix for more information.

    4. See Richard Monastersky, "Anthropocene: The Human Age," *Nature* 519, no. 7542 (2015).

    5. P. J. Crutzen and C. Schwägerl, "Living in the Anthropocene: Toward a New Global Ethos," *Yale Environment 360*, January 24, 2011, http://e360.yale.edu/feature/living_in_the_anthropocene_toward_ a_new_global_ethos/2363/.

    6. *The UNESCO Courier*, October–December 2011, 2.

    7. John Rawls, *Political Liberalism* (New York: Columbia University Press, 1996), 14.

    8. For more discussion of value configuration, see my "Cultural Configurations of Values," *World Affairs: the Journal of International Issues* XII, no. 2 (2008): 28–49.

    9. For a detailed account of the Confucian philosophy of harmony, see my *The Confucian Philosophy of Harmony* (London/New York: Routledge, 2014).

    10. *Thirteen Classics with Commentaries* ("*TTC*")《十三經注疏》(Beijing: Zhongguo Shuju, 1985), 90; cf. Richard Wilhelm and Cary F. Baynes, *The I Ching or Book of Changes* (Princeton: Princeton University Press, 1967), 351–52.

    11. See Chenyang Li (2014) as in Note 9.

    12. John Knoblock, trans., *Xunzi: A Translation and Study of the Complete Works*, vol. II, books 7–16/17–32 (Stanford: Stanford University Press, 1990/1994) (*Xunzi* 9.16a; Knoblock: 103–4).

    13. Fung, Yulan《中國哲學史》*A History of Chinese Philosophy* (Beijing: Zhonghua Shuju, 1961), 55.

    14. Tu Weiming, "An 'Anthropocosmic' Perspective on Creativity," in *Dialogue of Philosophies, Religions and Civilizations in the Era of Globalization: Chinese Philosophical Studies, XXV*, ed. Zhao Dunhua (Washington, DC: Council for Research in Values and Philosophy, 2007), 147. For more discussion of the concept of "heaven," see my "Is the Confucian Concept of 'Heaven' Still Relevant Today?," in Zhao, *Dialogue of Philosophies, Religions, and Civilizations*, 161–64.

    15. *Xunzi* 17.6; Knoblock 1994, 17; modified.

    16. *Xunzi* 17.14; Knoblock 1994, 20.

    17. The *New York Post* reported that more than 100,000 people have applied to take a one-way trip to Mars to colonize the Red Planet; see "More Than 100,000

Apply for Mission to Colonize Mars in 2022; 40 Picked Will Never Return," *New York Post*, August 10, 2013, http://nypost.com/2013/08/10/more-than-100000-apply-for-mission-to-colonize-mars-in-2022-40-picked-will-never-return/.

18. *TTC* 17; cf. Wilhelm and Baynes: 382–83.

19. Chan Wing-tsit, *A Source Book in Chinese Philosophy* (Princeton: Princeton University Press, 1963), 98.

20. Tu, "An 'Anthropocosmic' Perspective on Creativity," op. cit.

21. The term "mega-humanism" has been used by Rudi Roth to describe a universal belief system of a post-theistic era after the end of the Abrahamic religions in which natural humanistic beliefs have replaced traditional religious beliefs *After God??: A New Approach for Secular Humanism* by Alan Gordon. The mega-humanism expounded in this chapter, however, calls for revisiting and reviving the traditional philosophy of Confucian triadic harmony and similar world traditions in contributing to the making of a mega-humanism.

22. I read 能 as capacity rather than merely as "can."

23. Fred Dallmayr, *Return to Nature? An Ecological Counterhistory*, Lexington, KY: The University of Kentucky Press, 2011, xi.

24. Ibid., 178.

Chapter 5

The Problem of Secularism

Rawls, Taylor, and Dallmayr

RONALD BEINER

I

As is abundantly evident in the work of Fred Dallmayr, political philosophy is an essentially dialogical enterprise. The theorist endeavors to put him- or herself in dialogue with thinkers who engage in the most ambitious reflection on human affairs and human experience, and endeavors to put such thinkers in dialogue with one another. In this chapter, I pursue this kind of dialogical exercise with three leading philosophers of our time—John Rawls, Charles Taylor, and Fred Dallmayr—in relation to a theme that has engaged theorists throughout the whole modern theory tradition, namely the problem of how to regulate the relationship between religion and politics in a normatively appropriate way.

A universal commitment to a secularist conception of political community is far from being a given in contemporary liberal societies, and in some ways we seem to be receding from that vision rather than moving closer to it—a situation captured in the fact that many increasingly refer to our current dispensation as a "post-secular" one. An essay from the *The Atlantic* in 2017 cites a Public Policy Polling study according to which Republicans, by an astonishing two-to-one majority, "support establishing Christianity as the national religion."[1] This in a society whose Founders were committed Lockean secularists and where the Constitution entrenches an inviolable separation of church and state. President Donald Trump, unlike his predecessors Jimmy Carter and George W. Bush, is not a born-again Christian, yet he would have won neither the Republican nomination nor the presidency without the committed support of countless right-wing evangelicals. His vice president, Mike Pence, is, politically, a theocrat (in the sense that he believes that national policy should be at the service of faith). Trump possesses not a particle of piety, nor is it credible that millions of the evangelical Christians who voted for him think otherwise. Still, according to the *Washington Post*, he has an "evangelical advisor," Robert Jeffress, who assures his followers that if Trumpian rhetoric or Trumpian foreign policy decisions lead the United States into World War III, the president has divine sanction for doing so: "In the case of North Korea, God has given Trump authority to take out Kim Jong-un."[2] As these remarks indicate, theocratic politics is alive and well in the contemporary United States.[3]

A secular regime is one whose members are given sufficient breathing space vis-à-vis religion that the political agenda is not subject to compulsory dictation on the part of religious authorities, and citizens can conduct their deliberations about political matters in a distinctively political (citizen-to-citizen) idiom. We have a civic (not a moral) duty not to express contempt for the sincerely held beliefs of our fellow citizens.[4] We have no choice but to take our fellow citizens as we find them and to give them civic space to communicate their political opinions in a manner corresponding to their actual beliefs. There is some tension between the two sides of this issue: letting people give expression to their actual beliefs, and not allowing those beliefs to be leveraged on behalf of indefensible power and authority. Bridging this tension is something we're able to pull off politically through the kinds of *compromises* familiar to liberal democracies. We don't bar Mitt Romney from the political arena just because he's a former bishop of the Mormon Church[5] and may have strange ideas of how God revealed Himself and what He expects of us. But neither do we tolerate the idea of a Mormon bishop becoming U.S. president as a prelude to instituting a Mormon theocracy. That's the liberal compromise, and no one genuinely committed to liberal secularism would countenance rejecting either side.

One view of the relationship between religion and citizenship is that religionists should be disciplined to express themselves in ways that steer clear of philosophically controversial "comprehensive doctrines." This is the Rawlsian idea of "political liberalism" in its simplest form.[6] Rawls wants a political domestication of religion without presenting it as such or suggesting any kind of singling out of religion for special treatment. So he proscribes *all* comprehensive doctrines, whether secular or religious, in the public sphere. All comprehensive doctrines are in principle "sectarian" and therefore cannot be appealed to in underwriting a properly liberal regime. Hence (despite the paradox), it is illegitimate to appeal to a liberal philosophy of life in founding a liberal polity. If Catholics can't legitimately found the state on a Catholic view of life (because its laws and policies will also apply to *Protestant* co-citizens), and if Protestants can't found the state on a Protestant view of life (because its laws and policies will apply to *Catholic* co-citizens), then the conclusion might seem equally compelling that one *also* cannot found the state on a *liberal-secular* philosophy of life, because (again) those who don't subscribe to this philosophy of life will be bound by its laws and policies. Political liberalism claims to solve this problem by subjecting all comprehensive doctrines, whether religious or secular, to the test of public reason.[7]

I reject that Rawlsian view. One has to take fellow citizens as one finds them and allow them to articulate themselves politically in a way that actually expresses who they conceive themselves to be. Rawls's attempted ban on comprehensive doctrines in the political sphere is misguided, not just because it will be applied in ways that are necessarily non-neutral (hence defeating what Rawls intended), but also because no one can properly be expected to check his or her existential commitments at the doorstep when he or she enters the sphere of civic life. How can we not find very odd a political philosophy that demands that we drive a wedge between our identity as human beings and our identity as citizens? A better doctrine, in my view, is to say that *the illegitimacy of theocratic politics is an entailment of a strong doctrine of citizenship*. There's a sense in which Rawls is saying something quite similar, but his ban on comprehensive doctrines within the sphere of public reason makes it harder to affirm philosophically the primacy of citizenship in relation to other aspects of human identity, even if that is in fact an underlying Rawlsian theoretical commitment.[8] Rawls objects to this because it commits the anti-liberal sin of telling people how to be human, which all versions of perfectionism do in one way or another.

II

Charles Taylor's approach to the problem of secularism and citizenship is much closer to that of Rawls than those familiar with the liberal-communitarian debates of the 1980s might have expected. This proximity is especially evident in Taylor's essay "Why We Need a Radical Redefinition of Secularism."[9]

What defines a secular regime on Taylor's account is (1) the right not to be coerced in one's religious beliefs or lack of such; (2) the equality of citizens, irrespective of their beliefs or non-beliefs; and (3) the assurance that all voices will be heard and respected. We must exert ourselves "to maintain harmony and comity between the supporters of different religions and Weltanschauungen."[10] But what is the reigning conception of secularism that needs to be "radically redefined"? Taylor seems to have two primary targets in mind: Atatürk's Turkey[11] and contemporary French republicanism. The latter continues to be animated by the "Jacobin" impulse (inspired by Rousseau) that there must be a more unitary foundation for peoplehood than can actually be squared with the realities of life in a radically multiculturalized world.[12] Taylor rightly acknowledges the historical fact that "in the French case, laïcité came about in a struggle *against* a powerful church."[13] But for Taylor, this historical background doesn't excuse the excesses of Jacobinism.

If one takes these miscreant regimes—Atatürk's Turkey and "hyper-republican" France[14]—as somehow defining *archetypes* of the properly secularist regime, then it might be possible to speak of a need for "redefining" secularism in light of the challenges of addressing contemporary multicultural realities. But of course there's no reason for regarding *those* two regimes as archetypically secularist, relative to, say, the founding of the American republic. I agree with Taylor that there is no need to posit one uniform institutional template for defining the separation of church and state, hence making allowance for the pluralism that's so important to him. However, unlike Taylor, I think it is reasonable to ask of a country like the UK, where by law only an Anglican can be head of state, why *doesn't* that impugn the civic status of non-Anglicans?

The perhaps surprising proximity between Taylor's and Rawls's views is also apparent in the 2011 book he coauthored with Jocelyn Maclure: *Secularism and Freedom of Conscience*. The normative core of Taylorian secularism is expressed thus:

> In a society where there is no consensus about religious and philosophical outlooks . . . the state must avoid hierarchizing the conceptions of the good life that form the basis of citizens' adherence to the basic principles of their political association. In the realm of core beliefs and commitments, the state, to be truly everyone's state, must remain "neutral." This implies that the state should adopt a position of neutrality not only toward

religions but also toward the different philosophical conceptions that stand as the secular equivalents of religion.[15]

Taylor's appeal to the idea of the state being "truly everyone's state"[16] is one with which I heartily agree. But this principle, which prohibits a state philosophy founded on a sectarian basis, is enveloped in a Rawlsian vocabulary. Taylor's reference to "philosophical conceptions that stand as the secular equivalents of religion" is obviously an allusion to the Rawlsian conception of "comprehensive doctrines."[17]

Not only is Taylor's Rawlsian turn a bit jarring for someone schooled in the debates of the 1980s,[18] but this Rawlsian vocabulary needs some unpacking. For example, what the "state neutrality" idea is intended to convey is not only that theocracies of all descriptions are illegitimate *but also* that the liberal state should not use the idea of secularism as a rationale for pursuing a war against religion (as arguably has been the case with some of the secularist regimes that most trouble Taylor). I have no disagreements here, but the appeal to "neutrality" is nonetheless problematic, for as Taylor himself has helped to teach us, nothing in life is neutral.

What drives Taylor toward Rawlsianism is the worry that if we concede that there's a comprehensive doctrine (a view of life) embodied in the liberal state, that will provide a mandate for (what Taylor sees as) the "bad" versions of secularism, such as the one we see in France, which leans on Muslim schoolgirls to shed their hijabs and requires both them and their parents to profess an allegiance to a French-republican "civil religion" of robust *laïcité*.[19] It is, in short, Taylor's multiculturalism that pushes him toward Rawlsianism. But putting to one side this more militant French version of secularism, surely even the "good" secularism that Taylor prefers embodies non-neutral conceptions of the good. If our state is founded on notions of liberty, equality, and upholding the common dignity of all citizens, then there are definite conceptions of the good instantiated in the liberal state. Following William Galston, Taylor calls this a "minimal perfectionism."[20] But a minimal perfectionism is still perfectionism, not neutralism. It may be "neutral" between Christian liberals, Muslim liberals, and agnostic liberals; but it's certainly not neutral between a liberal vision of life (including civic life) and various non-liberal visions of life (including civic life).[21] And if it's not neutral in the latter sense, it's not neutral. The notion of more neutrality or less neutrality makes little sense. "The neutral state" *either is or isn't* neutral. It isn't.

The famous liberal-communitarian debate of the 1980s was substantially defined by Rawls's commitment to "the priority of the right to the good" and the largely Taylor-inspired insistence that conceptions of the good are never absent and never lose their ultimacy.[22] This (along with much else) is one of the things that I learned from Taylor. Rawlsian neutralism never went away—in important ways, that neutralism became more radical.[23] But Taylor's commitment to a style of theorizing oriented to ambitious conceptions of the good and their centrality to moral life (at least in their *political* relevance) seems to have weakened. Or at least that's what his rapprochement with Rawls suggests to me. The unmistakable implication of chapters 1 and 2 of *Secularism and Freedom of Conscience* seems to be that Rawlsian political liberalism gives a better account of Taylor's multicultural commitments than does the doctrine of the ultimate primacy of conceptions of the good. If Taylor is being drawn to a Rawlsian self-understanding, I want to urge a return to Taylor's erstwhile commitment to a conception of political philosophy fundamentally oriented to conceptions of the good. To borrow a formulation suggested by Cécile Laborde, one might speak of a Rawlsian "temptation" that needs to be resisted.

If, for example, a liberal civic community takes its stand on the principle of full civic equality, it's hard to see how it can fail to acknowledge the claim to equality instantiated in same-sex marriage (which is why this particular political cause has seen notable gains in the last few years). Abiding by Rawlsian strictures, we declare this change in civic norms to be "philosophically neutral," related neither to a religious nor to a non-religious vision of life. It is, so to speak, metaphysically and existentially agnostic. It's simply the playing out of the freestanding *political* commitments of citizens of a liberal polity. But the evangelical Christian (or a conservative Catholic) reacts to this claim of neutrality with understandable incredulity: surely there is *some* vision of life at play in affirming a robust conception of civic equality for nonheterosexual citizens. As I have said elsewhere,[24] we can't expect a comprehensive doctrine to be trumped by something that's *less* than a comprehensive doctrine.

My alternative to Rawlsian philosophical neutralism is what I've called citizenship—or civicism—as a comprehensive doctrine (namely, an existential commitment to a life of equal citizenship),[25] and secularism both as I define it and as Taylor defines it is part and parcel of this comprehensive doctrine. I'm not convinced that appeal to a mere "overlapping consensus" would ever have gotten us to an acknowledgment of the justice of same-sex marriage. But I *am* convinced that such an acknowledgment is *required* by a robust conception of shared citizenship. We're not likely to do full justice to the relationship between citizenship and secularism within Rawlsian parameters.

Taylor radically understates problems of philosophical coherence in Rawlsian political philosophy. If I spontaneously privilege the idea of ecumenical citizenship—of being fair to all citizens just in their capacity of being fellow citizens—then *liberalism* is my comprehensive doctrine. If there are non-liberal aspects to my view of life or to my view of the good, and I *subordinate* these to the imperatives of shared citizenship, then the idea of shared citizenship has trumping power within my philosophy of life—hence the notion of *citizenship* as a comprehensive doctrine, that is, as a privileged existential commitment. Either way (ecumenical citizenship subordinated to other comprehensive doctrines, or those other comprehensive doctrines subordinated to ecumenical citizenship), there is no philosophical neutrality.

What matters is not just the fact that prior to "The Idea of Public Reason Revisited" Rawls wanted to gag religious believers, and subsequent to that he became willing to let them speak and contribute as citizens. The idea of neutralism—of not politically privileging conceptions of the good—is at the heart of the *very conception* of political liberalism. What "political liberalism" fundamentally means is that grand reflection on the ends of life is *redundant* for purposes of political philosophy in the way that Rawls practices it or tries to practice it—because the sociological coming-to-be of a liberal society provides the overlapping consensus needed to sustain a liberal society. In fact, such reflection is potentially *subversive* of a liberal society because, insofar as it encourages people to focus on the philosophically deep commitments that divide them, it may actually *disrupt* the overlapping consensus that has already been achieved. Hence the philosopher reins in his or her natural inclination to pursue and debate these deep questions and instead invents a new way of doing political philosophy (viz., political liberalism) that circumvents or steers clear of the philosophically deep commitments that threaten to reawaken existential conflicts between citizens of a liberal society.

It strikes me that forgoing this whole dimension of ambitious reflection on the ends of life—an exercise in self-reflection that helps to constitute our humanity, after all—is a very large price to pay for the embrace of Rawlsian liberalism. In any case, the idea that one could affirm a vision of politics without endorsing any particular conception of ultimate human flourishing is chimerical. A society centered on liberal-egalitarian ideas of decency and mutual respect is obviously very different from societies fundamentally geared toward warrior honor, or Sparta-like republican virtue, or piety, or contemplative communing with nature, or other non-liberal views of the human good. So non-neutral conceptions of the good are inscribed in the liberal experience of life, whether Rawlsians want to acknowledge this or not.

There are, of course, larger issues here, such as whether it's appropriate to look for normative anchors and whether political philosophy is the discipline tasked with locating and articulating these anchors.[26] Or is respect for cultural and religious pluralism the primary—one could say, the overriding—normative concern? I think that Taylor's philosophical inclinations—akin to those of his teacher, Isaiah Berlin—lean toward this latter view. By contrast, I'm of the view that the upholding of secularism as a political ideal ties into firm normative principles and, as such, traces a limit to normative pluralism. I'm not opposed to mutual understanding—between different religions, and between believers and non-believers. But this strikes me as a *civic* task, not a *philosophical* task.

Although Rawls is not committed to cultural pluralism in quite the same way as what Taylor inherited from Berlin, similar issues apply to his approach to theory. This reveals a quite important commonality between Rawls and Taylor concerning their respective conceptions of the purpose of political philosophy, which are surprisingly convergent; and this too is very much relevant to the problem of defending the politics of secularism against the politics of piety. The task of philosophy is the pursuit of truth. And pursuing truth uncompromisingly is as likely to lead to intractable *limits* to mutual understanding as to the *promotion* of mutual understanding. This indeed is why a theorist like Rawls (for *civic* reasons not unlike those that animate Taylor) is concerned with inventing a way of doing political philosophy that (paradoxically) *moves away from* the preoccupation with truth characteristic of philosophy as such. For both Rawls and Taylor, the tasks of liberal citizenship are *imported into* philosophy, thereby diminishing the radicality of philosophy in its proper vocation. Hence both Taylor and Rawls, unexpected as this may be, belong to a common movement that is content to see the proper purposes of philosophy trumped, or subsumed, by what is thought to be the more urgent business of promoting better and more tolerant citizenship. This enables us to see that Taylor makes his "new" conception of secularism out to be more novel and more controversial than it really is. What he offers, in my view, is the standard understanding of a secular regime, accompanied by a more emphatic determination to be welcoming of religious and culturally marginal voices in the civic conversation.

III

What can Dallmayr contribute to this conversation? He, perhaps counterintuitively, emerges as the "outlier" among the three theorists whose views are being sketched. Two provocative essays on secularism by Dallmayr serve to bookmark this account. The first, published in *Review of Politics* in 1999, is titled "Rethinking Secularism (with Raimon Panikkar)."[27] Panikkar (1918–2010) was a very accomplished Spanish-Indian Catholic (or perhaps Catholic/Hindu) theologian and philosopher committed, as both Dallmayr and Taylor emphatically are, to interreligious dialogue. What is notable about Panikkar's thinking about secularism (if it makes sense to call it secularism) is its enthusiastic advocacy of a grandly metaphysical attunement to Being. Panikkar calls this a "cosmotheandric" philosophy—where nature, the human, and the divine compose a kind of interlacing and mutually reliant "symphony."[28] God is not "other," and faith is entirely bound to the quest for earthly justice. The spiritual and the political are fully reciprocal: "religion is impregnated with politics and politics with religion."[29] Dallmayr refers to their relationship or "rapprochement" as one of "constitutive interdependence"—a "differential entwinement equally opposed to both fusion and separation."[30] When Dallmayr reviewed Taylor's *A Secular Age* thirteen years later, he again took Panikkar as his intellectual touchstone.[31] In this later essay even more than in the earlier one, Dallmayr joins Panikkar in his firm rejection of binaries such as human/divine and immanent/transcendent.

Across these two essays, Dallmayr makes explicit his steadfast repudiation of any politicization of religion marked by theocratic ambitions,[32] and he rightly acknowledges "the liberating effects of secular modernity."[33] Yet Dallmayr equally disavows the liberal separation of religion and politics. He affirms Panikkar's paradoxical construction of a "sacred secularity."[34] But there does seem to have been a shift in some aspects of Dallmayr's relationship to Panikkar over this time. In the 1999 essay, he distances himself from Panikkar's more exuberant hopes concerning the present age as an especially propitious moment for an epochal convergence of the spiritual and the political.[35] But by the later essay, he seems to have overcome his hesitations about embracing Panikkar's metaphysical faith. As one would expect, the Panikkar-Dallmayr vision of sacred secularity is admirably ecumenical, never sectarian. Still, one wonders whether Dallmayr needs to say more about why we should be confident that this proposed non-secular secularity—committed to a specific theology, however syncretic—won't open the door to a repoliticization of religion that (as Dallmayr knows) has proven perilous in the past and that remains perilous today. A reciprocity of religion and politics would be fine, provided that we could be assured that the agents of this religiously animated politics will be souls as generous, as peace-loving, as justice-loving, and as tolerant as Dallmayr himself is. No such assurances are available, of course, and less encouraging outcomes from any annulment of the liberal separation of religion and politics are not difficult to envisage. The hard question that must be faced by anyone who welcomes our seemingly post-secular dispensation is how we will cope with the tough realities of interreligious conflict and interreligious intolerance that rendered secularism politically imperative in the first place.

One has to admire Dallmayr philosophically for his refusal to expel comprehensive doctrines from the business of philosophy, and one has to admire him politically for his determination to put different comprehensive doctrines into receptive dialogue with each other. Still, even if one is skeptical that Rawls's political liberalism represents a viable solution to the problem of religion and politics, one can see that this is animated by a concern running throughout the liberal tradition right from its very beginnings: namely, a legitimate anxiety about the politicization of religion and its potential for undermining shared citizenship among members of the polity with very different existential commitments. No one could accuse Dallmayr of being an unconscious or covert Rawlsian. The metaphysical vision he draws from Panikkar is, and knows itself to be, far more ambitious, both theologically and politically, than what defines Taylor's modestly "Rawlsian" articulation of secular citizenship. As I've tried to make clear, my view is that Rawls is mistaken in thinking that we can have a civic space denuded of comprehensive doctrines. And Dallmayr and Panikkar indeed give us a comprehensive doctrine—a stunningly ambitious one. But it doesn't seem excessively Rawlsian to point out that it's hard to see how a specific doctrine of the unity of God, nature, and humanity can supply a shared charter of citizenship for a multireligious society populated by both believers and agnostics.

Notes

1. Kurt Andersen, "How America Lost Its Mind," *The Atlantic*, September, 2017, 89.

2. Sarah Pulliam Bailey, "'God Has Given Donald Trump Authority to Take Out Kin Jong-un,' President's Evangelical Advisor Says," *Washington Post*, August 9, 2017.

3. For a fuller account of my views concerning the perils of theocracy, see my "Secularism as a Common Good," in *Citizenship and Multiculturalism in Western Liberal Democracies*, ed. David Edward Tabachnick and Leah Bradshaw (Lanham, MD: Lexington Books, 2017), 37–55.

4. If one really thinks that a particular belief is nonsense (for instance, religiously-motivated rejection of the theory of evolution), it's not obvious that one shows respect for other people by displaying more respect for their beliefs than one thinks those beliefs actually merit. Perhaps feigned respect of this sort is simply patronizing. Yet it's hard to see how one can sustain healthy civic relations within a political community if groups of citizens are denouncing each other not only for embracing the wrong policies but also for being credulous fools. But perhaps this betrays insufficient trust in the capacity of citizens to be honest about their philosophical differences. Perhaps here, too, feigned respect is merely patronizing. I'm less confident than adherents of Rawls's political liberalism (as well as multiculturalists) tend to be about what respect for the beliefs of fellow citizens truly requires. For a good discussion of this, see Terry Eagleton, *Reason, Faith, and Revolution* (New Haven: Yale University Press, 2009), 147–48.

5. See Sheryl Gay Stolberg, "For Romney, a Role of Faith and Authority," *New York Times*, October 15, 2011.

6. Rawls was forced to develop increasingly convoluted versions of this doctrine on account of the indignation and pushback aroused, understandably, by his initial formulations.

7. As Taylor nicely expresses it, the original impulse in Rawls's political liberalism was for "religious views [to be left] in the vestibule of the public sphere"; Charles Taylor, "Why We Need a Radical Redefinition of Secularism," in *The Power of Religion in the Public Sphere*, ed. Eduardo Mendieta and Jonathan VanAntwerpen (New York: Columbia University Press, 2011), 49, cited hereafter as "Radical Redefinition." And because this was a manifestly non-neutral requirement put upon *certain* citizens, Rawls felt impelled to require that *all* "comprehensive doctrines" be left in that same vestibule. Taylor goes on to write ("Radical Redefinition," 53) that Rawls entertained such an idea only "for a time"; cf. Jocelyn Maclure and Charles Taylor, *Secularism and Freedom of Conscience* (Cambridge, MA: Harvard University Press, 2011), 110. However, without some version of this doctrine, political liberalism would not be political liberalism.

8. For a fuller version of this critique, see Ronald Beiner, *Civil Religion* (New York: Cambridge University Press, 2011), chap. 23.

9. An expanded version (entitled "What Does Secularism Mean?") has been published in Taylor, *Dilemmas and Connections: Selected Essays* (Cambridge, MA: Belknap Press, 2011), 303–25.

10. "Radical Redefinition," 35.

11. "Radical Redefinition," 37: Atatürk's regime was not "genuinely secular" because it was "fixated on" (i.e., discriminated against) religion. Such a regime doesn't leave people at liberty in their chosen religious identities, but aggressively challenges

those identities. Hence secularism "in its polemical sense of non- or antireligious" (39) is not really secularism.

12. For the reference to "Jacobin" *laïcité*, see 'Radical Redefinition," 35; cf. *Secularism and Freedom of Conscience*, 17. On p. 40 of "Radical Redefinition," Taylor calls this "hyper-Republicanism."

13. "Radical Redefinition," 39. Cf. *Secularism and Freedom of Conscience*, 14: "The temptation to make secularism the equivalent of religion is generally stronger in countries where secularism came about at the cost of a bitter struggle against a dominant religion [such as France or Turkey]. It may be because of the fairly widespread sense that secularism was achieved in Quebec in a pitched battle against the Catholic church that some Quebecers today are sympathetic toward a certain version of French and Turkish secularism." (See the next note.)

14. In 2013, the Parti Québécois government proposed a "Charter of Quebec Values" that was "hyper-republican" in precisely Taylor's sense. This project died when the PQ lost the provincial election in 2014; however, a version has since been legislated by the Coalition Avenir Québec government. This raises the question of whether Quebec deserves to be added to Taylor's list of miscreant regimes. Taylor himself has been vocal in condemning this legislation.

15. *Secularism and the Freedom of Conscience*, 13. Of course, this is a coauthored book, so with respect to any particular sentence, there's uncertainty about whether it's Taylor's or Maclure's. However, all the ideas in the book discussed here are affirmed in other related texts by Taylor, including the single-authored "Radical Redefinition" article.

16. Cf. *Secularism and the Freedom of Conscience*, 20: "the state must be the state for all citizens."

17. Cf. "Radical Redefinition," 37. I have explained in *Civil Religion*, chap. 23, why I do not find Rawls's assimilation of religious and non-religious comprehensive doctrines persuasive. See especially 299, n. 37. Taylor, in his debate with Habermas transcribed in *The Power of Religion in the Public Sphere*, carries another step forward Rawls's suggestion—inscribed in the very notion of comprehensive doctrines—that there is in principle no difference between basing one's view of life on religious beliefs and basing it on a secular philosophy. This is another aspect of Taylor's Rawlsian turn.

18. Rawlsian categories are appealed to throughout *Secularism and the Freedom of Conscience* (see, for instance, 86, 97, and 107); and they figure equally prominently in the "Radical Redefinition" essay: see, for instance, "Radical Redefinition," 37, on "state neutrality" (citing "the value of the late-Rawlsian formulation for a secular state"); and 48, on "overlapping consensus." Taylor tends to present Rawls, and Habermas too, as having modified their earlier harder-line philosophical rationalism in a way that brings them closer to Taylor's views ("Radical Redefinition," 35 and 53; *Secularism and Freedom of Conscience*, 110). But I think this tells only half the story. If Rawls has moved closer to Taylor, Taylor has also moved closer to Rawls.

19. "Radical Redefinition," 47; *Secularism and Freedom of Conscience*, 14–15.

20. *Secularism and Freedom of Conscience*, 112, n. 4.

21. My suggestion would be just to call it "the liberal state." See *Secularism and Freedom of Conscience*, 16–17, which acknowledges limits to the idea of state neutrality while remaining committed to the language of neutrality.

22. It was Taylor-inspired in the fairly obvious sense that contestation over "the priority of the right to the good" became central to Michael Sandel's critique of Rawls. The basic Rawlsian idea was that as philosophers we shouldn't attempt to *adjudicate* competing conceptions of the good, because we know in advance that this will never lead anywhere. Instead, we should content ourselves with formulating principles of civic coexistence that will help to advance our ends, whatever they turn out to be. It's hard to see any difference between that Rawlsian view and the Taylorian view discussed here.

23. This more radical neutralism is captured in familiar Rawlsian slogans of "apply[ing] the principle of toleration to philosophy itself," "stay[ing] on the surface, philosophically speaking," etc. For relevant citations, see *Civil Religion*, 296, n. 28, and 298, n. 34. Rawls feels that in the interests of civic peace, he needs to emasculate philosophy as the pursuit of ultimate truth about the ends of life, and this in turn has the consequence that he emasculates his own version of liberalism. Putting it like this should help make clear why I don't regard Rawls as a political-philosophical model.

24. *Civil Religion*, 298–99.

25. See the texts cited in notes 3 and 8 as well as "Citizenship as a Comprehensive Doctrine," *The Hedgehog Review* 10, no. 3 (Fall 2008): 23–33.

26. For an extended discussion, see "Hermeneutical Generosity and Social Criticism," in Ronald Beiner, *Philosophy in a Time of Lost Spirit* (Toronto: University of Toronto Press, 1997).

27. Fred Dallmayr, "Rethinking Secularism (with Raimon Panikkar)," *Review of Politics* 61, no. 4 (Autumn 1999): 715–35.

28. "Rethinking Secularism," 735.

29. Ibid., 730.

30. Ibid., 727–28.

31. Fred Dallmayr, "A Secular Age? Reflections on Taylor and Panikkar," *International Journal for Philosophy of Religion* 71, no. 3 (2012): 189–204.

32. "Rethinking Secularism," 716, 725, 727, 733–34; "A Secular Age?," 200, 202.

33. "Rethinking Secularism," 720.

34. "Rethinking Secularism," 724, 731, 732, 734; "A Secular Age?," 196, 199.

35. "Rethinking Secularism," 731.

Chapter 6

Between Berlin and Königsberg

Toward a Global Community of Well-Disposed Human Beings

Herta Nagl-Docekal

Analyzing the conditions of modern life from the perspective of political theory, many authors highlight one problem in particular: the propensity toward an atomistic isolation of the individual that leads to a disintegration of social bonds and dwindling solidarity. There is an unfortunate recombination of two different conceptions of liberalism, with the rights of the individual, which are protected by the liberal state, being exploited for the sake of the competitiveness promoted by economic liberalism. The social integration of communities has come under persistent pressure because the language of the market has intruded into all spheres of interpersonal relationships. Obviously, many people who express a general condemnation of "Western ways of life" today are targeting these social pathologies.

From early on, Fred Dallmayr has addressed the inner tension of the modern world, noting, for instance, that "in the process of modernization or rationalization, society is wrenched away from traditional moorings and quasi-natural conventions, and thus is set adrift in the turbulent sea of competition and agonistic struggle."[1] He has made it a prime task of his work to elaborate a political theory that suggests ways "to counteract social atomization and excessive divisiveness"[2] while simultaneously averting any suggestions for a return to premodern forms of social order. With this concern in mind, Dallmayr turns to Hegel's *Philosophy of Right*, arguing that this book—even though based on systematic premises that may have become obsolete—does provide the current discourse with a "multifaceted edifice that makes room both for free individual initiative (civil society) and for shared moral bonds."[3] Devoting particular attention to the concept of *Sittlichkeit*, Dallmayr maintains that Hegel "holds out the promise of reconciliation."[4]

As Dallmayr wrote *G.W.F. Hegel: Modernity and Politics* in the early 1990s, he employed his findings in particular in challenging dominant discourses of that era, such as poststructuralism and the controversy of liberalism versus communitarianism. Furthermore, Dallmayr criticizes the mode in which Habermas, while emphasizing Hegel's importance as the chief instigator of the "discourse of modernity," proposes to replace the concept of *Geist* by means of "recourse to the process of communicative action leading to a quasi-contractual agreement among participants." As Dallmayr contends, "in relying on individual will-formation, his [Habermas's] proposal threatens to upset or unhinge Hegel's mediating balance between individual and community in favor of modern predilections for radical individualism."[5]

My reflections take up this latter issue, focusing on theories elaborated in recent years that, while indebted to Habermas's approach in general, seek to overcome its deficits. Concepts of social life typically maintained by younger representatives of Frankfurt School thought tend to fail to get rid of the problem of "a quasi-contractual agreement." In searching for a way out of this problem, my claim is that Kant's moral philosophy provides important elements for conceiving a truly human, cosmopolitan community. While resonating with Dallmayr's consideration that "in our time, marked by consumerism and private self-satisfaction, Kant's prioritizing of duty seem[s] indeed desirable as a corrective,"[6] I suggest that Kant provides even more than a corrective.

Relational Institutions

In *Das Recht der Freiheit*, Axel Honneth advocates adopting the core argument of Hegel's *Philosophy of Right*, according to which we need to distinguish different "spheres of action." Beyond the spheres of the liberal state and individual morality, Honneth argues, we need to focus on the social institutions, based on shared values, in which we find ourselves embedded. Highlighting that the experience of being part of such a community is commonly expressed by the term "we," he claims that, today, we typically are embedded in three different modes of "We": the "We" of personal relations,[7] the "We" of interactions in terms of market economy,[8] and the "We" of the formation of the democratic will.[9] Each of these contexts is based on specific ideals that have been incorporated in social practices that are captured appropriately by the term *Sittlichkeit*, as defined by Hegel.

Considering dominant constellations of life in the current world, Honneth addresses three different forms of personal relations: friendship, intimate relations, and families. Their decisive common feature is that the individuals involved "meet one another in an attitude of mutual recognition that implies viewing their own actions as providing the respective others with the preconditions for reaching their aims."[10] Thus he sees these relations as based on an attitude of "reciprocal considerateness" that allows each individual to "count on" the other to act in a way "that brings his/her actions to full realization."[11] These reciprocal expectations "are institutionalized in the form of social roles" that, under normal circumstances, ensure smooth processes of interaction. "Only when the complementary roles are performed appropriately," he argues, "can the shared intentions of the involved individuals be fully implemented."[12] Talking to an interviewer, Honneth poignantly notes that, in personal relations, individuals seek the "realization of their own freedom through cooperation with another person."[13]

This assertion, however, gives rise to questions regarding the consistency of his approach. Two topics seem intertwined here that need to be disentangled. While it is certainly appropriate to describe some of our practices in the context of social institutions in terms of taking complementary roles, with the aim of achieving a shared goal, this perspective does not provide a concept of "love" that would meet our common understanding of the term. Honneth's view differs clearly from Hegel's in this respect—in fact, it seems to take the opposite direction. Whereas for Honneth the ultimate point of intimate relationships is to bring the freedom of the individual partners to full flourishing, Hegel, employing his dialectical method, claims rather that lovers, while remaining separate individuals, develop a shared identity:

> Love is a distinguishing of two who, nevertheless, are absolutely not distinguished for each other. The consciousness or feeling of the identity of the two—to be outside myself and in the other—this is love . . . , and both the other and I are only this consciousness of being-outside-ourselves and of our identity; we are only this intuition, feeling, and knowledge of our unity.[14]

Based on his concept of the dialectical process of "Spirit" that also shapes his understanding of the Christian community, Hegel contends that loving individuals are united in such a manner that their bond can be described as "the worldly religion of the heart."[15] This thesis implies that Hegel's approach is in line with the common ideal of an unconditional commitment to the beloved person that is not based on a perspective of reciprocity.

Honneth, on the contrary, explicitly notes that he is not taking up Hegel's dialectical concept of "Spirit" and reads Hegel in a way that emphasizes individual enhancement. Referring to Luhmann, he portrays personal relations, such as friendship and intimate love, as "emotional experiences in which the subject can see in the other the precondition of his/her self-realization."[16] Significantly, language addressing what the partners can "expect" from one another, or which modes of action they can mutually "count on," is used frequently. Thus it is obvious that his reflections are shaped by the logic of the contract even where he claims to move beyond the sphere of the law by focusing on personal relations. One consequence is that his concepts of friendship and love tend to bypass issues of fallibility that are part of such relations in everyday life. What happens, one might ask, when the individuals fail to meet the expectations of their respective others? We miss, for instance, the topic of forgiveness, as emphasized by Hegel and Hannah Arendt, and also a focus on the potential that our sense of humor has for overcoming feelings of disappointment and estrangement.

Contractual Approaches to Morality

Recent studies by representatives of the Frankfurt tradition tend to follow the logic of the contract also when it comes to defining morality. There is, of course, good reason for addressing moral issues in the context of a theory of *Sittlichkeit*. From a contemporary perspective, the shared values and traditional practices that have shaped the communities in which we find ourselves embedded turn out to be flawed in important respects, in particular when they generate social asymmetries such as gender disparities. Therefore, critical examination is called for and has indeed been under way for many years. Obviously, this critique needs to appeal to moral principles that have an independent basis rather than ones derived from traditional social values. From this angle, Hegel's theory of *Sittlichkeit* appears to be inconsistent. As many critics contend, Hegel's claim to employ the concept of *Aufhebung* (which represents the core structure of the dialectical process, defined by the triad negation/preservation/elevation) in a way that demonstrates the priority of *Sittlichkeit* over morality has failed.[17]

This ambivalence also shapes Honneth's way of dealing with morality. While emphasizing the need to expose and overcome the hierarchical implications of traditional social practices,[18] Honneth nevertheless views these very practices as a necessary precondition of moral action. As he notes, they provide "the socio-cultural conditions that precede, as *moral* givens, every individual act of self-legislation."[19] However, which concept of the "moral" is employed here? The term "self-legislation," while alluding to Kant's moral philosophy, is clearly used in the sense of "individual self-determination." This ambivalence calls for a distinction to be made: whereas it is obvious that our self-determination depends on options provided within the framework of historically grown social practices, there is good reason to doubt that, by meeting the normative expectations of the respective social entity, our actions are *eo ipso* qualified in terms of morality. Emphasizing this difference, Kant distinguishes "between a human being of good morals . . . and a morally good human being."[20]

As regards morality as a specific sphere, Habermas's approach—which locates moral judgment in public discourse—is widely shared. According to Habermas, "Moral judgments explain how conflicts among different actors can be resolved on the basis of a rationally motivated agreement."[21] A similar line of thought shapes Rainer Forst's concept of the "right to justification."[22] Forst, who also views moral issues as conflict based, emphasizes the right of persons who are irritated or offended by the actions of others to "request reasons." Correspondingly, he maintains that each person must be granted the equal right to justify his or her way of acting. Advocating a "discourse-theoretical transformation of the categorical imperative," he contends that "each person must, on principle, be recognized as a person with the right to justification according to the criteria of reciprocity and universality, [i.e.] as a normative authority who is my equal."[23] Specifying this kind of authority, Forst notes that "morally autonomous persons regard themselves and others as the authors and addressees of moral validity claims."[24]

Regarding what is required to provide good reasons for a contested action, these "post-metaphysical" theories argue that it is imperative to refer to universally accepted normative principles. As Habermas claims, the validity of norms depends on processes of a "joint will- and opinion-formation concerning the norms of communal life." He further explains: " 'Correctness,' in the moral sense of a well-founded norm, means that the respective norm 'deserves' to be universally acknowledged in the light of good reasons."[25]

This thesis corresponds to Honneth's characterization of what he calls "the moral sphere." This sphere, he explains, is constituted as a specific "type of social interaction" by the mode in which "the subjects concede to each other the chance of moral justification. The one considers the other capable of judging, in a case of conflict, in terms of . . . universalizable reasons."[26]

As this brief summary clearly indicates, these authors agree—regardless of the differing claims their studies may otherwise defend—on a concept of morality that is shaped by the logic of contract. This shared understanding fails, however, to correspond to our everyday perception; in fact, it falls short of our ordinary way of looking at morality in several respects. As we seek to locate these points of incompatibility, Kant's moral philosophy provides a valuable basis.

First, as Kant emphasizes, contractual agreements are, by definition, incapable of generating a moral attitude. Agreements on rules of action can only concern the "external" aspect: the action as an observable process. Accordingly, Kant defines "juridical laws" as being "directed merely to external actions and their conformity to law."[27] However, as regards the "internal" aspect—the agent's perspective—it is obvious that I cannot be bound by contract to making a certain end "my end."[28] Second, a circular argument is at work here. The thesis that moral principles represent a matter to be decided in an unrestricted public discourse fails to take into consideration that moral principles are required in the first place to make such a discourse possible. Taking a Kantian route of argument, Otfried Höffe addresses this issue lucidly as he challenges Forst's attempt to explain "human rights and the sovereignty of the people" by referring to one and the same discursive process. Human rights, Höffe contends, are "precedents, such as the protection of life and limb, which make equal access to the discourse possible in the first place, and therefore cannot then be suspended in specific discourses."[29]

Third, the thesis locating the origin of moral issues in conflicts among actors fails to take adequately into account what is commonly called "conscience." It does not reflect, for instance, that we may view some of our actions as morally wrong even if no one has observed or contested them. Significantly, Kant's approach takes the opposite direction, as he locates the source of morality primarily in the acting subject. Defining the *differentia specifica* of humans, Kant highlights "the original moral disposition in us."[30] To explore this shared ability to distinguish good and evil is the core concern of his theory of the categorical imperative. The exclusive addressee of this imperative is the subject: "So act that you use humanity, whether in your own person or in the person of any other, always at the same time as an end, never merely as a means."³¹ Kant's prime aim is to demonstrate that the duty to respect and treat every human being as a person is what morality is all about.

As regards the others who are affected by our actions, there is a need for differentiation. To implement the moral duty properly, we certainly have to cultivate our sensitivity as to whether others might be offended or harmed by our actions. In this respect, it is obvious that we need to engage in discourse wherever possible.³² Critical responses voiced by others can provide invaluable incentives for our self-examination. The importance of such consultations does not, however, provide evidence for the claim of a "procedural transformation of the categorical imperative." On the basis of this sweeping claim, the moral evaluation of actions would be committed to the public, ultimately denying the relevance of the agent's conscience. We also need to consider the danger of pretense: it is evident that public pressure on individuals to justify their actions may induce individuals with a talent for sophistry to hide their actual intentions behind "good reasons" that agree with widely accepted norms, whereas less sophisticated persons might find it impossible to verbalize adequately their true motivation. In general terms, Kant expresses a clear warning, stating that "it is the pure attitude of the heart that represents true moral value, yet this is never fully perceived by others, very often even misjudged."³³

Solidarity and the Ethical Community

In the common understanding, one crucial feature of a moral attitude is the commitment to provide unconditional help and support to others. Because of their focus on reciprocity, contractualist approaches fail to properly capture this. From their perspective, auxiliary burdens must be distributed according to the principle of mutual benefit. This principle, although it provides a sound foundation for regulations enacted in the liberal state, proves insufficient with regard to a comprehensive concept of auxiliary obligations in moral terms. Kant introduces an important distinction: reciprocity, he argues, is a core element of an ideal moral community. While this is something to hope for in the long run, it does not justify the thesis that, from a moral point of view, we ought to make symmetry a precondition of our present actions. In general, the moral law rather imposes on us a unilateral duty. I am obliged to respect and treat others as persons, even when I have good reasons to doubt that they would behave likewise toward me.³⁴ Emphasizing that this claim is convincing well beyond the academic discourse, Kant cites the Christian demand that one should love one's enemies.[35] Poignantly phrased, he contends that the moral imperative appeals to the subject *to make a beginning*.

Examining the manifold duties implied in the moral imperative, and seeking a structured assessment, Kant first of all distinguishes duties of narrow and wide obligation. His elaboration on the latter, in particular his theory of "duties of wide obligation toward others," proves highly relevant with regard to the current quest for ways to "counteract social atomization." As the concept of "solidarity" has gained increasing significance in the recent debate on this challenge,[36] it is important to note that—*avant la letter*—Kant demonstrates that this concept has a solid moral foundation. Let us recall his theory of the "duty of love to other men,"[37] which includes the "duty of beneficence," in a briefly summarized manner.[38]

The core demand that one should respect others as ends in themselves implies that we ought to consider their capability to act individually, that is to say to choose their own paths to happiness; this also implies that we ought to be aware of the finiteness that inescapably characterizes human beings—their vulnerability and their need for support on their individual paths of life. Consequently, acts of charity and support are part of our moral obligation. As Kant explains, "When it comes to my promoting happiness as an end which is also my duty, this must . . . be the happiness of other men, whose (permitted) end I thus make my own end as well. It is for them to decide what they count as belonging to their happiness."[39] Kant takes into account here that we are unable to answer everybody's call for help, let alone to promote everybody's happiness. With regard to this limitation, he introduces the concept of duties of wide obligation. Contradicting the view that the obligation we perceive in this manner fails to represent moral duty in the proper sense of the term, Kant emphasizes that wide duties are veritable duties too,[40] yet duties that impose on us a specific burden. Because it is up to the individual agent to decide, for instance, how much help and support he or she will grant to others, wide duties are more challenging than narrow ones. "The law," he explains, "cannot specify precisely in what way one is to act and how much one is to do."[41]

In this context, the concept of "supererogatory deeds," which has been widely accepted in the contractualist discourse on morality, needs to be addressed. Explicitly challenging Kant's approach, this concept claims that we must distinguish two types of moral actions: actions representing the moral common sense and those representing moral excellence by going "beyond the call of duty."[42] This distinction suggests viewing a unilateral commitment of care for others as being based on the personal preference of outstanding individuals rather than on the sense of moral obligation shared by everyone.[43] However, the concept of "moral duty" that is at play here fails to accommodate the ordinary perception of most people. As Kant seeks to spell out this common perception, he maintains that all human beings find themselves continually confronted, by their own practical reason, with the call to "go the extra mile." Concrete acts of charity represent individual ways of implementing the one moral law. Arguing in this manner, Kant provides a sound basis for the claim that it is a duty of every individual to cultivate an attitude of solidarity and to act accordingly as far as possible.

Kant further reflects that moral duties, while calling on the individual agent, often require cooperative efforts of implementation. Joint endeavors are needed not only in the temporally limited mode of responding to given needs, but also in a persistent way. It is our duty, he argues, to participate in establishing two types of social order: in addition to promoting a liberal constitutional order, on the global as well as the national level, we ought to take part in shaping a community based on the moral law. With regard to today's pressing issues, it seems worthwhile to focus on the second demand.

Kant's theory of the "ethical community" is based on the thought that, while each human being has the duty to strive for his or her moral improvement, these efforts will face enormous obstacles unless the individuals cooperate in establishing a community ruled by the laws of virtue:

> [T]he highest moral good will not be brought about solely through the thriving of one individual person for his own moral perfection but requires rather a union of such persons into a whole toward that very end, i.e. toward a system of well-disposed human beings in which, and through the unity of which alone, the highest moral good can come to pass.[44]

Transferring Hobbes's concept of the *bellum omnium contra omnes* from the political sphere to that of morality, Kant argues that as long as the individual remains in circumstances defined by the "ethical state of nature," he is exposed to moral perils generated by other human beings to whom he is related:

> Envy, addiction to power, avarice, and the malignant inclinations associated with these, assail his nature . . . as soon as he is among human beings. Nor is it necessary to assume that these are sunk

in evil and are examples that lead him astray: it suffices that they are there, that they surround him, and that they are human beings, and they will mutually corrupt each other's moral dispositions and make one another evil.[45] These observations certainly sound familiar: maybe the moral perils Kant describes are even more prevalent today than was the case in his era.

Examining how we might overcome the "ethical state of nature," Kant maintains that "the dominion of the good principle is not otherwise attainable [. . .] than through the setting up and the diffusion of a society . . . solely designed for the preservation of morality by counteracting evil with united forces."[46] In fact, he argues, our moral reason specifies the duty that "the human being ought to leave the ethical state of nature in order to become a member of an ethical community."[47] Emphasizing the social implication of this duty, Kant contends: "In addition to prescribing laws to each individual human being, morally legislative reason also unfurls a banner of virtue as rallying point for all those who love the good, that they may congregate under it."[48]

With regard to a common (mis-)understanding, it is important to underscore that these reflections do not suggest any modification of the concept of the constitutional state. Kant rather insists on the need to establish both the "political" and the "ethical state" alongside, yet clearly distinguished from, each another. Examining the relation between these two types of "community," he points out that the "ethical community . . . can exist in the midst of a political community and even be made up of all the members of the latter. . . . It has however a special unifying principle of its own (virtue)."[49] The issue of membership reveals a further difference: Because the "ethical community" is based on the duty to implement the moral law as consistently as possible, its scope cannot be limited to the citizens of a certain state (or to a group of people defined by other criteria). Referring to the universal character of the one moral law, Kant argues that "since the duties of virtue concern the entire human race, the concept of an ethical community always refers to the ideal of a totality of human beings."[50] From this perspective, there exists a tension between the two types of community: because the "ethical community" abstains from any logic that draws a line between "we" and "they," it clearly has a critical potential with regard to practices of exclusion.[51]

The question remains open as to where we might find an "ethical community," at least in a rudimentary form, or how we might go about building one. Kant introduces a link between the spheres of moral life and religion, stating that "the concept of an ethical community is the concept of a people of God under ethical laws,"[52] and continues with the thesis that "the idea of a people of God cannot be realized (by human organization) except in the form of a church."[53] This seems to indicate that Kant's thinking is tied to a monotheistic perspective to such an extent that it could not gain relevance with regard to other religious traditions. However, referring to the epochs of world history, from early on, Kant contends that the great diversity of religious narratives and practices may be viewed as so many efforts to realize, within the respective particular cultural contexts, humanity's most demanding moral task. This thesis certainly is of interest with regard to the current debate on religious conflicts: Kant's prime focus is not on addressing the disparities—or similarities—of religious confessions on the surface but on considering their shared moral basis. Significantly, from this perspective, every creed, since humanity's earliest religious ideas, has intrinsic value, and the task is to examine which contribution each has made to create a community whose members jointly seek to support and improve their moral lives.

Kant's approach does open up a critical perspective as well. In his observations on the institutional realities of religious communities, including the Protestant church he belonged to, he applies the traditional distinction between "invisible" and "visible" church,[54] noting that "the sublime, never fully attainable idea of an ethical community is greatly scaled down under human hands."[55] The most serious problem he addresses concerns the fact that, as institutions shaped by humans, churches commonly have adopted political models of structuring. In this manner, "statutory laws,"[56] laid down by church authorities, have tended to get in the way of the moral law.[57] This allows us to read Kant as claiming that the genuine moral teachings contained in each traditional confession can be fully brought to light, and made available as practical guidelines, only by detaching them from hierarchical pressures that seek to establish a heteronomous form of acting. Read in this manner, Kant's view on "church" suggests that, in the context of modernity, it is appropriate to approach religious creeds in a carefully reflecting manner rather than to uphold traditional teachings and practices unreflectingly.

In many parts of the world religion has lost its appeal for substantial segments of the population. From this perspective, Kant's concept of the "ethical community" is widely considered obsolete today, even among Kant scholars. However, with regard to the current social pathologies, rereading Kant's thoughts on our moral obligation to contribute to establishing an inclusive global community of well-disposed human beings might open up an important perspectivea prospect that corresponds to Dallmayr's reflections on the meaning of the *adveniat* of the "coming reign."[58]

Notes

1. Fred R. Dallmayr *G.W.F. Hegel: Modernity and Politics* (Newbury Park: Sage, 1993), 249.
2. Ibid. See also Fred Dallmayr, *On the Boundary: A Life Remembered* (Lanham, MD: Hamilton Books), 85.
3. Dallmayr *G.W.F. Hegel*, op. cit., 5.
4. Ibid., 250.
5. Ibid., 7–8.
6. Dallmayr, *On the Boundary*, op. cit., p. 74.
7. Axel Honneth, *Das Recht der Freiheit. Grundriß einer demokratischen Sittlichkeit* (Berlin: Suhrkamp, 2011), 233–316.
8. Ibid., 317–469.
9. Ibid., 470–624.
10. Ibid., 222. All quotations from Honneth 2011 are my translations.
11. Ibid., 224.
12. Ibid., 225.
13. Axel Honneth, "Das Recht der Freiheit. Daniela Zumpf im Gespräch mit Axel Honneth," *Information Philosophie* 3 (2013), 29.
14. Georg Wilhelm Friedrich Hegel, *Lectures on the Philosophy of Religion*, vol. III, ed. Peter C. Hodgson (Berkeley: University of California Press, 1985), 276.
15. Georg Wilhelm Friedrich Hegel, *Vorlesungen über die Ästhetik II, Werke*, vol. 14 (Frankfurt a.M.: Suhrkamp, 1970), 186, my translation.
16. Honneth, *Das Recht der Freiheit*, op. cit., 233–34.
17. See Siep Ludwig, *Aktualität und Grenzen der praktischen Philosophie Hegels* (Munich: Fink, 1992), 217–39.
18. Honneth, *Das Recht der Freiheit*, op. cit., 297–84.
19. Ibid., 183; emphasis added.
20. Immanuel Kant, *Religion within the Boundaries of Mere Reason*, ed. Allen Wood and George di Giovanni (Cambridge: Cambridge University Press, 1998), 54.
21. Jürgen Habermas, *Erläuterungen zur Diskursethik* (Frankfurt a.M.: Suhrkamp, 1991), 11, my translation.
22. Rainer Forst, *The Right to Justification* (New York: Columbia University Press, 2014).
23. Rainer Forst, "Rechtfertigung in der praktischen Philosophie: Stellungnahmen," *Information Philosophie* 4 (2015): 22. All quotations from Forst are my translations.

24. Rainer Forst, *Kontexte der Gerechtigkeit* (Frankfurt a.M.: Suhrkamp, 1994), 403.

25. Jürgen Habermas, "Kommunikative Vernunft. Ein Interview mit Christoph Demmerling und Hans-Peter Krüger," *Deutsche Zeitschrift für Philosophie* 64/5, 806–27. My translation is from page 818.

26. Honneth, *Das Recht der Freiheit*, op. cit., 193.

27. Immanuel Kant, *The Metaphysics of Morals*, trans. Mary Gregor (Cambridge: Cambridge University Press, 1991), 42.

28. Ibid., 187.

29. Höffe Otfried, "Kant ist kein Frankfurter. Rainer Forst begründet das Recht auf Rechtfertigung, allerdings nicht ganz zureichend," *Zeit Online*, no. 45 (November 1, 2007), 3, my translation.

30. Kant, *Religion within the Boundaries of Mere Reason*, op. cit., 69.

31. Immanuel Kant, *Groundwork of the Metaphysics of Morals*, trans. Mary Gregor (Cambridge: Cambridge University Press, 1996), 38.

32. See Herta Nagl-Docekal, "Learning to Listen or Why Morality Calls for Liberal Politics," in *Ethics or Moral Philosophy*, ed. Guttorm Fløistad (Dordrecht: Springer, 2014): 109–30.

33. Kant, *Reflexion* 6858 (1776–78), *Materialien zu Kants Kritik der praktischen Vernunft*, ed. Rüdiger Bittner and Konrad Cramer (Frankfurt a.M.: Suhrkamp, 1975), 125. My translation.

34. For an in-depth critique of contractualist concepts of moral judgment, see my *Innere Freiheit. Grenzen dernachmetaphysischen Moralkonzeptionen* (Berlin: De Gruyter, 2014).

35. Kant, *Groundwork*, op. cit., 13.

36. See, for instance, Fred R. Dallmayr, *Freedom and Solidarity* (Lexington, KY: University Press of Kentucky, 2016).

37. The German gender-neutral term "*Mensch*" is used rather than a misleading term like "man," as introduced by the translator of the English edition cited here.

38. Kant, *Groundwork*, op. cit., 38; Kant, *The Metaphysics of Morals*, op. cit., 243–54.

39. Kant, *The Metaphysics of Morals*, op. cit., 192.

40. For an in-depth examination of Kant's concept of wide duties, see Christine M. Korsgaard, *The Sources of Normativity* (Cambridge: Cambridge University Press, 1996), 106–23.

41. Kant, *The Metaphysics of Morals*, op. cit., 194.

42. David Heyd, *Supererogation: Its Status in Ethical Theory* (Cambridge: Cambridge University Press, 1982).

43. James Opie Urmson, "Saints and Heroes," in *Moral Concepts*, ed. Joel Feinberg (London: Oxford University Press, 1962), 60–73.

44. Kant, *Religion within the Boundaries of Mere Reason*, op. cit., 109.

45. Ibid., 105.

46. Ibid., 106.
47. Ibid., 108.
48. Ibid., 106.
49. Ibid.
50. Ibid., 107.

51. Kant's argument clearly supports Dallmayr's objection to Chantal Mouffe's claim that every community is defined by a "constitutive outside." "Die Heimkehr des Politischen" (review of Chantal Mouffe, *The Return of the Political*), *Deutsche Zeitschrift für Philosophie*, 44/3, 522.

52. Kant, *Religion within the Boundaries of Mere Reason*, op. cit., 109.

53. Ibid., 111.

54. A lucid comment on the distinction of two types of church is provided in Anderson-Gold Sharon, "God and Community. Religious Implications of the Highest Good," in *Kant's Philosophy of Religion Reconsidered*, ed. Philip Rossi and Michael Wreen (Bloomington Indianapolis: Indiana University Press, 1991), 113–32.

55. Kant, *Religion within the Boundaries of Mere Reason*, op. cit., 111.

56. Ibid., 110.

57. For an elaborate discussion of this issue, see Immanuel Kant, *The Conflict of Faculties*, trans. Mary J. Gregor (Lincoln: University of Nebraska Press, 1979), 31–139.

58. Dallmayr, *On the Boundary*, op. cit., 86–88. See also Fred R. Dallmayr, "The Relation of Heaven and Humanity: Beyond Monism and Dualism," in Songshan Forum on Chinese and World Civilizations (ed.), *The Unity of Humanity and Heaven* (Beijing, China: PKU, 2014), 54–84. See page 68.

Chapter 7

Learning and Scholarship

Unearthing the Roots of Humanism and Cosmopolitanism in the Islamic Milieu

Asma Afsaruddin

Islam is frequently characterized as a "religion of the Book," the Book in question being the Qur'an, the central revealed scripture of Islam. According to Islamic tradition, the first word uttered by the angel Gabriel in roughly 610 CE that initiated the series of divine revelations to the Prophet Muhammad was *Iqra*! ("Recite" or "read"). The full verse (96:1) commands: "Read in the name of your Lord Who has created [all things]." The act of reading or reciting, in relation to Islam's holy book and in general, thus took on an exceptionally sacrosanct quality within Islamic tradition and practice, as did the acquisition of particularly religious knowledge by extension. "Are those who know and those who do not know to be reckoned the same?" asks the Qur'an (39:9). The Qur'an depicts knowledge as a great bounty from God granted to His prophets and their followers through time.[1]

Believers also took to heart the Prophet's counsel, "Seek knowledge even unto China," which sacralized the journey, often perilous, undertaken to supplement and complete one's education, an endeavor known in Arabic as *rihlat talab al-'ilm* ("journey in the search for knowledge"). The "seeker of knowledge" (Ar. *talib al-'ilm*) remains until today the term used for a student, normally in its abbreviated form (*talib* [masc.]/*taliba* [fem.]) for all levels of education. Another equally well-known statement of the Prophet exhorts, "The pursuit of knowledge is incumbent on every Muslim," a statement that has made the acquisition of knowledge mandatory for the Muslim individual irrespective of gender. Sanctioned by both the word of God and the words of His prophet (the latter recorded in what is known in Arabic as *hadith*, lit. "speech"), the pursuit of knowledge (Ar. *'ilm*) is regarded as a religious obligation on a par with prayer, charity, and so forth. It is customary to find these proof-texts extolling the merits of *'ilm* and recorded in many treatises on learning and education in both the premodern and modern periods to exhort the believer to embark on the noble pursuit of knowledge.[2] This chapter focuses on the traditions of learning and scholarship that developed within the Islamic milieu in the premodern period based on this scriptural exhortation to acquire knowledge and the ethos of humanism and cosmopolitanism that it fostered. It then reflects briefly on how this legacy can be appropriately resurrected and adapted to the exigencies of the modern world.[3]

Classical Centers of Learning

The earliest venue of education was the mosque, the place of formal worship in Islam. During the Prophet Muhammad's time, his mosque in Medina served as the locus both of private and public worship and of informal instruction of the believers in the religious law and related matters. The mosque continued to play these multiple roles throughout the first three centuries of Islam (seventh through ninth centuries of the Christian or the Common Era). Typically, instruction in the religious and legal sciences would be offered by a religious scholar to students who sat with him (and, not infrequently, with her) in teaching circles (Ar. *halaqa, majlis*) either inside the mosque or outside in its courtyard. By the tenth century, a new feature, the hostel (*khan*), was increasingly being established next to "teaching mosques" in Iraq and the eastern provinces of the Islamic world, which allowed students and teachers from far-flung areas to reside near these places of instruction. The emergence of the mosque-khan complex is a consequence of the lengthier and more intensive period of study required to qualify as a religious scholar. Religious learning had expanded by this time, and study of the religious law (Ar. *al-Shari'a*) became more detailed and sophisticated, reflected in the eventual establishment of the four prominent Sunni schools of law (Ar. *madhahib*; sing. *madhhab*) by the tenth century.

In the tenth and eleventh centuries of the Common Era, another important institution developed and proliferated known as the *madrasa*, literally meaning in Arabic "a place of study." The *madrasa* was a logical development of the mosque-khan complex, being both a teaching and residential institution. In addition to the impetus of the greater systematization of knowledge, particularly of the legal sciences, which led to the emergence of the *madrasa*, the development of this institution has also been attributed in part to a reassertion of Sunni Muslim identity in the wake of the collapse of the various Shi'i dynasties that had ruled much of the Islamic world in the tenth and eleventh centuries. In the tenth century, a Shi'i dynasty called the Buwayhids (or Buyids) established their control over 'Abbasid Iraq and Iran, with the Sunni 'Abbasid caliph remaining as the nominal ruler. The Buwayhids retained their control until the eleventh century, when they were beaten back by the Sunni Saljuqs, a Turkic-speaking people from Central Asia. In 969 CE, another Shi'i dynasty from North Africa later called the Fatimids gained power in Cairo, Egypt, and ruled the Sunni population until 1171, when they were defeated by the Ayyubids. One of the Fatimids' enduring intellectual legacies was the establishment of what has been called the oldest continuing university in the world—the al-Azhar *mosque-madrasa* complex in Cairo—in 972 to propagate Fatimid-Shi'i doctrine and learning. With the fall of the Fatimids, there was a concerted Sunni effort to roll back the Shi 'i influence of the past two centuries. The *madrasa* became in many ways the locus classicus for waging this campaign of religious and intellectual reclamation. This is dramatically reflected in the transformation of al-Azhar into the foremost Sunni center of higher learning in the twelfth century, a position it still enjoys today.[4]

In addition to mosques, mosque-*khan*s, and *madrasa*s, other institutions developed over time that played important, supplementary roles in the dissemination of learning. Among the most significant were the libraries (*maktaba*) that burgeoned from the ninth century on. The larger mosques often had libraries attached to them containing books on religious topics. Other semipublic libraries would additionally have books on logic, philosophy, music, astronomy, geometry, medicine, astronomy, and alchemy. The first academy in the Islamic world, known in Arabic as *bayt al-hikma* (lit. "House of Wisdom"), was built by the 'Abbasid caliph al-Ma'mun (813–33) and had a library and an astronomical observatory attached to it, about which more is said below.

Sometimes wealthy private individuals, such as 'Ali b. Yahya (d. 888), endowed a library in their residences. Known as *khizanat al-hikma* (Ar. "Treasury of Wisdom"), such libraries allowed students to study all branches of learning in them without fees. At all times, informal and formal instruction were offered by men and women in their own homes or in the private homes of scholars and wealthy individuals. In most areas of the medieval Islamic world, such modes of private education were more the norm than formal, collective education in a *madrasa*.[5]

Organization and Curricula of Madrasas: The Parameters of Religious Education

Religious education was based on what is termed in Arabic *al-'ulum al-naqliyya* (lit: the "transmitted sciences"), which consists primarily of the Qur'anic sciences, the *hadith* sciences, and jurisprudence (Ar. *fiqh*). In addition to the "transmitted" or religious sciences were *al-'ulum al-'aqliyya* ("the rational sciences"), which included logic, philosophy, mathematics, and the natural sciences. The rational sciences were also termed the "foreign sciences" or "sciences of the ancients," pointing to their largely classical Greek provenance.

In the pre-'Abbasid period, *madrasas*, like the "teaching" mosques before, were primarily devoted to religious learning based on the study of the transmitted sciences (study of the Qur'an, *hadith*, and the religious law), supplemented by the ancillary sciences of grammar and literature. George Makdisi, who has done pioneering work on Islamic education and demonstrated the influence of the *madrasa* on the development of the medieval European college, has given us a comprehensive idea of medieval curricula of study and the organizations of learning.[6] As far as the traditional or religious sciences were concerned, it was customary for the student to learn in sequence: the Qur'an; *hadith*; Qur'anic sciences, which included exegesis; variant readings of the text; and *hadith* sciences, which involved the study of the biographies of the *hadith* transmitters. The student would then proceed to study two "foundational sciences:" *usul al-din*, referring to the principles or sources of religion, and *usul al-fiqh*, the sources, principles, and methodology of jurisprudence. The student would additionally learn the law of the *madhhab* (school of law) with which he[7] was affiliated, the points of difference (Ar. *khilaf*) within the same *madhhab* and between the four schools of law, and dialectics (Ar. *jadal*), also called disputation (Ar. *munazara*).[8]

Following dialectics came the study of *adab* or belles lettres, including poetry, prosody, and grammar. These subjects in essence constituted the curriculum and were meant to be sequentially studied as indicated here—at least as preferred by the educational theorists of the time. In reality, however, the method and course of study tended to be informal and unstructured and were often dependent on the proclivities of the teachers and sometimes of the students. Thus a typical day of instruction for the famous jurist Muhammad b. Idris al-Shafi'i (d. 820) would involve teaching a course on Qur'an before any other topic in the day, then one each on *hadith* and disputation in that order, followed by a late morning course on the classical language, grammar, prosody, and poetry until about noon.[9]

In his famous *Prolegomena* written in the fourteenth century, the fourteenth-century historian Ibn Khaldun (d. 1406) lists a similar curriculum for the religious sciences, with an emphasis on the Qur'an and its sciences; *hadith* and its sciences, including the study of specific *hadith* terminology; jurisprudence (*fiqh*), with an emphasis on the complex law of inheritance and the sources of jurisprudence but with the addition of theology (*al-kalam*), Sufism (Islamic mysticism; called in Arabic *al-tasawwuf*), and the science of the interpretation of dreams or visions (*ta'bir al-ruya*).[10]

The Rise of Humanism and Paidea

In the study of law, the scholastic method of disputation (*munazara*) prevailed, a pedagogical method that originated quite early in the Islamic milieu. The 'Abbasid caliph Harun al-Rashid (d. 809) encouraged the holding of disputations at his court. The famous early jurist Malik b. Anas (d. 795) used to deputize his contemporary 'Uthman b. 'Isa b. Kinana (d. 797) to engage another well-known jurist, Abu Yusuf (d. 798), in *munazara*. Al-Husayn b. Isma'il (d. 942), a *hadith* scholar and jurisconsult (*mufti*), who was the judge of the Iraqi town of Kufa for sixty years, held regular sessions of legal disputations at his home during his period of judgeship, often attended by other prominent jurisconsults. Other examples of regular disputation sessions abound in the legal literature. These sessions tended to be very popular and often attracted large audiences, frequently running from sunset to midnight.[11]

Rationalism and the method of disputation had their eloquent proponents outside juridical circles as well. The famous "free-thinking" poet of the eleventh century Abu al-'Ala al-Ma'arri (d. 1057) took well-aimed shots at the traditionalists in elegant verse:

> In all you do you follow some tradition, even when you say
> "My Lord is One, Unique."

> But He's ordered us to reflect on His creation, yet when we
> do we're dubbed as heretic.
> Save for natural rivalry, there would not be such books of
> disputation as the *'Umad* or *Mughni*.

Al-Ma'arri is clearly making the point that the Qur'an itself exhorts the believer to reflect on the signs of God and thus to make use of his or her rational faculties. Rationalist disputation may thus be understood to be scripturally mandated, which has led to the composition of beneficial works of intellectual scholarship, such as the well-known *'Umad* and *Mughni*.

In another set of verses, al-Ma'arri makes clear that his preference is for a kind of religious humanism that occupies a middle road between pure intellectualism and traditional religiosity. He said: "They all err—Muslims, Christians, Jews and Magians. Two make humanity's universal sect: One man intelligent without religion, and one religious without intellect."[12] The tension between traditionalism and rationalism would continue through much of the medieval period, with traditionalism slowly gaining ground and becoming predominant in the Late Middle Ages. But rationalism never faded away, as some, particularly Orientalist scholars, have mistakenly and polemically alleged;[13] one could say it ultimately triumphed in forcing traditionalism to reckon with it, adopt its methodology of rational dialectic, and absorb many of its premises while attempting to refute them.

The "Ancients" as a Source of Learning and Wisdom

As early as the middle of the eighth century during the Abbasid period, strong interest began developing in the learning of the ancient world, particularly its Greek sources, but to a lesser extent in its Persian and Indian ones as well. The intellectual awakening that this interest spawned has rendered this age especially illustrious in the annals of Islamic and world history. Because of the political and territorial expansion of Islam beyond the original Arabian peninsula, Muslims became the heirs to the older and more cultured peoples whom they conquered or encountered in other ways.

At the time of the Arab conquest of the Fertile Crescent, the intellectual legacy of Greece was unquestionably the most precious treasure at hand. Under the Abbasid caliph al-Ma'mun (d. 833), the previously mentioned Bayt al-Hikma (the House of Wisdom) was established in 830. This House of Wisdom was a combination library, academy, and translation bureau.

The Bayt al-Hikma may be described as the most important educational institution since the foundation of the Alexandrian Museum in the first half of the third century BCE. Under al-Ma'mun, the Bayt al-Hikma became the center of translation activity. This era of avid translation would last through the early tenth century.[14] The chief of the translators was Hunayn b. Ishaq (d. 873), one of the greatest scholars of the age. Hunayn was a Nestorian Christian from Iraq who was appointed by al-Ma'mun as the director of the famous Bayt al-Hikma. Hunayn is reported to have translated Plato's *Republic*, several works of Aristotle, and almost all of Galen's scientific output. During the heyday of the translation movement, practically all the works of Aristotle that had survived to that day had been translated into Arabic. This intellectual floruit in the Islamic world was taking place while Europe was almost totally ignorant of Greek thought and science. One modern historian has remarked, "While al-Rashid and al-Ma'mun were delving into Greek and Persian philosophy, their contemporaries in the West, Charlemagne and his lords, were reportedly dabbling in the art of writing their names."[15] As these works available in translation progressively took intellectual circles by storm, Muslim scholars, like Patristic Christian theologians before them, had to grapple with "the problem of how to assimilate the 'pagan' knowledge of the Greeks to a conception of the world that included God as its creator."[16]

In the early 'Abbasid period, the rational sciences were taught in special institutions called *dar al-'ilm* (lit. "house of knowledge"), which flourished until about the middle of the eleventh century, when they began to cede ground to the *madrasa*. Like the *madrasa*, the *dar al-'ilm* was also often a *waqf* institution, that is, an endowed institution established by a private Muslim individual using his or her private property for a public charitable purpose. In addition to these institutions, the rational sciences were typically taught in private homes and in other non-institutional locations. Because of the largely non-institutional nature of this kind of education, it has been assumed by some historians that instruction in the rational sciences considerably declined and then disappeared after the twelfth century, just as Europe was beginning to experience a surge in learning inspired by its contacts with the Islamic world. It appears that these historians had been looking for *'ilm* in all the wrong places, because once the *madrasa* with its mandated curriculum of religious sciences became the predominant institution of formal learning, the rational subjects were taught primarily in informal study circles in private homes, libraries, and the *dar al-'ilm* institutions until they disappeared. Because most modern scholars have tended to focus on the *madrasa* as the locus classicus of Islamic education, non-formal and non-institutionalized modes of learning tended to be ignored.

Research based on unpublished manuscripts, charitable foundation deed documents, and biographical works on scholars yields a revised picture. In favorable circumstances, the rational sciences continued to be taught and studied openly even in *madrasa*s, sometimes even in mosques, and certainly in informal study circles and libraries. This was a natural consequence of the fact that the broadly educated person who had acquired mastery in several fields, including the Hellenistic subjects, remained the ideal throughout the premodern period, in contradistinction to our era of specialization. Thus biographical dictionaries from the Mamluk period (1256–1571) refer to *shaykhs* (professors and learned notables) in Damascus who had achieved enviable mastery (Ar. *riyasa*, *imama*) in a number of subjects, including theology, belles lettres, medicine, mathematics, natural science, and the Hellenistic sciences. A Hanafi jurist is described in one biographical entry as having taught logic and scholastic dialectic in the Umayyad mosque in Damascus during the Mamluk period.[17]

George Makdisi, who remains after his death the preeminent scholar on Islamic education, has pointed to the fact that the "ancient sciences" remained accessible and avidly pursued through the High Middle Ages, even by "conventional" scholars such as the Shafi'i jurisconsult Sayf al-Din al-Amidi (d. 1234). In regard to these sciences, he remarked that "[n]ot only was access easy, it was in turn concealed, condoned, allowed, encouraged, held in honour, according to different regions and periods, in spite of the traditionalist opposition, the periodic prohibitions, and autos-da-fé."[18]

Humanistic studies (*Adab*)

A very important part of education in the Islamic milieu was the humanistic sciences, termed in Arabic *adab*, which was based primarily on the study of literature (poetry, belles lettres, prosody) and the linguistic sciences (grammar, syntax, philology). In addition to religious or sacred literature, "profane" or secular literature was also being produced since the Umayyad period (661–750). In the field of literature and the arts, the Persian contribution was the strongest. The earliest literary prose work in Arabic that has come down to us is *Kalila wa-Dimna*, a translation of a wisdom tale from Pahlavi (Middle Persian), which in turn was a translation from the Sanskrit. It was rendered into Arabic by Ibn al-Muqaffa' (d. 759), a

Persian Zoroastrian convert to Islam, whose life spanned the late Umayyad and 'Abbasid periods.

The attraction toward "foreign," "un-Islamic" literary traditions was, unsurprisingly, not to everyone's liking. There is no need to recapitulate here the *Kulturkampf* that would ensue for the next two centuries (ninth through the tenth) pitting Persian ethno-cultural sentiments against similar Arab sensibilities.[19] At the end of it, a much more cosmopolitan Islamic cultural identity emerged that was not necessarily predicated on a particular (specifically Arab) ethnic affiliation. Some have described this multicultural, multiethnic, and multireligious civilization as "Islamicate" rather than Islamic, underscoring the fact that Islam as a religion was but one seminal component of the rich constellation of values, ideas, imaginaries, and perspectives that shaped such a civilization.[20]

As a consequence of these intellectual and cultural trends, a specifically Islamic humanism emerged based on the concept of *adab*. According to probably the most famous premodern belle-lettrist in Arabic literature, Amr b. Bahr al-Jahiz (d. 869), *adab* may be defined as "1) the total educational system of 2) a cultured Muslim who 3) took the whole world for his object of curiosity and knowledge."[21] *Adab*, according to the first part of this definition, is the equivalent of the Greek notion of *paideia*, according to which a holistic education contributes to the moral development of the individual.

One may even speak of a multiplicity of humanistic trends (humanisms) in this period of extraordinary intellectual and cultural floruit. These trends may variously be characterized as:[22] 1) philosophical humanism, referring to the humanism of the Muslim philosophers of the tenth and eleventh centuries who held that philosophy, rather than religion, was the ultimate guide to perfect conduct of both the state and the individual; 2) intellectual humanism, practiced mainly by the Mu'tazilites (the Rationalists) predicated on the belief that Islam is a rational religion in full accordance with the laws of logic; 3) literary humanism, which has been described as the product of an "aristocracy of the mind,"[23] resulting from a formal, broad-based humanistic education with an emphasis on language studies that led to the acquisition of refined cultural and social ideals appropriate to the courtier, statesman, religious dignitary, and diplomat, for example; 4) religious humanism, which may be characterized as a "serene contentment with the non-transcendental aspects of Islamic life alongside an unreserved acquiescence to all the conditions of the faith, thus integrating a human and satisfying earthly existence with the hope of eternal salvation;"[24] and 5) legalistic humanism, engendered by the fact that the repository of ethical and legal principles known as the Shari'a, being as comprehensive as it is in its scope, requires the jurist and other legal practitioners to be concerned with the complexities of human nature at the spiritual and temporal levels, allowing for the emergence of a certain humanist perception and insight.

Adab in the broad sense of humanistic studies became an integral part of the curriculum in mosques, *madrasa*s, and libraries. The sciences of the Arabic language (*'ulum al-'Arabiyya*) were necessary ancillaries to the religious sciences from the very beginning. According to the well-known philologist al-Anbari (d. 1181), a full range of offerings in the Arabic sciences would include grammar, lexicology, morphology, metrics, rhyme, prosody, history of the Arab tribes, Arab genealogy, as well as the science of dialectic for grammar and the science of grammatical theory and methodology.[25] Secular belle-lettristic works were sometimes taught even in mosques; the fourteenth century biographer al-Safadi (d. 1363) mentions that a shaykh taught al-Hariri's famous *Maqamat* and other literary works in the Umayyad mosque.[26]

Being a polymath was a matter of pride, and scholars won renown for their breadth of learning in various religious and secular subjects rather than for a narrow specialization. Thus the elder Taqi al-Din Subki (d. 1355), father of the famous biographer and chronicler Taj al-Din Subki (d. 1370), is described by his son as not atypically having mastery over jurisprudence, *hadith*, Qur'anic exegesis and recitation, didactic and speculative theology, grammar and syntax, lexicography, belles lettres and ethics, medicine, scholastic dialectic, *khilaf* (points of difference among the law schools), logic, poetry, heresiography, arithmetic, law, and astronomy.[27] Physicians were also commonly learned in *adab* and the legal sciences, just as many jurists were also learned in medicine.[28] Mastery of the Arabic language in fact became equated with moral superiority so much so that the scholar Ibn Hubayra the senior (d. 1165) declared that the pious man who correctly spoke Arabic possessed greater merit both in this world and the next than the pious man who did not.[29]

The master narrative on Islamic education in both Islamic (Arabic, Persian, Urdu, etc.) and Western languages has traditionally minimized the role of women in scholarship, creating the impression that their influence has been slight. Yet, not-as-frequently consulted sources like biographical dictionaries establish that women's contributions, particularly in the transmission of *hadith* and in other areas of religious scholarship, have been considerable and recognized as such by their contemporaries.[30]

The participation of religious minorities, mainly Christians and Jews, in the intellectual and academic life in Islamic societies is also well documented in various sources. We have already referred to the noteworthy contributions of Jacobite and Nestorian Christians to the efflorescence of Islamic civilization starting in the eighth century through their translation activities funded by their Muslim patrons. Interfaith dialogue and dialectics were sometimes conducted at the caliphal court to promote a critical understanding of the other's religion. For example, the Abbasid caliph al-Mahdi (d. 785) convened formal discussions on theological matters with the Catholicos Timothy, leader of the Nestorian church in Iraq in the eighth century. One source mentions that a certain Muslim scholar learned in grammar and the rational sciences held study sessions in his house attended not only by Muslims but also by Jews, Christians, "heretics," and Samaritans,[31] while another shaykh (leading scholar), 'Izz al-Din al-Hasan al-Irbili (d. 1262), is said to have read rational sciences and philosophy with fellow Muslims, the "People of the Book," and philosophers.[32]

Other such examples occur in works of biography and prosopography of the period. Lessons in non-Muslim scriptures were also sometimes given by Muslim scholars. According to one source, a professor in Damascus convened study circles on the New Testament, which were attended by Christians, and others on the Old Testament, which were attended by Jews.[33] The celebrated Jewish philosopher Moses Maimonides, called in Arabic Musa ibn Maymun, served as Saladdin's court physician and wrote most of his philosophical treatises in Arabic. Highly respected for his scholarship, he moved easily in learned Muslim and Jewish circles. His death in 1204 was officially mourned by Jews and Muslims alike for three days in his birthplace, Cairo. In Persia, the Syrian Jacobite Catholicos Abu al-Faraj Ibn al-'Ibri (d. 1286) lectured in the thirteenth century at the famous Il-Khanid observatory and library of Maragha on Euclid and Ptolemy.[34] This kind of ecumenical scholarly collegiality was a major ingredient in the formidable edifice of learning in the medieval Muslim world.

Looking Ahead: Making the Case for Liberal Religious Education in the Islamic Milieu

This survey in broad strokes of Islamic educational patterns and systems from the classical and medieval periods allows us to make the following remarks. At its best and most confident, medieval Islamic civilization came the closest to the modern conception of a vibrantly diverse, multicultural, and tolerant society as was possible in the premodern period. The usual caveats apply—tolerance and diversity in the twenty-first century are different in quality and scope from its facsimile in the ninth, and we must be aware of the pitfalls of anachronism. But the early and high 'Abbasid periods, the period of *convivencia* ("co-existence") in Muslim Spain (al-Andalus), and the Ottoman era were the high benchmarks of a medieval civilization that was generally tolerant of religious minorities and inclined to be receptive to a diversity of beliefs and thought at a time when such notions were unheard of in most other parts of the world. During the early 'Abbasid period, an avidity for knowledge, whatever its source, and tolerance of various religious groups (first Jews and Christians, then later Zoroastrians and Hindus as well) as mandated by scripture were among the reasons that Muslims were able to develop a cosmopolitan, intellectually vibrant, and, at the same time, an intensely religious civilization that left its indelible mark on the course of world history. A constellation of values similar (but certainly not identical, given the disparities in time and historical circumstances) to what we now prize in the modern liberal educational system may be identified in the premodern Islamic modes of education. The revival of classical Muslim education at its best, with its appeal to both faith and reason wedded to the practical curricular needs of the modern classroom, will make the educational systems of various Muslim-majority societies robust and relevant today, particularly for nurturing an ethic of responsible global citizenship.

In *Being in the World: Dialogue and Cosmopolis*, Fred Dallmayr remarks that such cosmopolitan endeavors "must be in tune with cultural, ethical, and spiritual or 'symbolic' dimensions of human life."[35] Central to this enterprise is a renewed emphasis on the humanities or liberal arts broadly conceived for the "formation of 'citizens of the world.' "[36] On this critical topic, al-Jahiz and Dallmayr—bridging a temporal chasm—are of one mind.

Notes

1. For example, Qur'an 2:151–52; 4:113; 5:110; 12:22; 28:14.

2. Two of the best known of such treatises are Ibn 'Abd al-Barr's *Jami' bayan al-'ilm wa-fadlihi* (Beirut: Dar al-kutub al-'ilmiyya, 2000); and Ibn Qayyim al-Jawziya's *Fadl al-'ilm wa-'l-'ulama'* (Beirut: al-Maktab al-Islami, 2001).

3. This topic is a fitting tribute to Dallmayr, who embodies the virtues of humanism and cosmopolitanism in his worldview and prolific scholarship.

4. For a comprehensive account of al-Azhar's prominence as an educational institution, see Bayard Dodge, *Al-Azhar: A Millennium of Muslim Learning* (Washington, DC: Middle East Institute, 1961).

5. See, for example, Michael Chamberlain, *Knowledge and Social Practice in Medieval Damascus, 1190–1350* (Cambridge: Cambridge University Press, 1994), 69ff.

6. See his classic study *The Rise of Colleges: Institutions of Learning in Islam and the West* (Edinburgh: Edinburgh University Press, 1901).

7. Law tended to be the preserve of the male scholar, although some women clearly received training in jurisprudence as well; see also footnote 29.

8. Makdisi, *The Rise of Colleges*, 80ff.

9. Yaqut al-Hamawi, *Irshad al-arib ila ma'rifat al-adib*, ed. Ahmad Farid al-Rifa'i (Cairo: Dar al-Ma'mun, 1936–38), 17:304.

10. Ibn Khaldun, *al-Muqaddima*," trans. F. Rosenthal (New York: Pantheon Books, 1958).

11. Makdisi, *Rise of Colleges*, 133ff. For a discussion of the influence of the medieval Islamic *madrasa* on the rise of colleges in medieval Europe and the adoption of the scholastic method there, see George Makdisi, "The Scholastic Method in Medieval Education: An Inquiry into Its Origins in Law and Theology," *Speculum* 49 (1974): 640–61; idem, "Interaction between Islam and the West," in *Mediaeval Education in Islam and the West*, ed. George Makdisi and Dominic Sourdel, eds. (Paris: Paul Guethner, 1977); and "On the Origin of the College in Islam and the West," in *Islam and the Mediaeval West: Aspects of Intercultural Relations*, ed. K. I. H. Semaan (Albany: State University of New York Press, 1980).

12. R. A. Nicholson, *Studies in Islamic Poetry* (Cambridge: Cambridge University Press, 1921), 268.

13. One of the most notorious examples of such a polemicist is Ernest Renan, who in the nineteenth century pilloried Islam as a religion opposed to rationality; see Albert Hourani, *Arabic Thought in the Liberal Age: 1798–1939* (Cambridge: Cambridge University Press, 1983), 120–21.

14. See Dimitri Gutas, *Greek Thought, Arabic Culture: The Graeco-Arabic Translation Movement in Baghdad and Early 'Abbasid Society (2nd–4th/8th–10th Centuries)* (London: Routledge, 1998).

15. Philip Hitti, *History of the Arabs*, rev. 10th ed. (New York: Palgrave Macmillan, 2002), 321.

16. Makdisi, *Rise of Colleges*, 77.

17. Al-Safadi, *al-Wafi bi al-wafayat*, ed. H. Ritter et al. (Istanbul: Franz Steiner Verlag, 1931), 21:88; cited by Chamberlain, *Knowledge and Social Practice*, 84, n. 76.

18. Makdisi, *Rise of Colleges*, 78.

19. For an account of this culture war, see Roy Mottahedeh, "The Shu'ubiyah Controversy and the Social History of Early Islamic Iran," *International Journal of Middle East Studies* 7 (1976): 161–82.

20. Marshall Hodgson, *The Venture of Islam: Conscience and History in a World Civilization* (Chicago: University of Chicago Press, 1974), 1:58–59.

21. Tarif Khalidi, *Classical Arab Islam: The Culture and Heritage of the Golden Age* (Princeton: Darwin Press, 1985), 57.

22. These categories are taken from Michael G. Carter, "Humanism in Medieval Islam," in *Humanism, Culture, and Language in the Near East*, ed. Asma Afsaruddin and Mathias Zahniser (Winona Lake, IN: Eisenbrauns, 1997), 27–38.

23. This is a phrase used by Muhammad Arkoun in his *L'humanisme arabe au Ive/IXe siècle, Miskawayh, philosophe et historien* (Paris: Maisonneuve et larose, 1982), 357.

24. Carter, "Humanism," 32.

25. Al-Anbari, *Nuzhat al-alibba' fi tabaqat al-udaba'*, ed. A. Amer (Stockholm: Almqvist and Wiksell, 1962), 55; cited by Makdisi, *Rise of Colleges*, 79.

26. Michael Chamberlain, *Knowledge and Social Practice in Medieval Damascus: 1190–1350* (Cambridge: Cambridge University Press, 2002), 85, n. 82.

27. Al-Subki, *al-Tabaqat al-shafi'iyya al-kubra*, ed. Mahmud Muhammad al-Tanahi and 'Abd al-Fattah Muhammad al-Hilu (Cairo: Matba'a 'Isa al-Babi, 1964–76), 6:146–47, 150, 168–69; also in Chamberlain, *Knowledge and Social Practice*, 86.

28. See, for example, Ibn Abi 'Usaybi'a, *'Uyun al-anba' fi tabaqat al-atibba'* (Beirut: Dar Maktabat al-Hayat, 1965), 646–51.

29. Recorded by Yaqut al-Hamawi, *Irshad al-arib ila ma'rifat al-adib*, ed. D. S. Margoliouth (New Delhi: Kitab Bhawan, 1982), 1:23.

30. Asma Sayeed, *Women and the Transmission of Religious Knowledge in Islam* (Cambridge: Cambridge University Press, 2015); Asma Afsaruddin, "Knowledge, Piety, and Religious Leadership in the Late Middle Ages: Reinstating Women in the Master Narrative," in *Knowledge and Education in Classical Islam*, ed. Sebastian Guenther (Leiden: E.J. Brill, 2019).

31. Al-Yunini, *Dhayl Mir'at al-zaman* (Hyderabad: Da'irat al-ma'arif al-'uthmaniyya, 1954–61), 2:165.

32. Al-Safadi, *al-Wafi*, 12:247; cited by Chamberlain, *Knowledge and Social Practice*, 84, n. 80.

33. Ibn Khallikan, *Wafayat al-a'yan wa-anba abna' al-zaman*, ed. M. 'Abd al-Hamid (Cairo: Matba'at al-Sa'ada, 1948), 4:397.

34. Hitti, *History of the Arabs*, 691.

35. Fred Dallmayr, *Being in the World: Dialogue and Cosmopolis* (Lexington, KY: University Press of Kentucky, 2015), 4.

36. Ibid., 5.

Chapter 8

Where to Explore the Political in Islamic Political Thought

AHMET OKUMUŞ

Students of contemporary political theory are well aware of the distinction between politics and the political, where the former comprises the daily and conventional practices, processes, and procedures of politics, while the latter signifies the founding dimension that structures and integrates the social whole and its various subdomains, including politics. In this respect, politics, just like economics or culture, is one subsphere of society among others, whereas the political is the mode of institution and overall configuration of all those subspheres, including politics. As Fred Dallmayr articulates it, "politics designates overt political activities and power strategies amenable to empirical research, whereas the political has a more elusive, quasi-transcendental or metaphysical status."[1] It is important to approach classical Islamic political thought with this distinction in mind, because this edifice of thought on politics (*siyasa*) is predicated on a range of assumptions and practices that are considerably different from the set of assumptions and practices we commonly associate with politics today. In other words, historico-semantically speaking, the references of the term *siyasa* hardly overlap with the references of the term "politics." Therefore, it seems more promising to raise questions concerning the founding dimension, the fundamental distinctions, and the

---

*I am grateful to Engin Deniz Akarlı and Özgür Kavak for their comments on an earlier version of this text.

basic "categories in which the political . . . makes itself available to us"[2] in Islamic political thought.

Drawing inspiration from Dallmayr's searching or *Zetetic* exercises, I pursue the question concerning political forms or regimes. Does Islamic political thought have any systematic body of reflection on the types of state, or on different political forms? What patterns of thought are there concerning the diverse forms the political whole could assume? What resources are available to address the question of "regime"? These questions are worth pondering in order to confront yet another question or challenge that global politics poses to Muslims today: "What is the character of *political* agency in the Islamic world?"[3]

I

Since Plato and especially Aristotle, the nature and the ethical quality of an order (or *cosmion*) and the way justice is instituted there have been elaborated with reference to the notion of *politeia* or regime, leading to several major types of regime classification, such as monarchy, aristocracy, and polity or democracy. Many scholars have underlined the polysemy of the term *politeia*. Usually translated as "constitution," its significations go far beyond this narrowly juridical and institutional sense to comprehend the entire form of life of a people. *Politeia* or regime not only designates the manner in which benefits and burdens are distributed, offices and entitlements assigned, and positions of power organized within the normative scope of a basic law; it also indicates the form of life this whole scheme of offices and institutions sustains.[4] In a sense, life takes on a different guise under every regime.

In the recent past, several influential political thinkers occupying divergent positions on the ideological spectrum have attempted to retrieve this dimension of the notion for contemporary politics. Among them, Leo Strauss stands out. He placed particular emphasis on the concept of regime as a rendition of the ancient *politeia* and as a potential corrective for the distortions caused by positivistic political science (and the social sciences in general). The concept of regime, according to Strauss, is incomprehensible to the new political science, which is preoccupied with generating and working with value-free terms based on the positivistic principle of separating facts from values. What are deemed to be value neutral here are supposedly general and homogenous categories of human and social reality, such as the invariant laws of human behavior or power, which came to displace the classical notion of regime as the new universals of political science.[5] While this normatively or evaluatively neutral orientation of the new political science was celebrated as a great advance in many quarters, it was incessantly criticized by Strauss as a detrimental turn that was gradually enervating our capacity for judgment in the face of political questions. In his view, those who sought, for instance, to compare political phenomena by means of homogeneous variables like power could not discern any qualitative difference between liberal democracy and communism; they could only perceive a difference of degree.[6] It was no wonder, then, that political thought, incapable of evaluating contemporary political formations, was mute and crippled when confronted with the tragedies of the age.

As Pierre Manent points out, political philosophy suffered its first trial in the twentieth century in the face of totalitarianism and struggled to make sense of this novel phenomenon because it no longer possessed an evaluative vocabulary of regimes.[7] Accordingly, the prevalent inability to name the totalitarian phenomenon, to apprehend the evil in it, and to diagnose new forms of political evil in general were all manifestations of this retreat of, or from, truly political thinking.[8]

II

Did the tradition of Islamic political thought establish any acquaintance with this central theme of classical political philosophy? Speaking about the Abrahamic tradition in comparison with the Greco-Roman one, or Jerusalem vis-à-vis Athens, Strauss proclaims that owing mainly to the centrality of a higher and divine law in the former, the question of regime had been sidelined. As he remarks, while "there are a number of Biblical terms which can be properly translated by 'law,' there is no Biblical equivalent to 'regime.'" While the regime was the axis and the laws were derivative or subsidiary to the regime in classical political philosophy, in the Abrahamic tradition the conception of the divine law came to center stage, earning the laws primacy over and independence from the regime.[9] Could we make a similar assessment regarding Islamic political thought?

Now, the relative silence of Ibn Sina (Avicenna), the towering figure of Islamic philosophy, regarding ethics and politics, largely because of his affirmation of the predominant role of the law (*shariah*) in these fields,[10] on the one hand, and the hardly silent Ghazali's definition of the same fields within the purview of the law (*min-al-fiqhiyyat*),[11] on the other, could both lend some credence to an affirmative answer. In addition, one could further support such an argument by relying on the widespread view of Islam as a "nomocracy."[12] What is more intriguing, however, is the idea propounded by some of the seminal experts on Islamic philosophy that even a figure like Farabi, commonly recognized as perhaps the most important direct contributor to political philosophy in the history of Islam, did not pursue a line of thinking premised on the discourse of regimes in the true sense of the term. Dimitri Gutas argues that Farabi did not quite capture the significations of the term *politeia*, primarily because his historical horizon of concepts and his political repertoire of experiences did not incorporate any such entity. In the context of tenth-century Baghdad, it was hardly possible to speak about *politeia* in any meaningful way in the legal and political senses of the term as regime, political form, or constitution.[13]

Gutas also specifies that in the Arabic translation of Aristotle's *Nicomachean Ethics*, the term *politeia* was mistranslated as *sîra* (plural *siyar*), that is, "way of life," thereby unsurprisingly impeding Farabi's grasp of the political contents and implications of the term. As he says, "al-Farabi approached the subject of human societies from an ethical point of view, primarily because of the mistranslation of the concept of constitution in the last paragraph of the Nicomachean Ethics as 'a way of life,' as *bios*."[14] In his view, it is equally mistaken to translate another key phrase in the philosophical literature, namely, *madaniyyun bit-tab'i*, as "political animal," misleadingly ascribing a political connotation to Farabi's thought. Even though Farabi's *madanî*, which literally means pertaining or belonging to the city (or "of the city"—from Arabic *madîna*, "the city"), covers the Aristotelian sense that "we are by nature programmed to communal living," this still lacked any clear or straightforward political connotation. Instead, it is more accurate to understand the phrase in its narrower and literal sense as "city animal," in line with the historical and conceptual possibilities of the time. As a corollary to this, the best option, according to Gutas, to retain the sense of *al-siyasa al-madaniyya* in Farabi is to translate it as "governance of the city," in contrast to its rendition as "political regime" by a number of scholars.[15] Otherwise, we are misled into thinking that Farabi has had a *political* philosophy concerned with regimes, whereas his precise focus was ethical and thus oriented to the autarkic organization of the city as a biosocial community in a manner favorable to the cultivation of human perfection. Gutas sums up the whole exposition with the contention that "Man, in other words, is a 'city' animal, and not a 'political' animal."[16]

However, to what degree could this essentially philological account settle the question?[17] As previously indicated, *politeia* covers not only the juridical and institutional ordering of offices and powers across society, but also the form of life animated by any such ordering; and this is an aspect of, or a layer of meaning in, the concept that an important group of political thinkers in the recent past have tried to reactivate. On the other hand, such recent interest in this aspect of the concept cannot simply be attributed to the peculiar concerns and predicaments of contemporary political philosophy. On the contrary, scholars of antiquity reveal a *politeia* tradition with roots antedating Plato and Aristotle and enduring after them—a tradition, again, dealing with every aspect of a style of living. As Malcolm Schofield enumerates, for instance, Xenophon's *The Politeia of the Spartans* and *The Politeia* of the Stoic Zeno both incorporate an extensive range of topics: "eugenics and the role of women; education (including diet, clothing and pederasty); the conduct of adolescents; choruses and athletic contests; public common meals and the use of drink; relations between parents and children; money and the accumulation of wealth."[18] As can readily be seen, the scope is not restricted to questions like who rules, in whose interest, and how offices relate to one another; rather, it encompasses almost every aspect of a shared life. In the *politeia* tradition, then, the concept takes on a depth of meaning pertaining to the common ethos of a people. On this ground, one can assert that any substantial analysis of regimes would endeavor to disclose the distinctive ethos of each type of regime and identify the motivational (or psychomotivational) underpinnings of each. This is why at a much later moment Montesquieu distinguishes two dimensions in every regime, one being its structure and the other its principle (or spirit), where the spirit is broadly interpreted as the animating motive or the psychomoral spirit of the regime.[19]

Seen against this background, translating *politeia* as *sîra* (form of life) and Farabi's concern with mores, customs, and the ethical dispositions prevailing in different cities seem quite in tune with this tradition. One could even argue that such an ethically inflected translation constitutes a perfect match to the notion, because, as some students of ancient political philosophy state, the "political analog of moral virtue" is *politeia*. In Jill Frank's words, "just as virtue is composed of sedimented habits, with no precise and identifiable source, that are generated by actions and that themselves generate but do not fully determine activity, so too is constitution [*politeia*] . . . a product of long and unvarying habit, 'a way of life of a people.'"[20] Just as virtues are relatively stable character traits, a regime is an ongoing crystallization of relatively stable patterns of human interaction and characteristic modes of civility, or the lack thereof. A regime serves as an ethical framework, facilitates ethical formation, and is thus a context of habituation into a form of life guiding and guided by its characteristic set of excellences. It does not suffice to concede only that *politeia* contains these meanings in its semantic space as a linguistic possibility, as Gutas does, because this falls short of recognizing the filiation of Farabi's usage of *sîra* to this broader tradition and its philosophical importance.

One might grant, following Gutas, that "governance of the city" is indeed a better counterpart to *al-siyasa al-madaniyya* than is "political regime." Nevertheless, what is a "city" and what is "governance"? Recalling that the city is one of the most ancient political forms[21] we know, should not we understand from governance here something more than municipal administration, something corresponding to the administrative affairs of a politically organized collectivity? Even if Farabi's *madîna* is not Aristotle's *polis*,[22] does not the governance of *madîna* bear on issues of war and peace, the rich and the poor, justice and injustice, and friend and enemy, which are all political in essence? Does not this *madîna* harbor ranks, groups, social strata, interests, and conflicts, which are all contingent on regime qualifications and politically implicated? Could we ever regard the city as a biosocial sphere, or somehow as a kind of pure sociality devoid of political dimensions? Could construing the *polis*, *madîna*, or the city as a biosocial whole detract from its political character in any way? Any sociality, especially if attains the stage of autarky, as both the *polis* and *madîna* do, stands under the auspices of the political. The delimitation of a sphere as "the social" or "society" is itself "shaped by our insertion into a historically and politically determined framework"; it rests on "the question of the constitution of the social space, of the *form* of society, of the essence of what was once termed the 'city.'"[23] In this regard, dissociating Farabi from political philosophy would run counter to the basic categories of his thinking, because what is supposedly missing from *sîra*[24] is in fact already embedded and encapsulated in *madîna*.[25] One could also notice that identifying the "city" with the social would amount to reading back into the past the modern distinction between society and state, or the social and the political, which was conspicuously absent from the classical world.

III

The preceding discussion delineates the contours of the question at hand so as not to misjudge the character of Islamic political thought in general and Farabi's thought in particular. Before embarking on the task of judging if there is genuinely *political* thinking on politics in this heritage or discriminating the specific modalities of any such thinking therein, one needs to ponder the categories of evaluation at one's disposal. Given the above considerations about the political, the regime, and the city, it seems difficult to banish Farabi from the tradition of political philosophy, though one might grant that in his analyses of regimes some of the more explicitly institutional and perhaps formal-procedural aspects of the matter are somewhat circumvented by the metaphysical and ethical élan of his thought. Farabi's classification of regimes is certainly not as detailed as we find in Aristotle's *Politics*, which remained, as is well known, inaccessible to Muslim philosophers throughout centuries. Farabi mainly dealt with the forms of the city in terms of their ethico-metaphysical promises. This was in accordance with his understanding of "theoretical politics" (*siyasa nazariyya*) as an inquiry about the universals (or universal principles) of politics rather than their historically varying particular instantiations, which were in turn the subject matter of practical politics (*siyasa amaliyya*).[26] Farabi's contribution was located on the level of "the political," which is, as indicated above, quasi-transcendental and metaphysical in status, rather than on that of practical politics. He was in fact the first to coin and use the term *falsafa siyasiyya* (political philosophy) in Arabic, by which he primarily intended the metaphysical moorings and ethical possibilities of politics. In this respect, even in the case of Farabi, who was the most emphatic of all the Muslim scholars regarding the importance of the question of regime, or of the ethico-political forms the city could assume, the political element in Islamic political thought might appear overshadowed by its ethical overtones.

However, the search for a new political ethic or perhaps for a new ethico-political turn has gained some prominence in political philosophy and in some corners of sociological theory today. While significant groups of political theorists are seeking the possibility of an ethico-political reorientation, others in the social sciences (or social theory) are fusing political philosophy and the social sciences together in interdisciplinary programs of research. In an endeavor to transcend the proceduralist bent of much of today's normative political theory, these political thinkers try to shift the accent toward the question of "ethos" (which can also be rendered as *sîra*) so as to envision an ethically invigorated public life or a public ethos (*sîra madaniyya*) animated by civic virtues.[27] A comparable attempt at reorientation is led by the research program known as the "sociology of action regimes," which aims to rework the conception of regimes in political philosophy within a sociological framework of analysis so as to generate models of individual and collective action operating alongside each other in a single society. Here the ethical contents (or the underlying ethical principles) of every regime are distilled as alternative models of justification simultaneously available in the social background where each regime (or, in this particular literature, "polity") offers a distinctive "grammar of justification." Traditionally treated as separate forms in political philosophy, regimes or cities transform into distinct action repertoires, or repertoires of ethical action, crisscrossing each other within society.[28] Farabi's ethically modulated conception of regimes allows useful comparisons with these more recent lines of social and political thought.

Overall, we can identify three main dynamics restricting the debate on political forms in the history of Islamic political thought. The first is the primacy of a tradition of jurisprudence (*fiqh*) with underpinnings in revealed law (*sharia*) over the question of regimes. The second is the philosophers' assent or acquiescence to the primacy and regulatory role of *sharia* in practical matters and their treatment of the topic of regimes mostly in terms of the universals of theoretical politics, as in the case of Farabi, who actually devoted considerable space to the topic in his works. The third is the entrenchment of hereditary absolute rule as a functioning and perhaps the only viable political option during most of history.

We need to try to dispel a couple of likely misunderstandings regarding the dynamics identified above. One concerns the preeminent position of *fiqh* in Islam, about which, as previously mentioned, there is a large consensus among scholars, despite some significant recent arguments to the contrary. Many have rightly detected an underlying and enduring tension between *siyasa* (politics) and *sharia* (law) in Islam, a tension that becomes manifest especially in representations of *sharia*, widespread throughout Islamic history, as the true or authentic politics that would realize justice, on the one hand, and of *siyasa* as at best its simulation, on the other.[29] In our contemporary context, this tension has found a new expression in charges of the "tyranny of legalism" and calls for rehabilitating the primacy of political philosophy.[30] While these more recent indictments are understandable in their own settings, one should not misconstrue the so-called legalist attitude assumed by

Muslim scholars in earlier times, because such attitudes were often themselves meant to restrain unlawful and arbitrary uses of power by or the tyrannous tendencies of the rulers.[31] Besides, although the preeminent position of *fiqh* may have contributed to a deficit of discourse on political forms, this did not preclude it from inspiring powerful images of good and principled rulers on its own. Addressing real persons or agents of responsibility rather than corporate persons or institutions, *fiqh* in a sense does not deal with the "reified" entities we are familiar with today; it aims, for instance, to stipulate the qualifications of the "caliph" rather than the "caliphate."[32] While this general stance tends to marginalize some core issues that deserve consideration in any rigorous account of regimes, it nevertheless offers images of a just ruler and proper principles of administration. One may wish to elaborate on this to draw a more satisfactory account of political forms from within the relevant literature of *fiqh* itself.[33]

The second misunderstanding relates to the hereditary absolute rule mentioned above. The entrenchment of this type of rule was thematized by Muslim scholars, as in the case of Ibn Khaldun, who held the conversion from caliphate to *mulk* (broadly, kingship) as one of his primary subjects of examination. However, although entrenched, kingship was not simply the result of some haphazard development or of a kind of historical drift. As Marshall Hodgson points out, "before the advent of modern technical conditions, a strong monarchy was by and large the most satisfactory form of supra-local government in any agrarianistic society," and it was "everywhere the acknowledged political ideal."[34] Nor is it comprehensible by recycling the age-old stereotype of Oriental despotism. Caution is also needed in lumping together all the historically varied formations scattered over diverse geographies under a summary label like hereditary absolute rule. The rule of the Abbasids was not the same as that of the Ottomans, just as Ottoman rule in the fifteenth century was not the same as that in the eighteenth century. In fact, Hodgson distinguishes five types of solution offered under the banner of Islamic legitimacy to the problem of durable government with varying degrees of adaptability to large-scale organization in an agrarian context: the Khārijī-Zaydī solution of face-to-face community under a caliph responsible to the community of the faithful at large; the Ismailī (*batinī*-gnostic) one of hierarchical legitimation; the solution of the "philosophically-conceived state" pursued by the *falasifa* (e.g., Farabi); the pro-absolutist solution of the *adib* (broadly, "the man of letters"), who advocated a polity of hierarchical privileges and distinctions along the old Iranian monarchic lines; and last, the juridical (or *sharia*) solution of the *ulema* (Muslim scholars) supporting a sort of egalitarian approach against any special privileges, with caliph being only "the first among essentially equal Muslims."[35] Although each solution seems to sketch an alternative form of regime, only the last two, the absolutist and juridical ones, survived as widely practicable options throughout much of Islamic history, intertwining in a tensional yet accommodative way. In any case, the question concerning political forms remained in a tenuous position up until the age of revolutions.[36]

IV

Political thought in the Muslim heritage springs from a highly diversified and complex historical background and has flourished in a rich variety of forms and produced several offshoots. Yet how and in what way this rich and diverse legacy would inform today's Muslims is an enduring puzzle. Is it amenable to retrieval and recovery, or is the situation more radical, the line broken, thus requiring a more aesthetic treatment? These questions are especially challenging for Muslims today, who live under the amplifying influence of a more cosmopolitan question: "What kind of political thinking is appropriate to our turbulent age?"[37] Encountering this bewildering range of issues, we need to rework the wealth of materials and contents in Islamic political thought through multiple readings from varying standpoints and with diverse methodologies. Approaching traditional contents with suggestive questions might help us chart a new course in this direction. In this chapter, I have aimed to identify a small set of such questions and focus on one of them. We lately have seen an increasing number of initiatives to ground similar inquiries relying on the classical corpus of Islamic jurisprudence and political thought. However, to augment the fecundity of such studies, what I would like to call a "healthy presentism" might be rewarding by anchoring our strivings in our lived experiences today. In Dallmayr's words, "political thought cannot escape nostalgically into the past nor project itself into a utopian future, but has to take its stand in the present—a present not conceived, however, as a point in a linear sequence, but rather as a lived moment lodged in the interstices of competing temporalities."[38]

The present is thus never merely an empty now; it is already sedimented by the past and remains pregnant with future possibilities. Dallmayr often reminds us that "human societies and cultures live not only in space but also in time"[39] and that we are always situated in this dialectical-dialogical meeting zone of temporalities. In this regard, the past, or tradition, can call us into question, just as we can raise questions concerning the relevance of the past in relation to our present troubles. We do honor the integrity of the past, but we do this better by reading the past, or interpreting the classics, in ways that they can still speak to us in new, fresh ways in our own times. We have to determine, or, perhaps more properly, beware of the questions we raise today. Ultimately, we have to learn to think on our own in the present.

Notes

1. Fred Dallmayr, "Post-metaphysical Politics: Heidegger and Democracy?," in *The Other Heidegger* (Ithaca: Cornell University Press, 1993), 87–88. Also see, in the same book, his "Rethinking the Political: Some Heideggerian Contributions," 49–76. For his more recent take on the same topic, see "The Concept of the Political: Politics between War and Peace," in *Integral Pluralism: Beyond Culture Wars* (Lexington: The University Press of Kentucky, 2010), 23–44.

2. Tracy B. Strong, "Politics and the Political in the 'Berkeley School' of Political Theory," *Political Studies* (July 2017): 801–2, at 802.

3. Fred Dallmayr, *Peace Talks Who Will Listen* (Notre Dame, IN: University of Notre Dame Press, 2004), 212.

4. This is why for Aristotle a *polis* is not the same *polis* if its *politeia* changes. See Aristotle, *Politics*, 1276a17–1276b13. On the notion of *politeia*, see Malcolm Schofield, *Plato* (Oxford: Oxford University Press, 2006), 28–43. See also Christian Meier, *The Greek Discovery of Politics*, trans. David McLintock (Cambridge, MA: Harvard University Press, 1990).

5. Leo Strauss, "What Is Political Philosophy," in his *What Is Political Philosophy and Other Studies* (Chicago: The University of Chicago Press, 1988 [1959]), 9–55, at 33–35; also, *Natural Right and History* (Chicago: The University of Chicago Press, 1950), 135–45. See also Claude Lefort, *Democracy and Political Theory*, trans. David Macey (Minneapolis: University of Minnesota Press, 1988), 2–3, 11–12, 218.

6. Leo Strauss, *Liberalism Ancient and Modern* (Ithaca: Cornell University Press, 1989 [1968]), 214–15.

7. Pierre Manent, "The Return of Political Philosophy," *First Things* (May 2000). See also Lefort, *Democracy and Political Theory*, 10. I am using "regime" and "political form" as interchangeable notions in contrast to Manent, who distinguishes the two.

8. Furthermore, because they had similarly undermined evaluative distinctions regarding political forms in their own ways, even revolutionary ideologies and ontologies of decline fell into the grip of the same conundrum. As Bernard Flynn makes the point in an exposition of Claude Lefort's thought, the Left's paralysis

in confronting the Stalinist terror, on the one hand, and Heidegger's disinclination to see any significant difference between the Soviets under Stalin and the United States under Roosevelt, on the other, both derived from the closure of their universe of thoughts to "the notion of a regime and the difference between regimes." See Bernard Flynn, *The Philosophy of Claude Lefort: Interpreting the Political* (Evanston, IL: Northwestern University Press, 2005), 152–57.

9. Leo Strauss, "What Is Political Philosophy," 34. See also his more detailed account of the matter in *Natural Right and History*, 135–45.

10. M. Cüneyt Kaya, "In the Shadow of 'Prophetic Legislation': The Venture of Practical Philosophy after Avicenna," *Arabic Sciences and Philosophy* 24 (2014): 269–96.

11. Ghazali, *al-Iqtisad fi'l-I'tiqad* (Beirut: Dâru'l-kutubi'l-ilmiyya, 2004), 127.

12. The omnipresence of *fiqh* is perhaps most emphatically expressed by George Makdisi in his description of the Islamic vision of the good order as "nomocracy"—Islam is "nomocratic and nomocentric." Such "legal-supremacist conceptualizations of Islam" have later been contested on a number of grounds. Recently, for instance, the late Shahab Ahmed criticized legal-supremacist views of Islam as falsely restricting the rich texture of Islamic discourse of normativity to *fiqh* alone. See George Makdisi, "Hanbalite Islam," in *Studies on Islam*, ed. and trans. Merlin L. Swartz (New York: Oxford University Press, 1981), 264; Shahab Ahmed, *What Is Islam? The Importance of Being Islamic* (Princeton, NJ: Princeton University Press, 2016).

13. Dimitri Gutas, "The Meaning of *madanî* in al-Fârâbî's 'Political' Philosophy," *Mélanges de l'Université Saint-Joseph*, LVII (2004), 259–82.

14. See Gutas, "The Meaning of *madanî*," 270.

15. Farabi, *The Political Writings: "Political Regime" and "Summary of Plato's Laws,"* trans. and annot. C. E. Butterworth (Ithaca: Cornell University Press, 2015).

16. Gutas, "The Meaning of *madanî*," 266. Gutas argues that the same holds true for Aristotle despite, as readers of "Marx and Gramsci and Strauss," our being "prone to read back into Aristotle things he never quite meant that way." Then, again, man, for Aristotle, is a "city" animal "biologically programmed to communal living in order to survive," but not a "political" animal. See Gutas, 266, footnote 20.

17. Gutas's primary target here is those who approach Islamic philosophical texts with the interpretive concerns of the so-called Straussian school. I am particularly interested in Strauss's attempts at reviving the regime question rather than any kind of esotericism or narrow textualism.

18. Schofield, *Plato*, 32.

19. Charles Louis de Secondat, Baron de Montesquieu, *The Spirit of the Laws*, trans. Anne M. Choler, Basia Carolyn Miller, and Harold Samuel Stone (Cambridge: Cambridge University Press, 1989), 21 (bk. 3, chap. 1).

20. Jill Frank, *A Democracy of Distinction: Aristotle and the Work of Politics* (Chicago: The University of Chicago Press, 2005), 136. Frank continues that "if

virtue 'preserves' practical wisdom and so produces (even as it is guided by) good judgment and thereby lawfulness, the polity's proper constitution, by introducing predictability, pattern, and order into individual practices, safeguards and preserves lawfulness to produce (even as it is guided by) the common judgment of the community, its common sense or consensus."

21. See Pierre Manent, *Metamorphoses of the City: On the Western Dynamic*, trans. Marc LePain (Cambridge, MA: Harvard University Press, 2013). Whether one could approach primitive chiefdoms as political forms in their own right is also debatable. See Pierre Clastres, *Society Against the State: Essays in Political Anthropology*, trans. Robert Hurley and Abe Stein (New York: Zone Books, 1989 [1974]).

22. Said Amir Arjomand says, ". . . the Greek or even the Hellenistic *polis* had long ceased to exist. Nor could the Greek idea of *polis*, faithfully rendered as *madina*, have any 'demonstration effect' as the Byzantine Empire was by then a Christian monarchy. Its impact depended on the trans-historical property of the Greek civilizational complex, which made possible its inter-societal transmission and rediscovery in medieval Islam and medieval Christianity. Such inter-civilizational transmission would, however, be inevitably selective." See "Perso-Indian Statecraft, Greek Political Science and the Muslim Idea of Government," *International Sociology* 16, no. 3 (2001): 470.

23. Lefort, *Democracy and Political Theory*, 11.

24. Regarding the term *sîra*, it might be interesting to note with Arjomand that although as a term referring to the way of life of the Prophet it became part of the normative vocabulary of Muslim scholarship from the very beginning, it was also being used by the works on statecraft to relate the stories and customs of the ancient kings. Arjomand contends, "the customs and the traditions of the ancient kings were given a *similar* normative status by the use of identical vocabulary," that is, a similar status to the customs and traditions of the Prophet. As far as I know, however, the same works on statecraft usually refrained from referring to the customs and traditions of the kings who came *after* the Prophet in time and who were non-Muslim. In a sense, they did not recognize post-prophetic *and* non-Islamic kings as normative in their evaluations. See Arjomand, "Perso-Indian Statecraft, Greek Political Science and the Muslim Idea of Government," 460–61. In the end, three uses of the term *sîra* appear as relatively established: the customs, the traditions, and the way of life of the Prophet (*siyar an-nabî*), of the kings (*siyar al-mulûk*), and of the cities (*siyar al-mudun*).

25. Farabi's arguments range over some broader-scale collectivities as well, such as *ma'mura*, the inhabited world (like *oikumene*), and the *ummah*. As Tarif Khalidi reveals, from the very beginning Muslim scholars have displayed a profound curiosity about the structure, character, and history of cities and urban settlements. See *Arabic Historical Thought in the Classical Period* (Cambridge: Cambridge University Press, 1994), 119.

26. See Şenol Korkut, *Farabi'nin Siyaset Felsefesi* (Ankara, Turkey: Atlas Kitap, 2015); and Hümeyra Özturan, *Akıl ve Ahlak: Aristoteles ve Farabi'de Ahlakın Kaynağı* (Istanbul: Klasik Yayınları, 2013).

27. For an explicit statement of this reorientation in contemporary political theory, see Stephen K. White, *The Ethos of a Late Modern Citizen* (Cambridge, MA: Harvard University Press, 2009).

28. See Luc Boltanski and Laurent Thévenot, *On Justification: Economies of Worth*, trans. Catherine Porter (Princeton, NJ: Princeton University Press, 2006).

29. Tarif Khalidi, *Arabic Historical Thought in the Classical Period*, 195–97.

30. Muqtedar Khan, "The Primacy of Political Philosophy," in Joshua Cohen and Deborah Chasman, eds., *Islam and the Challenge of Democracy* (Princeton, NJ: Princeton University Press, 2004), 63–68.

31. Asım Cüneyt Köksal, *Fıkıh ve Siyaset: Osmanlılarda Siyaset-i Şer'iyye* (Istanbul: Klasik Yayınları, 2016).

32. I thank Özgür Kavak for bringing these aspects of the matter to my attention.

33. Ovamir Anjum's recent work can partly be read as an attempt in this direction. Although he shares the view that law trumped politics in medieval Islam, drawing on Ibn Taymiyya's opus, he distinguishes a "community-centered" ("*ummah*-centric") conception of politics, which was based on consultation ("*shura*-centric"), from a ruler-centered conception. Anjum argues that the "Taymiyyan moment" needs to be recovered. See his *Politics, Law and Community in Islamic Thought: The Taymiyyan Moment* (Cambridge: Cambridge University Press, 2012). Anjum also advocates a change of focus in studying Islamic political thought in favor of more foundational regions of discourse like *kalam* (roughly, Islamic theology) and *fiqh* before working on the "aggregate concepts" of politics like caliphate and *mulk*. This perfectly reasonable suggestion can be read together with ontological and political theological turns in recent political theory, but with a caveat usually underscored by Dallmayr: "there can be no simple derivation of practice from ontological or other theoretical insights." See Stephen K. White, "Introduction," in Stephen K. White, ed., *Life-World and Politics: Between Modernity and Postmodernity* (Notre Dame, IN: University of Notre Dame Press, 1989), 12.

34. Hodgson says, "In our day, when representative democracy is regarded as the only proper principle of national government, the monarchical ideal is easily misunderstood. Too readily we speak with a certain scorn of 'Oriental despotism.' We are sometimes surprised to find that most wise men, in both Christendom and Islamdom, in all ages down to recent centuries regarded monarchy as unquestionably the most excellent form of government." See Marshall G. S. Hodgson, *The Venture of Islam: Conscience and History in a World Civilization*, vol. 1 (Chicago: The University of Chicago Press, 1974), 281.

35. Hodgson, *The Venture of Islam*, vol. 1, 473–74.

36. Ali Yaycıoğlu, *Partners of the Empire: The Crisis of the Ottoman Order in the Age of Revolutions* (California: Stanford University Press, 2016). A comparable eclipse of regime discourse in early modern Europe is also noted. Especially in the seventeenth century, what Eric Nelson calls "the Hebrew revival" exerted an influence to displace the "constitutional pluralism" of earlier times in favor of the republican form as the only legitimate constitutional form—hence "republican exclusivism." See Eric Nelson, *The Hebrew Republic: Jewish Sources and the Transformation of European Political Thought* (Cambridge, MA: Harvard University Press, 2010). On the other hand, according to David Runciman, Hobbes's theoretical construction was wholly projected to discourage consideration of alternative regimes. See *Politics* (London: Profile Books, 2014).

37. Dallmayr, *The Other Heidegger*, 49.

38. Dallmayr, *The Promise of Democracy: Political Agency and Transformation* (Albany, NY: State University of New York Press, 2010), 86.

39. Dallmayr, *Dialogue Among Civilizations: Some Exemplary Voices* (New York: Palgrave Macmillan, 2002), 85. See also "Borders or Horizons: An Older Debate Revisited" in his *Small Wonder: Global Power and Its Discontents* (Lanham, MD: Rowman & Littlefield, 2005), 176–98; "Liberating Remembrance: Thoughts on Ethics, Politics, and Recollection" in his *Alternative Visions: Paths in the Global Village* (Lanham, MD: Rowman & Littlefield, 1998), 145–65; and "Why the Classics Today? Lessons from Gadamer and de Bary" in his *In Search of the Good Life: A Pedagogy for Troubled Times* (Lexington, KY: The University Press of Kentucky, 2007), 141–53.

Chapter 9

"*Docta Ignorantia*" and "*Hishiryō*"
"The Inexpressible" in Cusanus, Dōgen, and Nishida

MICHIKO YUSA

What is beyond readily knowable—something hidden—has always exercised a fascination over the human psyche. Cusanus's (Nicholas of Cusa, or Nikolaus von Kues; 1401–64) "*docta ignorantia*" ("learned ignorance")[1] and Dōgen's "*hishiryō*" ("beyond knowing") are two ways of talking about what is "beyond knowledge," and in this respect, their thinking moves in a similar direction. Following a close reading of Cusanus and Dōgen, I turn to Nishida Kitarō, whose philosophical vision starts out with the bold recognition of the realm of consciousness that is beyond knowledge. Part of the beauty of intercultural inquiry is to discover an idea that resonates beyond a particular historical and cultural conditioning. Fred Dallmayr wrote about Cusanus's "wise ignorance" in his thought-provoking book *In Search of the Good Life: A Pedagogy for Troubled Times*.[2] He should find in all three thinkers kindred spirits who behold human existence in both its particular and cosmic dimensions.

Nicholas of Cusa

I. THE ILLUMINATION OF "DOCTA IGNORANTIA"

Cusanus "received" a revelatory experience, based on which he formulated his famous "*docta ignorantia*" and "*coincidentia oppositorum*." He wrote about this experience to his former mentor and lifelong friend, Cardinal Giuliano Cesarini,[3] and appended it to *De docta ignorantia* (hereafter *DDI*), which reads:

> Accept now, Reverend Father, what for so long I desired to attain by different paths of learning but previously could not, until returning by sea from Greece when by what I believe was a celestial gift (*superno dono*) from the father of lights (*a patre luminum*)—from whom comes every perfect gift—I was led to embrace incomprehensible matters incomprehensibly (*incomprehensibilia incomprehensibiliter amplecterer*) in learned ignorance, by transcending those incorruptible truths that can be humanly known. This, now, in him who is the truth, I completed in these books, which can be compressed or expanded according to the same principle. ("*Epistola*," *DDI* III.263)[4]

Cusanus boarded the ship at Constantinople on November 27, 1437, to return to Venice. He had traveled there as part of the papal envoy dispatched by Pope Eugenius IV, who wished to win the support of the Greek patriarch of Constantinople, Joseph II, and the Byzantine Emperor, John VIII Palaeologus, and requested their presence at the "union council," which was to take place in Ferrara (and Florence) in 1438.[5] Cusanus traveled back on the same ship that carried the Greek entourage.[6] His charge while in Constantinople appears to have been collecting manuscripts of old Church council documents, which would give support to the deliberations at the Ferrara-Firenze council. He also collected philosophical manuscripts in Greek—probably out of his own interest.[7] At a monastery of the Minorite brothers in Constantinople, he came across a copy of the *Qur'an* in Arabic, whose Latin translation had already been available in Europe.[8] His stay in Constantinople, albeit barely two months long, became for him an occasion to witness firsthand the scenes of vibrant diverse religious practices.[9]

During his return voyage, Cusanus received the "divine illumination"—a kind of "*satori*"—concerning how "to embrace the incomprehensible things in an incomprehensible manner." The timing of this illumination seems crucial, as it directly followed his personal exposure to a wider and vibrant world full of rich diverse religious practices amid lively intercontinental commerce and exchange of goods. Cusanus composed "*De docta ignorantia*," or "*On the Learned Ignorance*" (1440), over the course of the next several months. I imagine him on board the ship, trusting himself to the undulation and rhythm of a sea voyage, witnessing daily the setting of the "sacred darkness" and the "stirring of rosy fingers of young Dawn"—to borrow Homer's lovely images (not to ignore the occasional hostile, stormy winds). A larger and holistic awareness (of "absolute maximum") *opened up to him* that allowed him to speak about the particulars in relation to the absolute maximum.

II. The Core Insight of "Docta Ignorantia" and "Coincidentia Oppositorum"

Cusanus applies the idea of *coincidentia oppositorum*—"the coming together" (*co-incidere*) of "the opposites"—to explain the underlying unity of the universe. "Because the maximum has nothing to oppose, the minimum coincides with it, and therefore the maximum is also in all things" (*DDI* I.5).[10] To illustrate this insight, he turns to mathematical demonstration and speaks about the flexible property of a straight line, which is at once "a circle," "a triangle," and "a sphere" (*DDI* I.33–42; for its application to the holy Trinity, see *DDI* I.42–73). He also recognizes that the intellect can never comprehend truth so precisely, but it could always comprehend it with ever more precision, as "the intellect is related to truth as a polygon to a circle" (*DDI* I.10). In Book Two, he explains how particular individuals in the universe are the "contraction" of the universal principle of absolute simplicity (*DDI* II.112–26). In Book Three, Cusanus applies his insight to his trinitarian vision, which is sustained by the intuition of "eternity" as suggested in the relationship of the begetter, the begotten, and the spirit that proceeds from the two (*DDI* I.87–88).

The guiding vision of his contemplation is framed in terms of the living reality of the Father as "unity," the Son as "equality," and the Holy Spirit *or* Love as "connection" of all things in the universe (*DDI* I.26, also I.28–29). Cusanus develops his Christology accordingly: in the person of Jesus Christ, the perfect union (*coincidentia oppositorum*) of humanity and intellect (i.e., divinity) is realized (*DDI* III.206). Cusanus gives an ontological reality to the *intellect*, which exists as a "certain divine being." The intellect is distinguished from "the sensory"—the latter remains "temporal and corruptible" (*DDI* III.205; also *DDI* III.182–207). Indeed Cusanus's anthropology retains the legacy of a medieval Christian understanding that "it is human nature that is raised above all the works of God and made a little lower than the angels" (*DDI* III.198). From the perspective of intercultural philosophy, the trinitarian references can be taken quite metaphysically. Through awareness of *docta ignorantia*, human beings can intuit the reality of the living universe.

III. On the Delimited Parameter of Intellectual Comprehension

Cusanus also applies this principle of *docta ignorantia* to explain "God" in his *Dialogus de Deo abscondito* (*A Dialogue on Hidden God*, hereafter *DDDA*, 1444–1445),[11] a dramatized exchange between a Christian and a pagan. The major points of philosophical interest of this dialogue may be summarized as:

1. "Knowledge" is defined as "the apprehension of truth (*veritas*)." (*DDDA* 3)

2. "Truth is one" and not many. (*DDDA* 5)

3. We do not know what the thing is ("quiddity") but *assume* that we know. (*DDDA* 5)

4. The knower is "the one who knows that one does not know." (*DDDA* 6)

5. One's existential desire to be in truth leads one to the act of "worship." (*DDDA* 6)

6. What one worships (i.e., "God") is ineffable truth itself (*DDDA* 6)—the absolute, pure, eternal, and ineffable truth. (*DDDA* 7)

7. Whatever one knows is not God; God transcends all human knowledge. (*DDDA* 8)

8. God is neither "nothing" nor "something," but above nothing and something. (*DDDA* 9)

9. "God is not ineffable but above all things effable." God is the cause of all nameable things. (*DDDA* 10)

10. God is not the root of contradiction but is real simplicity. (*DDDA* 10)

11. God is previous to being and non-being; God is "the fountainhead and the origin" of all the principles of being and non-being. (*DDDA* 11)

12. God is prior to every truth. (*DDDA* 12)

13. Christians call this fountainhead and origin "God" "on account of the resemblance of perfection." (*DDDA* 13)

14. "In the realm of color the act of seeing has no color," and as such seeing (*visus*) is "nothing" rather than "something." "God relates to everything just as seeing does to visible things." (*DDDA* 14)

15. God is not a composite thing, and thus unknowable within the realm of composite things. God is "hidden from the eyes of the wise." (*DDDA* 15)

IV. The Spirituality of *Docta Ignorantia*

Another significant theme in the "*Dialogus de Deo abscondito*" is the attitude of "reverence" (*adorare*, often translated as "worship"). A person in possession of the wisdom of "*docta ignorantia*" sees that the scope of human knowledge is circumscribed. Becoming aware of this fact translates into the existential posture of *awe* underlined with *humility*. The dialogue actually begins with these lines:

PAGAN: I see you are prostrating on the ground with greatest devotion and shedding tears of love that come from your heart, and not false tears. If I may, who are you?

CHRISTIAN: I am Christian.

PAGAN: What do you worship (*quid adoras*)?

CHRISTIAN: God.

PAGAN: Who is the god you adore?

CHRISTIAN: I do not know (*ignoro*).

PAGAN: How can you worship so earnestly that which you do not know?

CHRISTIAN: Precisely because I don't know, I worship (*quia ignore, adoro*).

PAGAN: It is amazing to see a person so devoted to that which he does not know.

CHRISTIAN: It is even more amazing to see a person devoted to that which he thinks he knows. (*DDDA* 1)[12]

To revere (or worship) what one knows is tantamount to idolatry. But the principle of the universe's unifying simplicity transcends an ego-centered perspective, and knowledge qua objectification. Genuine faith issues forth from the source of reality that is beyond human ratiocination. Thus for Cusanus, the religious act of "worship" is rooted in "*docta ignorantia*."

V. "DOCTA IGNORANTIA," THE "HORIZON" OF CONSCIOUSNESS, AND THE "INFINITE SPHERE"

Cusanus's experience of receiving the illumination during his sea voyage made me think about *docta ignorantia* in terms of the expanding and contracting *horizon of consciousness*. Indeed, the workings of consciousness can be likened to a horizon: (1) what we see is always within the delimited horizon (and this goes back to the ancient Greek meaning of this verb "*horidzein*"—to "limit," "bound," "divide," "separate"); but (2) this horizon is not a fixed boundary, but it constantly changes as we shift our perspective; and (3) a more comprehensive horizon can open up and embrace narrower horizons within it; in this way a horizon widens and gains its depths in accordance with the widening of our awareness.

Cusanus "discovered" that there is a way to talk about the "incomprehensible," going beyond the tradition of mystical (or negative) theology of Dionysius, who "did not think of God as truth, or intellect, or light, or anything that can be spoken" (*DDI* I.87). Cusanus's vision moves away from the *transcendent infinity* to the *immanent eternity*, imbued with the experience of this universe in its dynamic begetting, begotten, and issuing forth of energy that permeates all things (cf. *DDI* I.87). Cusanus's universe is an animated incarnating and engendering reality. He finds the expression of such a worldview in a mathematical model of the "infinite sphere" (*DDI* I.34, also I.70), which Meister Eckhart described as: "*Deus . . . est sphaera intellectualis infinita, cuius centrum est ubique cum circumferentia, et cuius tot sunt circumferentiae, quot puncta.*"[13] (God is an infinite intellectual sphere, whose center is everywhere with its circumference; and of which there are as many circumferences as there are points.)

Dōgen

I. On Zazen (Seated Meditation) and "Hishiryō"

For the eminent Japanese Zen master Dōgen (1200–1253), the practice of seated meditation (*zazen*) is *the* authentic Buddhist practice handed down from the time of Śākyamuni Buddha. I focus on his *"Zazenshin"* ("A Zazen Pointer" or "The Heart of Zazen"),[14] which he wrote in 1242, while still at Kōshōji Temple near Kyoto, but which he gave as his "dharma talk" (or sermon) in November of the following year in Echizen, where he moved to establish a new monastic center, away from Kyoto, deep in the mountains.

Dōgen begins "Zazen Pointer" with the following dialogue (or "*mondō*," literally, "question and answer"), attributed to Master Yakusan Igen (Ch. Yaoshan Weiyan).[15] This dialogue revolves around the three key terms: *shiryō* 思量 ("thinking"), *fushiryō* 不思量 ("non-thinking"), and *hishiryō* 非思量 ("beyond thinking"),[16] and it is usually translated as follows:

> When Master Yakusan came out of his zazen, a monk asked him, "Assuming the immovable posture, what were you *thinking (shiryō)*?"
> The master said: "I was thinking about *non-thinking (fushiryō)*."
> The monk asked again: "How does one think about non-thinking?"
> The master said: "By what is beyond thinking (*hishiryō*)."

The meaning of this exchange is interpreted quite differently even among Dōgen specialists. The interpretations basically fall into three types.

Interpretation I: A Cautious View of Thinking in Arriving at Satori

This interpretation represents the mainstream classical Zen attitude toward thinking. Among the proponents of this view is D. T. Suzuki.[17] In his 1941 essay *"Zen to ronri"* [Zen and logic], Suzuki describes the discriminating activity of consciousness (including "logic") as "secondary" to the unbifurcated primary experiential reality and considers that one has to transcend the discriminating consciousness in zazen practice to come face-to-face with this primary living reality. For Suzuki, logical thinking is characterized by the subject-object dichotomy, and he takes the monk's question, "How does one think about non-thinking?," as clinging onto the dichotomous mental posture, which must be dropped to face the living presence of Master Yakusan, the "person." Therefore, Suzuki has Master Yakusan *shout*: "Beyond thinking!"—presumably to wake up the monk's mind.[18] Suzuki's point is that the living reality eludes intellectual scrutiny. A trace of this type of interpretation is found in "Authentic *hishiryō*" (*The Zennist*), in which we read: "When you are sitting in zazen, don't think. Don't use your frontal lobe."[19]

Suzuki's interpretation, standing on the view that zazen consists of going beyond the plane of logical discriminating thinking, is helpful insofar as it acknowledges the place assigned to logical thinking ("*shiryō*" or "*funbetsu*") in daily activities, but it would be unhelpful if it gave the impression that logical thinking is detrimental in the pursuit of contemplative life. I would propose with caution that discerning discriminating wisdom (*jñāna* or *prajñā*) would not "negate" logical thinking per se, but rather recognize the proper place of discriminating thinking and steer clear of the futile ego-centered arguments. The first interpretation of this *mondō* could roughly be translated as follows:

> MONK: "Master, what were you thinking while you were in zazen?"
>
> MASTER: "The realm beyond thinking."
>
> STUDENT: "How does one think about what is beyond thinking?"
>
> MASTER: "Don't think. Just be awakened to your real self!"

Interpretation 2: The Gradational States of Consciousness

The second interpretation takes a phenomenological approach, carried out, for instance, by Thomas Kasulis in *Zen Action, Zen Person*.[20] Kasulis resorts to the phenomenological apparatus of "noetic attitude" and "noematic content" and summarizes his findings as follows:

> (i) Thinking" (shiryō): its noetic attitude is positional (either affirming or negative), and its noematic content is conceptualized objects.
>
> (ii) Not-thinking (fushiryō): its noetic attitude is positional (only negating), and its noematic content is thinking as objectified.

(iii) Beyond thinking (hishiryō): its noetic attitude is nonpositional (neither affirming nor negating), and its noematic content is pure presence of things as they are.[21]

It appears that Kasulis was unwittingly influenced by the Dōgen scholars of the mid-twentieth century, who tended to interpret this *mondō* in terms of three "dialectical" stages of consciousness. Somewhat simply put: thinking is "negated" by non-thinking, which is supplanted by that which is beyond thinking and non-thinking. Although careful not to treat these three cognitive modes in this manner, Kasulis concludes with the observation that "*hishiryō*" is a "non-conceptual or prereflective mode of consciousness,"[22] implying that this *mondō* stands on three distinctive separate stages or modes of awareness. The translation of the dialogue along the second line of interpretation would run something like:

MONK: "What were you thinking while you were doing zazen?"

MASTER: "I was thinking about non-objectified thinking that negates thinking."

MONK: "How does one think about what negates thinking?"

MASTER: "By becoming one with the workings of prereflective consciousness."

Interpretation 3: "Perspectival" or Aspectual Reality of "Thinking"

According to the third interpretation, the three key terms are not "three modes of consciousness" but rather three ways in which the universe manifests itself in our awareness. Each cognitive reality of "*shiryō, fushiryō*, and *hishiryō*" is as real and authentic as the other, and these three realities are not pitted against one another. By the mention of "*shiryō*" or "*fushiryō*," "*hishiryō*" is already implied by the others—the three terms mutually contain one another. This type of interpretation does not treat progress in zazen in terms of "stages" or "gradations," but rather cognition (thinking) is understood in its "aspects," in terms of the dynamic activities of the universe itself.

Among the proponents of this view is Sakai Tokugen, who explains the import of this *mondō* as follows:

The monk's second question, "how are we to think about *fushiryō*," implies that actually "anything whatsoever *is* thinking." What Dōgen meant by "*hishiryō*" is this totality of life-activities carried out by all the embodied beings (*shintai*) of the entire universe . . . "*Hi*" of "*hishiryō*" is not a word of negation, but stands for the expansive truth of nature beyond any human activities. For Dōgen, sustained zazen practice (*shikan taza*, "just sitting") was the practice of universal truth itself that authenticates its truth. This is to put *hishiryō* into practice (*hishiryō no jissen*).[23]

Kawamura Kōdō's reading of this *mondō* goes as follows:

> All living individual things ("*dharmas*") are real and alive. This is what is meant by "*shiryō*"—the actual life-dynamism every individual manifests. "*Shiryō*" (qua individual's activities) is made possible by the primary activity (*hataraki*) of "*fushiryō*," which transcends cognitive operations altogether ("*zesshiryō*"). What is called "*hishiryō*" is like a "field" (*ba*), which is none other than the principle of life (*inochi*) itself, which enfolds each and every individual that embodies the original activity of the universe beyond its "ego." "*Hi*" of "*hishiryō*" is not a "negation" but it refers to "absolute reality that is face-to-face [with each individual]" (*zettai* 絶待). *Hishiryō* is the field where all activities of each and every being (*shiryō*) takes place. As such it is nothing but the very hallowed life of Buddha (*hotoke no on-inochi*).[24]

This third line of interpretation takes "*hishiryō*" as the very cosmos permeated with life and populated with sentient as well as non-sentient beings. Interestingly, Kasulis's phenomenological analysis in its "noematic content" points to this "pure presence of things as they are." Having dissolved the "noetic attitude," one is in that pure presence. That is why it is "beyond thinking" (*hishiryō*), and, moreover, it refers to dynamic nature, the source of all activities. Under the third interpretation, the *mondō* may be translated as follows:

MONK: "Assuming the immovable posture of zazen, what were you *thinking* (*shiryō*)?"

MASTER: "Freedom (*fushiryō*)."

MONK: "How does one *think* about freedom?"

MASTER: "On account of life (*hishiryō*)."

II. ZAZEN AS "DROPPING OFF THE MIND AND THE BODY"

What Dōgen understood by "zazen" was "dropping off the body and the mind" (*shinjin totsuraku*). This teaching comes from his Chinese master Rujing (Jp. Nyojō). In 1225, when Dōgen was assiduously practicing zazen under his guidance at Mount Tiantong,[25] Rujing explained to him that "in zazen the mind and the body drop off." He meant that "the five desires and five psychological impediments fall away." Dōgen's immediate reaction was that this was no different from what he had leant at the Tendai monastery in Japan. Rujing responded that zazen as the genuine practice of Buddhas is essentially one and places no artificial boundaries upon whether the teaching comes from the small or the large vehicle.[26] The very "body" from which both mind and body have fallen away (*totsuraku shinjin*) is the "one" who sits zazen, and this is the noetic attitude of "*shiryō-fushiryō*" for Dōgen.

III. "SHIRYŌ," "FUSHIRYŌ," AND "HISHIRYŌ"

To see how Dōgen himself understood this *mondō*, we need to read his "*Zazenshin*" as a whole text by going beyond the initial *mondō*. Dōgen's commentary on the *mondō* may come as a surprise, as he actually approves the monk's second question—"How can one think about non-thinking?"—by considering it a natural turn of the inquiring mind, and hence not something to be suppressed.[27] Dōgen says: "In zazen some thinking is present. Otherwise, how could one make progress in one's zazen practice? Unless one is an utter fool, one is endowed with the intellectual power that asks questions concerning one's own zazen practice."[28]

For Dōgen, then, the objective of zazen is not to "shut" one's intellectual mind "up," but "one must inquire, see, and understand."[29] The thing he discourages is "argumentations" (*jōron*),[30] which is not to be confused with intellectual reflections that deepen one's zazen practice. Certainly he saw it as necessary to cultivate awareness of the realm beyond thinking (*fushiryō*), the state in which the mind is liberated from self-centered viewpoints (*gaken*).[31] Proper zazen practice should make one increasingly aware of this reality of "*fushiryō*." There, the intellectual mind is not silenced but purified, as it were, and its reifying tendency is overcome, or "fallen away," so that the mind is in tune with the dynamic unfolding of nature. Dōgen maintains that the intellectual power to know (*chi*) is deeper than recognition (*kakuchi*). Genuine intuition transcends any human doings (*zōsa*).[32] He concludes his "*Zazenshin*" with these poetic words:

> The key point of zazen practice for Buddhas and great masters has been this:
>
> In non-thinking (*fushiryō*), reality is revealed as it is, without the subject-object dichotomy.
> Reality thus revealed in non-thinking is intimate to my being.
> Free of subject-object dichotomy, reality manifests as it is.
> In its intimacy to my being, it is free of mental contamination.
> Reality manifests itself as the authentication of my being; there is no need for the teaching of unity and differentiation of the mind.[33]
> This unspoilt intimacy requires no mental scrutiny; it is the state in which the mind and the body have fallen away.
> This authentication, free from the teaching of unity and differentiation, has nothing to do with the designing mind. Only the merit of zazen increases.
> In the clear water fish swim as they do.
> In the wide-open sky birds fly as they do.[34]

Nishida Kitarō on the Source of Infinite Creativity

Nishida Kitarō (1870–1945) was very much interested in Cusanus's thought, and delivered a presentation titled "*Coincidentia oppositorum* and love"[35] in October 1919.[36] One statement from this lecture captures the quintessential Nishidan insight: "For the establishment of knowledge, there has to be some X that cannot become knowledge. This is the intuition of the whole" (*Chishiki ga seiritsu suru ni wa, chishiki to narienai mono ga aru. Kore ga zentai no chokkaku de aru*).[37]

This X—that which cannot (or does not) become the object of logical judgment but forms its basis and establishes knowledge—operates on the same deep critical awareness of the limits of knowledge as Cusanus's "*docta ignorantia*" or Dōgen's "*hishiryō*." This X is the "storehouse" out of which intuition bursts forth, and thereby a new horizon of mental awareness emerges. Intuition thus widens the horizon of understanding and experience, and along the way a new conceptual paradigm ("a paradigm shift") is introduced into human understanding. And just as we saw the importance of the idea of the horizon for Cusanus, so Nishida found the imagery of the "infinite sphere" to depict his vision of the "dialectical world." His "logic of *basho*" (or *topos*) can be nicely described by the imagery of the "horizon."

This X comes very close to what Cusanus calls God, who is "previous to being and non-being; God is the fountainhead and the origin of all the principles of being and non-being" (*DDDA* 11). If we replace "God" with X, it reads as "X is previous to being and non-being; X is the fountainhead and the origin of all the principles of being and non-being." This is similar in spirit to Nishida's statement—"in order for knowledge to be established, there is something that does not become knowledge." And Dōgen's "*hishiryō*" can be read as this X, which is the root of all life and establishes all activities, including thinking.

A brief reflection on why Nishida speaks about "love" in relation to Cusanus's "*coincidentia oppositorum*" is helpful. By "love," Nishida understands that ontologically everything is "mutually inter-constitutive"; what we consider "discrete" individuals are actually ontologically *porous*—you and I are not separate entities, but "you are" constitutively at the root of "me," and so "I am" at the root of "you." Beings are radically interpersonal, social, and "inter-independent."[38] Thus Nishida observes that love is actually present even in the formulation of logic. Love renders discrete individual entities interrelated. In the world of religion, such love is the essence of God/Buddha. For Nishida, all knowledge ultimately concerns the personal (*jinkaku*) reality,[39] the built-in nature of which is *coincidentia oppositorum* (testified in the self-world interrelatedness). We know this reality of love not by way of knowledge but through our feelings, especially in our intimate personal experiences. *Coincidentia oppositorum* thus understood encompasses all activities, knowing, and loving.[40] Indeed, Cusanus in describing God's "gaze" writes: "Your seeing is your loving," which never abandons the faithful[41] (*De vision Dei*, 10).

Nishida's words concerning the deep unknown source of infinite creativity provide an appropriate conclusion to this chapter:

> At the depths of our mind is a world that transcends the realm of knowledge. The depth of our mind is so abysmally deep that no anchor is of use. In that realm there are no such things as conceptually conceived things (*mono*) or ego (*ga*) but pure activity

(*jun naru katsudō*). Therein, there is no fixed form (*katachi*) but the formless form that gives birth to infinite kinds of forms. There is no fixed color but the colorless color that gives rise to infinite spectrum of colors. In that realm, each stir is a creation, a pure activity of giving rise to shape and color.[42]

Be it "*docta ignorantia,*" "*hishiryō,*" or "deep bottomless abyss of the mind," these philosophers paid attention to the vital source of life that gives, nurtures, sustains, yet also takes away life. Even the suns and stars—the universe itself—is governed by this principle of dynamic "arising and passing."

Notes

1. My mentor, Raimon Panikkar, awoke my interest in Cusanus.

2. Fred Dallmayr, *In Search of the Good Life: A Pedagogy for Troubled Times* (Lexington: University Press of Kentucky, 2007), see chapter 3: "Wise Ignorance: Nicolaus of Cusa's Search for Truth," 58–79.

3. H. Lawrence Bond, trans. with introduction, *Nicholas of Cusa, Selected Spiritual Writings* (hereafter *Selected Writings*) (Mahwah, NY: Paulist Press, 1997), "Introduction," 4.

4. For the Latin text, see H. Lawrence Bond, "Nicholas of Cusa from Constantinople to *Learned Ignorance*: The Historical Matrix for the Formation of the *De Docta Ignorantia*," (hereafter "Historical Matrix") in Gerald Christianson and Thomas M. Izbicki, eds., *Nicholas of Cusa on Christ and the Church, Essays in Memory of Chandler McCuskey Brooks for the American Cusanus Society* (Leiden: E. J. Brill, 1996), 136 n. 8. The English translation, especially the last sentence, is altered. I thank my colleague E. Engelsing for his help in decoding Latin. For Bond's translation of this letter, see *Selected Writings*, "Introduction," 20; also 205–6.

5. For a detailed historical background of this council and Cusanus's papal visit to Constantinople, see H. L. Bond, "Historical Matrix," 135–63.

6. Bond, "Historical Matrix," 137–43.

7. Among the manuscripts Cusanus brought back home were *Adversus Eunomium* of Saint Basil, a Greek edition of the works of Dionysius the Areopagite, and the *Theologia Platonis* of Proclus. See Bond, "Historical Matrix," 141, 142 n. 34, 146, 149–50.

8. Bond, "Historical Matrix," 142.

9. H. L. Bond suggests that these encounters and discussions with Greek theologians formed the basis of Cusanus's later writing, *De pace fidei*, written at the wake of "the Fall of Constantinople" (1453), "Historical Matrix," 142.

10. *DDI* is customarily cited by the book and paragraph number(s): this passage is from Book 1, paragraph 5.

11. Nicolai de Cusa, *Opera Omnia* 1, ed. Ernst Hoffmann and Raymond Klibansky (Heidelberg: Felicis Meiner, 1959), 1–10. For an English translation, see H. L. Bond, *Selected Writings*, 207–13.

12. See Bond, *Selected Writings*, 209. Bond translates "Gentile" as "Pagan."

13. H. L. Bond, *Selected Writings*, 307, n. 56: Meister Eckhart, *In Ecclesiasticum* 24.20.

14. For Dōgen's text of *Shōbōgenzō*, see Mizuno Yahoko, ed., *Shōbōgenzō*, 4 vols. (Tokyo: Iwanami Shoten, 1990). (Hereafter the text is cited as SG, followed by the volume number and page number(s).) For the text of *"Zazen-shin,"* see SG 1.226–52.

15. Mizuno, SG 1.226.

16. These terms captured the heart of zazen practice for Dōgen. See his "Universal promotion of zazen" (*"Fukanzazengi"*) (1227), which he composed soon after his return from Song China. Toward the end of his life, he again mentions them in his sermon (1252), dedicated to honor his deceased parents (*Eihei kōroku*, *"Jōdō,"* #524).

17. He deepened his appreciation of the importance of "logical explanation," especially through his intimate, lifelong friendship with Nishida Kitarō. On Suzuki's approach to "logic," see M. Yusa, "D. T. Suzuki and the 'Logic of *Sokuhi*,' or the 'Logic of *Prajñāpāramitā*,'" in G. Kopf, ed., *Dao Companion to Japanese Buddhist Philosophy* (Springer Press, forthcoming 2018).

18. D. T. Suzuki, *"Zen to ronri"* [Zen and logic] (December 1941), compiled in *Suzuki Daisetsu Zenshū* [Collected works of D. T. Suzuki] (new edition), vol. 32 (Tokyo: Iwanami Shoten, 2002), 304–10.

19. http://zennist.typepad.com/zenfiles/2008/04/authentic-hishi.html, posted on April 15, 2008. Also see Norman Waddell and Masao Abe, trans. with annotation, *The Heart of Dōgen's Shōbōgenzō* (Albany, NY: State University of New York Press, 2002); the passages concerned read as: "What is thinking of not-thinking?" "Nonthinking!" (cf. 4, also 110).

20. T. P. Kasulis, *Zen Action Zen Person* (Honolulu: University Press of Hawaii, 1981), 65–86, and esp. 70–77.

21. Kasulis, *Zen Action Zen Person*, 73.

22. Ibid., 75.

23. Sakai Tokugen, *"Eihei Kōroku,"* in *Dōgen no chosaku* [Dōgen's works], ed. Kagamishima Genryū and Tamaki Kōshirō (*Kōza Dōgen* [Dōgen Studies], vol. 3) (Tokyo: Shunjūsha, 1980), 106–7.

24. Kawamura Kōdō, *"Shōbōgenzō,"* in Kagamishima and Tamaki, *Dōgen no chosaku*, 64. For the word, *"hotoke no on-inochi"* ("hallowed life of Buddha"), see Dōgen, *"Shōji,"* in *Shōbōgenzō*, Mizuno, SG 4.467.

25. It is recorded in his *Hōkyōki*, the record of his exchanges with Master Rujing during his study in China. See Dōgen, *Hōkyōki*, Ikeda Rosan, trans. into modern Japanese (Tokyo: Daitō Shuppansha, 1989), 50–56.

26. Dōgen, *Hōkyōki*, 50–56.

27. Ejō, *Shōbōgenzō zuimonki* [Records of Dōgen's teachings], 6.14. Dōgen encouraged his students to ask questions so that the master can clarify them; in fact, any master responds only after a disciple asks a question. See Ejō, *Shōbōgenzō zuimonki*, Watsuji Tetsurō with Nakamura Hajime, ed. (Tokyo: Iwanami Shoten, 1982), 143–44.

28. "*Zazen-shin*," Mizuno, SG 1.227.

29. Ejō, *Shōbōgenzō zuimonki*, 6.6, 135. 聞くべし、見るべし、得るべし。

30. Ejō, *Shōbōgenzō zuimonki*, 5.7, 111.

31. Ejō, *Shōbōgenzō zuimonki*, 4.3, 88.

32. Dōgen's commentary on Wanshi (Ch. Hongzhi), Mizuno, SG 1. 245: 知は覚知にあらず。

33. Here, Dōgen is referring to Tōzan Ryōkai (Dongshan Liangjie)'s exposition of "Five Ranks" (*Goi* 五位). "*Sei*" 正 (unity) refers to the world under the mode of equality of all things, and no objectification of consciousness is involved; "*hen*" 偏 (differentiation) refers to the world under the mode of differentiations, as consciousness is divided into subject and object; it thinks of sundry of things.

34. "*Zazenshin*," Mizuno, SG 1.250–51.

35. Nishida Kitarō, "*Coincidentia oppositorum to ai*" [*Coincidentia oppositorum* and love] (1919), in *Nishida Kitarō Zenshū* (hereafter NKZ) (Tokyo: Iwanami Shoten 1979), vol. 14, 293–300. For my English translation of this lecture, see K. Reinhardt and H. Schwaetzer, eds., *Cusanus-Rezeption in der Philosophie des 20. Jahrhunderts* (Regensburg: S. Roderer Verlag, 2005), 221–25 (a typographical oversight in this translation must be corrected on 224, line 6: "nor does it become" should read "*and yet it becomes*").

36. Nishida delivered this on the Founding Day of Ōtani University in Kyoto on October 13, 1919.

37. Nishida, "*Coincidentia oppositorum*," NKZ 14.298.

38. This is Raimon Panikkar's formulation of the similar insight; see *The Rhythm of Being* (Maryknoll, NY: Orbis Books, 2010), 53, 57 et passim.

39. "Person" (*jinkaku* 人格) has a specific meaning, laden with ethical, ontological, and religious dimensions. It refers to the ultimate mode of integrated authentic human existence qua individual imbued with spiritual consciousness.

40. Nishida, "*Coincidentia oppositorum*," NKZ 14.299–300.

41. H. L. Bond, *Selected Writings, On the Vision of God* (1453), 239.

42. Nishida Kitarō, "Hirasawa Tetsuo, *Chokugen geijutsu-ron, jo*," (August 1921), NKZ new edition (Tokyo: Iwanami Shoten, 2005), 11.264–65.

Chapter 10

Paradigms of the Perfect Human and the Possibility of a Global Ethos

Marietta Stepanyants

Threatening challenges in the world are urging us to rethink and reevaluate many fundamental issues so as to put the end to cruelty, violence, terror, wars, to all those phenomena where humans behave inhumanly. The time has come to relearn what the meaning of being human is. Who, if anyone, could we call a Perfect Human? History demonstrates the continued coexistence and confrontation of two main trends that are associated with models that can be labeled as "normative social" and "individualistic." The first is based on the adoption of the existing world as objective, natural, or given by the Creator. Hence there is an orientation to its preservation and maintenance by the implementation of generally accepted moral norms and rules. In the spirit of Fred Dallmayr's scholarship in comparative social and ethical thought, I review normative moral systems in three main traditional societies of the East: Indian, Chinese, and Muslim. I then briefly consider the more individualistic trends within each. Finally, I move to some reflections on the opportunities and obstacles associated with a global ethos. This too pays homage to Dallmayr's work, which is marked by his constant return to global ethics.[1]

India

In India, for the vast majority of the population who are Hindus, such a normative social model aims to observe *varna-ashrama-dharma*, a specific set of requirements that are considered sacred. *The Laws of Manu* (Chapter XII, 94) says: "The Veda is the eternal eye of the manes, gods, and men; the Veda-ordinance (is) both beyond the sphere of (human) power, and beyond the sphere of (human) comprehension; that is a certain fact."[2] The Veda's prescriptions are incomprehensible and immeasurable. The most widespread synonym for the word "man" in ancient Hindu texts is *manusya*, a derivative of the verb "to think." Yet the fundamental difference between humans and animals lies in the former's capacity to follow *dharma*, or the "moral law." "Only man is open for the 'ought' regardless of what he has in common with the animals, he finds himself faced with norms and duties, i.e., dharma."[3] Cosmogonic processes are not related to the arbitrary rule of gods or to natural mechanical causes, but rather to moral principles—or, to be more precise, to the moral state of the creatures inhabiting the cosmos.

One of the central concepts of Indian culture, religion, and philosophy is *samsara* ("passing through a sequence of states"), which means a rebirth, reincarnation, transmigration of souls. Samsara in combination with the idea of *karma* is often referred to as the law of moral causation: rebirth is moral retribution for karma. *Atman*, by transiting from one existence to another, only changes its "shell"—"body." Atman itself is not subject to samsara. This belief in rebirth makes possible the reincarnation of a human soul in the "body" of other creatures that has driven another very important concept of Indian culture—*ahimsa*. Ahimsa means to avoid killing and injuring by action, word, or thought all beings. It is the fundamental, first virtue of all Indian moral systems, the first stage in ethical training.

In the Hindu tradition people enjoy different "rights" regarding their participation in the dharmic process. They fulfill their dharmic duties in accordance with the *varna-ashrama* code, which strictly regulates their social life and the daily roles they are expected to play in it. The departure from one caste and move to another in this life is not possible. Ideal behavior means the strict observance of the relevant karma, which alone can ensure a higher social status in a future birth. Hinduism is referred to in Sanskrit as *sanátana-dhárma*, which literally means "eternal religion," "eternal way," or "eternal law." Yet Hinduism originated at certain times, under certain historical conditions. There is every reason to believe that the historical Vedic religion—the religion of the initial period of Aryan history—transformed into Brahmanism (seventh century BC–fifth century AD), then into Hinduism (the period of its formation—first and fifth centuries BC).

On the question of how and by whom an ancient civilization in India was created opinions differ. One is that Indus (Harappan) civilization developed in the Indus Valley in 1300–3300 BC as a result of the invasion of Aryans. The most significant centers were Mohenjo-Daro and Harappa. The population during the years of the heyday was about 5 million. Another view holds that the Indus civilization in northwestern India owes its origin to the Dravidians who came from the South of India, whose civilization originated fifty-one centuries ago. Many researchers have the Dravidians as a separate race, which is common among people of South India. They spoke the Dravidian languages. It is unlikely that any "meeting" of the two civilizations in antiquity could be exclusively peaceful. The oldest of the Indo-Aryan texts, the "Rigveda" (composed about 1700–1100 BC), reported persistent clashes between local tribes and Aryans. Dravidians in the hymns of "Rigveda" were portrayed as physically unattractive, rejecting the gods of the Vedas, and not knowing the rituals of sacrifice practiced by Aryan priests. There is also a version of reading the famous epic "Ramayana" as a long war between the two civilizations and ideologies. In Hinduism, it is considered that the actions of the "Ramayana" occurred about 1.2 million years ago. Modern scholars date the same epic from the fourth century BC. Although the "meeting" of the Aryans with the Dravidians took the form of a strong confrontation, in the long run it managed to spare the destruction of one civilization in favor of another.

Some believe that this "happy ending" was ensured by the spirit of tolerance that was laid in sacred texts of the North. I rather assume that a greater role was played by good judgment on both sides: survival has the advantage over the elimination of each other that usually happened during the encounter of civilizations when strategies of physical destruction had been chosen and "hostile" cultures were eradicated. Thus a preference was given to a gradual reconciliation through the tactics of inclusiveness. Inclusiveness is most evident in Hinduism. Here is a simple example. Artifacts found during excavations of the Harappa civilization demonstrate the typical farming culture honoring a female deity, symbolizing fertility (terracotta female figurines), of totemic and animistic beliefs and practices. In Hinduism all these cults have survived, albeit in a slightly transformed form. The female deity became not just a "spouse" of a particular God. It is his Shakti (Skt.—power, strength). "Shakti" has many meanings: it is called the great universal infinite energy, which is creating and executing the ocean of the divine consciousness. Shakti is goddess-mother. Shakti is the phenomenal world. Shakti is referred to as Mother Nature.

China

Neither ontology nor cognitive problems occupy as conspicuous a place in the speculations and reflections of Chinese thinkers as does the subject matter of the human being. The key notion, codified in the I-Ching (Book of Changes), has had a paradigmatic impact on the whole Chinese culture. According to Chen I-Chuan (1033–1107), one of the renowned commentators of the Book of Changes, "in ancient times, the sages instituted the system of the Changes in order to follow the principle of nature and destiny . . . (Each hexagram) embraced the three powers (Heaven, Earth, and Man) . . ."[4] Though the human being is but one of the "ten thousand things," he or she is at the same time considered to be the most valuable among mundane things. Referring to Confucius's maxim, "Of the creatures born from the refined essence of Heaven and Earth, none is nobler than man," who receives the mandate from Heaven and is therefore superior to other creatures.

The human being is distinguished from all other creatures by holding five gifts, which are endowed by nature. The fist is *Jen*, meaning humanity. It implies empathy and love for one's fellow human beings. The second is *I*, standing for "righteousness," justice. It is identical with *I*, denoting uprightness and duty. The third, *Li*, or "propriety," is identified with Li, meaning "to act," "ritual," to follow one's path in search of self-perfection. The fourth is *Chi*, or "wisdom," and is related to chi, meaning "to know," to have one's own vision and deep understanding. The fifth is *Hsing*, or "sincerity," which is identical with *chen*, standing for "truthfulness," meaning to give oneself wholly to a single goal without deviating from one's course.

Among these five gifts, *Jen* and *Li* are the central concepts of Confucian teaching. Jen means the self-making, self-transformation, self-perfection through which an individual becomes an exemplary person [*chun-tzu*]. There are five attitudes (respect, tolerance, living up to one's word, diligence, and generosity) that lead an individual to the state of being an exemplary person. Li stresses proper conduct, that is, "ritual action." "If you do not learn the Rituals," says Confucius, "you will not have the means to take a stance." The Confucian ideal is the harmony of the perfect individual and a well-ordered society based on the mutual moral obligations of the five human relations: those between ruler and minister, father and son, elder brother and younger brother, husband and wife, and one friend and another.

The Three Obediences and Four Virtues were a set of basic moral principles specifically for women in Confucianism. These two terms first appeared in the Book of Etiquette and Ceremonial and in the Rites of Zhou, respectively. A woman's three obediences were to obey her father as a daughter, her husband as a wife, and her sons in widowhood. The four feminine virtues were wifely virtue, wifely speech, wifely manner/appearance, and wifely work. In the centuries after Confucius, it became common to discuss gender in terms of *yin* and *yang*, with women being yin and men yang. Yin was soft, yielding, receptive, passive, reflective, and tranquil, whereas yang was hard, active, assertive, and dominating. Day and night, winter and summer, birth and death, indeed all natural processes occur though the interaction of yin and yang. Conceptualizing the differences between men and women in these terms stresses that they are part of the natural order of the universe, not part of the social institutions created by human beings. In yin yang theory, the two forces complement each other but not in strictly equal ways. The natural relationship between yin and yang is the reason that men lead and women follow. If yin unnaturally gains the upper hand, order at both the cosmic and social level is endangered.

During Han times (202 BCE–220 CE), the family head was generally the senior male, but if a man died before his sons were grown, his widow served as head until they were of age. The law codes of the imperial period enforced monogamy and provided a variety of punishments for bigamy and for promoting a concubine to the status of wife. Men could divorce their wives on any of seven grounds, which included barrenness, jealousy, and talkativeness, but could do so only if there was a family for her to return to. There were no grounds on which a woman could divorce her husband, but divorce by mutual agreement was possible.

It is often said that the status of women began to decline in the Song period, just when Neo-Confucianism was gaining sway. The two signs of this decline most frequently mentioned are the pressure on widows not to remarry and the practice of binding young girls' feet to prevent their feet from growing more than a few inches long. By the early Qing period (1644–1911), the cult of widow chastity had gained a remarkably strong hold, especially in the educated class. Childless widows might even commit suicide. Although most Confucian scholars and government officials disapproved of widow suicide and chaste fiancées, they often expressed great admiration for the determination of particular women they knew, thus helping to spread the custom. At the same time that widow chastity was becoming more prevalent, more and more women were learning to read and write. In the seventeenth and eighteenth centuries, a surprising number had their poetry published. As in much of the rest of the world, since twentieth-century

China, intellectuals and social activists have leveled many criticisms against the old family system and especially the ways it limited women's chances.

Islam

Muslim cosmology not only considers man God's most perfect creation, but also maintains that he is made in the image of God and possesses a fraction of divine spirit. There are five main basic acts of Islamic faith known as the Five Pillars of Islam: the *shahada*, or the declaration of faith ("There is no god but God, and Muhammad is the messenger of God"); five daily prayers (*salat* in Arabic), or (*amaz* in Persian); and fasting during the month of Ramadan. In the ninth month of the Islamic (lunar) year, *zakat*, or the tax equaling 2.5 percent of one's income that is used for alms giving to the poor; and the *hajj*, or pilgrimage to Mecca, which is to be performed at least once in a lifetime.

A believer's main virtues manifest in his or her relation with God (piety, reverence, etc.) as well as in following God's commandments. One may call them "Quranic Decalogue" (Quran 6:151–53):

> Say: "Come, I will rehearse
> What God hath (really)
> Prohibited you from": join not
> Anything as equal with Him (1);
> Be good to your parents (2);
> Kill not your children
> On a plea of want; —We
> Provide sustenance for you
> And for them (3); —come not
> Night to shameful deeds,
> Whether open or secret (4);
> Take not life, which God made sacred, except
> By way of justice and law (5).
> ....
> And come not nigh
> To the orphan's property,
> Except to improve it,
> Until he attain the age
> Or full strength (6); give measure

And weight with full justice (7); —
No burden do We place
On any soul, but that
Which it can bear; —
Whenever ye speak, speak justly,
Even if a near relative
Is concerned (8); and fulfil
The Covenant of God (9);
Thus doth He command you,
That ye may remember.

Verily, this is My Way,
Leading straight: follow it;
Follow not (other) paths:
They will scatter you about
From His (great) Path:
Thus doth He command you,
That ye may be righteous (10).⁵

The rigid norms embedded in the normative ethics in Islamic culture are based on the fatalistic notion about the limitless dependence on God's will. The predetermination of human destiny and behavior is asserted in numerous *ayats* of the Koran. However, the sacred Book also contains verses that could be considered a negation of such blind fatalism. Hence the disputes and contention among Muslims on the issue of predestination arose as early as the reign of the first caliphs. Yet the idea of fatalism was codified as a basis of the Islamic ethical system by the theologians. Normative morals in the world of Islam assume that Muslims' lives should be organized in accordance with *Shariah*—the law of God. The Law could not be changed, and the right of its interpretation and application belongs only to the *ulema* belonging to the limited number of four law schools—*mazhab*. Legislative bodies even in modern Muslim societies are considered not as state institutions for legislation but as ones that administer God's law. The "doors" of *idjtihad*—an independent judgment—has been "kept closed" since about the ninth century.

From the descriptions given so far of the normative moral systems in three main traditional societies of the East, it is evident that those systems could be defined as cosmocentric (that is the most typical for Chinese culture) or theocentric (emblematic for Islam). Cosmocentrism sees the world as an ordered cosmos. Hence, all of the phenomena of perceived reality, including the human being, are to be viewed through the prism of the cosmos. Theocentrism holds that God is understood as some "center" of the Universe, without which nothing can exist or be perceived. Both systems presuppose normative moral standards, excluding freedom of will and choice. The same approaches were characteristic of all societies in ancient times and the Middle Ages. Western civilization succeeded in making the transition from the cosmocentrism of antiquity and the theocentrism of the Middle Ages to anthropocentrism as the basis of the human worldview starting from the epoch of the Renaissance, when humans started to be seen as a unique type of creature capable of creating the world they inhabit. Non-western civilizations did not experience these transitions. Yet they had their own way of following an individualistic model of morality.

Eastern Individualisms

In India, the caste system, sanctioned by the sacred Vedas, so rigidly determined human life that it did not leave any hope for a chance to get rid of suffering other than by rupture of *samsara*-chains. If you cannot modify *karma*, you have to break free from it. It is the path of austerity and mystical search offered in the *Bhagavad Gita* and practiced by *sannyasi*—in Hinduism, it is the religious ascetic who has renounced the world by abandoning all claims to social or family standing. Sannyasi's ascetic behavior might be of a mystical nature, a way of seeking the divine truth. Sannyasis not only expressed indifference to the social moral code, but they even could actively protest against it, as was the case among the mystics belonging to other religious beliefs. One example is Sannyasi's anti-British peasant movement of 1760–75 in three Indian provinces: Bengal, Bihar, and Orissa.

The most comprehensive way to lead an ascetic life in mystical quest is offered in India by Buddhism. Perfection is understood not as loyalty to the normative moral code, but as an ability to apprehend one's own self. *The Dhammapada* (the most popular Buddhist text) portrays an ascetic beggar—*bhikshu*—who behaves in accord with the following moral maxima:

> Raise yourself by yourself, examine yourself by yourself.
> Thus guarded by yourself and attentive, you, mendicant, will live happy.
> For self is the lord of self, self is the refuge of self.[6]

In China, the "individualistic" model found its fullest expression in the Taoist tradition. It differs from Confucianism in its view of the human being as a social creature. The Taoists concentrated first and foremost on the natural aspects of the human being. According to Taoism, the human being appears to be endowed with two natures. The natural in him or her is ingrained, created, and determined by the universal Tao (and therefore is true). The other is artificial, generated, and determined by passions intrinsic to the human ego (and therefore is false). Drawing on this premise, the Taoists consider the human being ideal if he or she manages to make his or her true nature predominate over the false. "The sage man learns of Heaven and follows nature. He should not be tied by convention nor enticed by the sophism of man."[7] It was unworthy to make "outward adornment of benevolence and righteousness," for "the impressions conveyed by the senses of eye and ear" should have no influence on a perfect human being, for he "cultivates the Tao-method within" and "moves in tune with the soul and spirit."[8]

For all the dissimilarities between Eastern cultures, the "individualistic" model that evolved in their traditions has some common features. Perfection is determined not by comparing the merits of ideal human beings with those of other people, but by their relationship with the Absolute, the highest degree of their nearness to, for example, either Brahman, Buddha, Tao, or Allah, because the criterion of ideality lies outside, or at least far above, conventional standards and does not belong to the phenomenal world. The ideal is oriented toward the transcendental but realizable in the human self. Such a criterion becomes possible by transferring the emphasis from the biological and social nature of the human being toward his or her supernatural, divine essence.

An individual model of perfection in Islam has been most extensively developed in the context of Sufism. According to the great sheikh, Ibn Arabi, the human being as a species is the most perfect in the universe. Any other being is a mere reflection of one of the numberless attributes of the Absolute, whereas human beings synthesize all of the forms of God's manifestation. The human being is viewed as a "microcosm," a kind of measure of the world at large, or the "macrocosm." The Koran says that:

> We did indeed offer
> The Trust to the Heavens
> And to the Earth
> And the Mountains;

> But they refused
> To undertake it,
> Being afraid thereof;
> But man undertook it.[9]

Sufis consider it proven that the human being is predestined to be the "Receptacle of the Divine Essence." To justify their supreme predestination, human beings should strive for self-perfection. If the heart is like a mirror in which the Divine Light is reflected, this mirror has to be properly "polished" so that one might see in it God's image. To reach this goal, it is not enough to merely follow the standards of common conduct prescribed by society. A law is simply a "reference point" in the manifested world, but for those who have embarked on the Way to the temple of True Being, the role of "leading lights" is performed by saints or perfect men.

While common folk rely on the guidance and examples of saints, it is presupposed that human beings are themselves capable of becoming perfect by way of self-cognition and apprehension of their true selves; they can and should serve as models of morality, an indicator of good and evil: "The ultimate aim and meaning of the Way is to reveal the Absolute in one's own self" (Ibn al-Farid). The path of perfection is endless; it encourages the development of all human forces, irrespective of any predetermined, common scale.

A Global Ethos?

A new age has proclaimed the value of the moral autonomy of the individual. Human reason as an internal lawmaker frees from obedience to authority imposed from outside the self. Human beings have the autonomous ability of knowing their duty without any external instruction and are capable of championing the cause declared just by their own conscience. This promotes the orientation to a new paradigm of the human in the context of involvement in global processes of an unprecedented magnitude. Is the process of "unification" of the human community in the material, technological, communication, and even political spheres also a movement leading to the eradication of cultural and, in particular, moral differences? There is no doubt on this account among adherents to globalism. They consider a global ethos to be among the most pressing problems for which it is necessary to develop a clear public position. The idea of a global ethos is also supported by those whose religious beliefs are in tune with the idea of moral unity. It is well known that the world religions, especially monotheistic Christianity and Islam, were hatching their own global projects. As Russian philosopher Nicolay Berdyaev pointed out, the unity of God logically requires the unity of mankind.[10]

One of the most important books on this topic is *Global Responsibility: In Search of a New World Ethic* by Hans Küng.[11] He played a leading role in compiling the original text of the *Declaration Toward a Global Ethic*,[12] adopted by the Parliament of the World's Religions in Chicago in 1993. More than six thousand members of that Parliament voted in favor of this document, considering that it gives an ethical justification for the Universal Declaration of Human Rights (UDHR) of 1948. The Swiss theologian is deeply convinced that the world has a chance to survive only if no place remains for different, contradictory, or even antagonistic ethics. A unified basic ethics, developed on the basis of a consensus between people around the world on the issue of values and norms, is needed. Achieving this kind of consent is, according to Küng, possible because "a common set of core values" exists in the teachings of all the religions. The most important principle of a global ethics should be: "Every human being must be treated humanely." This principle in turn leads to four "Irrevocable directives": Commitment to a Culture of

1. "Non-violence and Respect for Life."
2. "Solidarity and a Just Economic Order."
3. "Tolerance and a Life of Truthfulness."
4. "Equal rights and Partnership between Men and Women."[13]

However, this position has many opponents, who denounce what they view as a manifestation of hegemony attributed either to the United States or the capitalist countries of the West, or to the Christian world in general. In opposition to the ideal of world citizenship, Iris Marion Young pointed out that this ideal, although morally appealing, has often forced marginalized or minority groups to assimilate to a dominant cultural and civic model neglectful of their situated needs. To correct this bent to conformity, she argues, "we need a group differentiated citizenship and a heterogeneous public where relevant differences are publicly recognized as irreducible"—though without abandoning concerns for the "common good" and the need "to decide together society's policies."[14]

Paradoxically, the idea of a global ethos is rejected even by those whose religious beliefs are not alien to the ideas of moral unity. There are major differences among members of the same denominations regarding the desirability and possibility of the moral unity of humankind through the establishment of a global ethos. Speaking in January 2004 at the Catholic Academy of Bavaria during a discussion with Jürgen Habermas, Cardinal Joseph Ratzinger (the future Pope Benedict XVI) claimed that there is no such rational, ethical, or religious formula with which the whole world would agree. Therefore, the so-called world ethos remains an abstraction.[15]

How do we explain such a skeptical, if not altogether negative, attitude toward the idea of a global ethos? Whatever is common to all people's "code of morality" is currently constructed on a secular worldview. The UDHR, although adopted by all UN members, certainly has a secular character. The rules of the relationship between the state and its citizens among all members of the international community stated by the UDHR confirm the principles of liberal axiology. However, liberal civilization standards, with their emphasis on individual freedom from conventions and restrictions, in addition to the limitations imposed by law, are often treated as hostile to traditional values, fully identified with religious ones.

Vladimir Shokhin, one of the most knowledgeable Russian experts on the philosophy of religion, claims that global ethics is a pseudoscientific idea. He is of the opinion that interreligious dialogue cannot be anything other than giving up one's own position by one of the parties because it is impossible to reconcile the irreconcilable. An attempt to find common denominators could be fulfilled only if one of the participants in the "dialogue" waives his or her own position.[16] Similar judgments are shared by followers of other religions, in particular Islam. A fundamentally analogous approach is expressed in the Cairo Declaration on Human Rights in Islam (CDHRI) adopted by the state members of the Organization of the Islamic Conference. It actually declares the rule of faith as the norm. After enumerating a set of rights and freedoms, largely repeating those in the UDHR, the CDHRI recalls that "all rights and freedoms set forth in this declaration shall be governed by the Islamic Sharia" (Art. 24) and "The Islamic Sharia is the only source of interpretation and explanation of any articles of this Declaration" (Art. 25).

If commitment to different religious beliefs prevents a global ethos, should we not work around these "confessional" limitations and try to build modern civilizational space beyond the religious and other traditional distinctions by basing this on rationality, which allows us to unite people of different beliefs?[17] Thus, for instance, distinguished Indian philosopher Daya Krishna, while being aware of the significance of differences between various cultures, claimed ". . . if philosophy is an enterprise of human reason, it is bound to show similarities across cultures to some extent and, similarly, as a human enterprise it is bound to be concerned with what man, in a particular culture, regards as the *summum bonum* for mankind."[18]

A global ethos cannot be achieved if it is not based on universally shared values. Yet do universal values really exist? If so, what is the relation between them and the essentials of different cultures? Is an opposition between them inevitable? What is the way to reduce tension and conflicts between them? These are some of the most urgent questions that need to be resolved. Some, who adhere to what is called metaphysical essentialism (associated with such different thinkers as Plato and Thomas Hobbes, Immanuel Kant and G. W. F. Hegel, Alfred North Whitehead and Jürgen Habermas), do not doubt the existence of universal values rooted in human nature as such. Those who oppose universalism mainly belong to such trends of thought as post-Nietzschean, post-Darwinian, or American pragmatism (William James, John Dewey, Hilary Putnam, Donald Davidson, and Richard Rorty). Thus Rorty argues, "There is nothing deep inside each of us, no common nature, no built-in human solidarity, to use a moral reference point." He is convinced that there is nothing that is necessary, nothing that escapes time and chance, no essential nature of what we really are. Consequently, so-called universal truths turn out to be the platitudes of entrenched vocabularies, only part of the rhetoric of our historically contingent vocabularies.[19]

There are difficulties in accepting the two extreme stands on the problem under consideration. Here is just one query to each. How do we explain from the point of view of metaphysical essentialism the striking diversity in the visions of "the end of our pursuit"? How is uniformity in values possible if what we desire in the long run is defined in a dissimilar way: *eudemonia* (Aristotle), unity with God (Saint Augustine and Saint Thomas Aquinas), knowledge (Benedictus de Spinoza), self-realization (Bradley), power (Friedrich Nietzsche), and so forth? Conversely, it is quite proper to ask adherents of relativist approaches: if there is nothing deep inside each of us to use a moral reference point, why do millions of individuals belonging to a particular culture demonstrate commonness in the approach to their pursuit? Is not Hindu *moksha*, which means to put an end to *sansara* (the migration of souls after death), or Chinese harmony of the human being with Heaven and the Earth, strikingly different from the Western pursuit of happiness associated with justice and prosperity at the same time?

Yet we are seeking not so much final answers as practical suggestions for how to deal with the diversity in values that provokes or justifies the tension, hatred, and aggressiveness that in the long run threaten the future. It seems helpful and reasonable to take into consideration at least the following few points. First, if there are universal human values due to a certain uniformity of human nature, they are still nominal. These values get their "fillings" from particular cultures. Second, along with nominally human universals, each culture has a set of its own universals that form its "backbone." Third, though it is not realistic (or admissible) to aspire to the uniformity of Weltanschauungen to achieve uniformity in understanding the meaning of human existence and the norms of human behavior, it is imperative to exert effort to work out common approaches to the issues of world order that determine the fate of humankind. This urgency results from the reality that humanity is truly going through the processes of globalization.

It is worthwhile mentioning the position of a prominent contemporary Iranian, Abdolkarim Soroush, who is convinced that there is a certain category of phenomena that require universal participation. He refers to a tradition from the prophet of Islam that says:

> We are all travelers on a ship; if one person pokes a hole in it, all of us drown . . . This is an excellent allegory, to see all the inhabitants of the globe as co-travelers on a ship. We Muslims have two kinds of problems, local problems and universal problems that are the problems of humanity as a whole. In my view, right now, problems such as peace, human rights, and women's rights have turned into global problems.[20]

To the list of such global problems should be added those connected with ecology and new technologies. All such problems demand collective efforts, which can be undertaken only as a result of intercultural dialogues.

Intercultural dialogue might bring us to understand that in every culture, with all its uniqueness, there is still something similar to the cultures of other people. As Hilary Putnam says, "We have to become more aware of the enormous value of cultural diversity, we have to recognize the need for and value of cultural roots."[21] Yet, as he points out, "pluralism should not be confused with naïve cultural relativism."[22] We can recognize the right to pluralism and at the same time a belief in a certain absolute ideal. We should be able to listen to each other, always continue to search, and seek to improve ourselves and society as a whole.

Dallmayr is a perfect example of a scholar who has been following the above-mentioned way of thinking and acting. These words open one of his recent coedited books, *A World beyond Global Disorder: The Courage to Hope*.[23]

> It is not Paris we should pray for.
> It is the world. It is a world in which Beirut,
> Reeling from bombings two days before Paris,
> is not covered in the press.
> A world in which a bomb goes off
> at a funeral in Bagdad
> and not one person's status update says "Bagdad"
> because not one white person died in that fire.
> Pray for the world
> that blames a refugee crisis for a terrorist attack.
> That does not pause to differentiate between the attacker
> and the person running from the very same thing you are.
> Pray for a world
> where people walking across countries for months,
> their only belongings upon their backs
> are told they have no place to go.
> Say a prayer for Paris by all means,
> but pray more,
> for the world that does not have a prayer
> for those who no longer have a home to defend.
> For a world that is falling apart in all corners,
> and not simply in the towers and cafes we find so familiar.

The poem is said to be anonymous, yet every time I reread it I hear Dallmayr's voice with its rooted cosmopolitanism in the best sense of this notion: an intellectual who combines a patriotic attachment to his country with openness to cultural diversity in our relentlessly globalizing world.

Notes

1. I remember fondly Dallmayr's participation in the Moscow First International Conference on Comparative Philosophy in 2003. He contributed a paper titled "Global Ethics: beyond Universalism and Particularism," which later was published in the original English and in translation in Russian. Моральная философия в

контексте многообразия культур. Сравнительная философия. Выпуск 2. Отв. ред. Степанянц М. Т. М: "Восточная литература," РАН, 2004; *Comparative Ethics in a Global Age*, ed. Marietta T. Stepanyants (Washington, DC: Council for Research in Values and Philosophy, 2007), 87–106.

2. *The Laws of Manu // Sacred Books of the East*, vol. 25, trans. George Bühler, 1886. The date of publication of *Manusmriti* is believed to be about 200 BC.

3. W. Halbfass, *Tradition and Reflection: Exploration in Indian Thought* (Albany: State University of New York Press, 1991), 278.

4. Selection from *Remarks on Certain Trigrams*, in *A Source Book in Chinese Philosophy*, trans. and comp. Wing-Tsit Chan (Princeton, NJ: Princeton University Press, 1963), 269.

5. *The Meaning of the Glorious Qur'an*, text, translation, and commentary by Abdullah Yusuf Ali, vol. I (Cairo: Dar al-kitab al-Masri, 1938).

6. S. Radhakrishnan, ed., *The Dhammapada* (Oxford: Oxford University Press, 1968), 175–76.

7. Evan Morgan, trans., *The Tao. The Great Luminant. Essays from Huai Nan Tzu* (London: Kegan Paul, Trench, Trubner & Co., 1933), 58.

8. Ibid., 44.

9. *The Meaning of the Glorious Qur'an*, 33:72.

10. V. S. Solovyov, *Muhammad, His Life and Religious Teaching* (Almaata: Kazahstan, 1991), 27.

11. Hans Küng, *Global Responsibility: In Search of a New World Ethic* (New York: Crossword, 1991).

12. Hans Küng and Karl-Josef Kuschel,, eds., *A Global Ethic. The Declaration of the Parliament of the World's Religions* (London: SCM Press/New York: Continuum, 1993).

13. Ibid.

14. Iris Marion Young, *Polity and Group Difference: A Critique of the Ideal of Universal Citizenship // Theorizing Citizenship*, ed. Ronald Beiner (Albany: State University of New York Press, 1995), 175–76, 181–84.

15. Jürgen Habermas and Joseph Ratzinger, *The Dialectics of Secularism on Reason and Religion* (Moscow: St Andrew's Biblical-Theological Institute, 2006), 103.

16. V. I. Tolstyh, ed., *A Global Ethics* (Moscow: Vostocnaya Literatura, 1999), 122.

17. A. A. Guseynov, "On Morality and Ethics," in *Philosophy. Morality. Politics* (Moscow: Academkniga, 2002), 139.

18. D. Krishna, *Comparative Philosophy: What It Is and What It Ought to Be // Interpreting Across Boundaries: New Essays in Comparative Philosophy* (Princeton: Princeton University Press, 1988), 71.

19. Richard Rorty, *Contingency, Irony and Solidarity* (Cambridge: Cambridge University Press, 1989), 177.

20. Abdolkarim Soroush, *Reason, Freedom & Democracy in Islam. Essential Writings of Abdolkarim Soroush* (Oxford: Oxford University Press, 2000), 25.

21. H. Putnam, "Can Ethics Be Ahistorical? The French Revolution and the Holocaust," in *Culture and Modernity: East-West Philosophic Perspectives*, ed. Eliot Deutsch (Honolulu: University of Hawaii Press, 1991), 304.

22. Ibid., 309.

23. Fred Dallmayr and Edward Demenchonock, eds., *A World Beyond Global Disorder: The Courage to Hope* (Newcastle upon Tyne, UK: Cambridge Scholars Publishing, 2017).

Chapter 11

Upholding Our World and Regenerating Our Earth

Calling for a Planetary *Lokasamgraha*

ANANTA KUMAR GIRI

Introduction

Fred Dallmayr has been an inspiring seeker of love, knowledge, wisdom, friendship, beauty, dignity, dialogues, and transformations in our world. His life and travel are an inspiration to many—humble fellow seekers and travelers. Dallmayr has traveled lightly and with light across many different traditions, religions, and philosophical movements with profound humility and a quest for learning that has gifted us with deep insights and wisdom as to the fundamental issues of the human condition as well as contemporary issues of survival and transformations, dialogues and peace, freedom and solidarity, mindfulness and letting be, cosmopolitanism and the good life, postsecular faith and a religion of service. Dallmayr has pursued his *sadhana* (strivings) and struggle with courage and *karuna* (compassion), fighting against apocalypse and striving to recover our wholeness—self, social, and humanity's. Dallmayr has pursued his life's journey of the search for knowledge and truth with a spirit of wondering and wandering rather than being a theoretical system builder as he also gently challenges us to realize such a mode of thinking and being. Dallmayr invites us to uphold our world in a spirit of co-creating it and taking it to the next evolutionary level without being a slave of narrow progressivism or linear Eurocentric evolutionism. This calls for action as well as meditation, acting as well as non-acting, dynamics that can be called meditative verbs of co-realizations.[1]

Upholding Our World:
Dharma, Sahadharma, and the Calling of an Integral *Pursurartha*

Upholding our world calls for a life of *Dharma*—right conduct and right living on the part of individuals as well as society. Dharma in Indic thought also has a cosmic dimension. *Dharma* is part of *Purusartha*—the fourfold end or goal of life characterized by *Dharma* (right conduct and right living), Artha (wealth as well as giving rise to the challenge of meaningful wealth), *Kama* (desire) and *Moksha* (salvation). *Dharma* refers to modes of right conduct and thinking, which is different from righteousness as a fixed system of classification between right and wrong, especially imprisoned within a political and religious system of classification between righteous self and unrighteous other. Upholding our world depends on living a life of *Dharma* and cultivating it in self and society. It challenges us to understand the relationship between *Dharma* and law as well as *Dharma* and justice,[2] as *Dharma* challenges us to go beyond an anthropocentric *reduction* of justice and dignity and realize our responsibility not only to human beings but also to non-humans.[3]

There is also a link between *Kama* (desire) and *Dharma*. We can critically rethink our epics such as Mahabharata and Gilgamesh to understand the violence of *Kama* when not guided by *Dharma*. The burning of the Khandava forest in Mahabharata is a manifestation of the destructive desire of Agni, the god of fire. In the epic, Krishna and Arjuna, instead of interrogating the desire of Agni to consume the forest of Khandava, became accomplices to this. This constitutes the originary violence in Mahabharata that led to subsequent violence, for example, the violence against Draupadi and the fratricidal war between Kauravas and Pandavas (Karve 1968).[4] Similar is the killing of Humamba, the guardian god of the forest in the epic Gilgamesh from the Sumerian civilization, the earliest epic of humanity.[5] Our dominant models and practices of development are accompanied by the destruction of forests and Nature that has brought us to the tipping point of climate change. It is a product of work of our *Karma* (action) and *Kama* (desire) not restrained and uplifted by the spirit of *Dharma*.

Purusartha was an important vision and pathway of life in classical India that provided paths of human excellence and social frame. But its implication for human development, social transformations, and upholding our world in the present day has rarely been explored. This is not surprising, as much of the vision and practice of development is Euro-American and suffers from an uncritical, one-sided philosophical and civilizational binding of what Dallmayr calls the "Enlightenment Blackbox." This cuts off our engagement with human development from our roots and especially our integral links with Nature and the Divine.[6] For upholding our world, we need to rethink and transform both *Purusartha* and human and social development. In traditional schemes, *Purusartha* is confined to the individual level and rarely explores the challenge of *Purusartha* at the level of society. In our conventional understanding, elements of *Purusartha* such as *Dharma* and *Artha* are looked at in isolation. But we need to overcome any isolated constitution of *Purusartha*'s elements and look at them instead in a creative spirit of autonomy and interpenetration. Much illness and ill-being both in traditional societies as well as in our contemporary ones emerge from isolating these elements—for example, *Artha* (wealth) not being linked simultaneously to *Dharma* (right conduct) and *Mokhsa* (salvation).[7] Integral *Purusartha* challenges us to realize and create transformational relationships among them.

Dharma as part of an integral Purusartha also challenges us to rethink and realize Dharma in an open way rather than as part of a logic of self-justificatory closure between self and other. Here we can engage the discourse of *swadharma* and *paradharma* in Shirmad Bhagavad Gita. Gita talks about *swadharma* (*dharma* of the self) and the need to protect one's *swadharma* from *paradharma* (*dharma* of others). So far in conventional religion, politics, and interpretative exercises, these concepts have been given a literal and group-linked categorical meaning. But *swadharma* is not only one's socially given religious identity; it is the dharma of one's being, the path of unfoldment, and the duty that one seeks and needs to follow. One needs to nurture and protect one's unique *dharma* and mode of self-realization from those forces that are not intrinsically significant for one's self-realization. For example, if one has an inclination to be an artist but is forced to be something else, one is not following the path of one's *swadharma*. If one is born into Hinduism, then one's *swadhama* is not only Hinduism in a superficial sense and Islam is the *paradharma*—the *dharma* of the other. This is a very superficial rendering of *swadharma* and *paradharma* at the level of caste, religion, and gender.

As we realize the deeper spiritual meaning and challenge of existing categories coming from our culture and religions, we also need to create new categories of reality, living, and realization. In the case of the existing discourses of self and other, *swadharma* and *paradharma*, which have been used in antagonistic battles, we need to create a new category of *saha* (together) and *sahadharma* (*dharma* of togetherness). *Sahadharma* emerges from what Martin Heidegger calls the "midpoint of relationships."[8] This is suggested in the concluding lines of Rigveda, where there is a call for Samagachadhwam, Sambadadhwam. For Daya Krishna, this path of togetherness is the call of the future, and the God to come is a God of togetherness. In his words:

> *Rta* and *Satya* provide the cosmic foundation of the universe and may be apprehended by *tapasa* or disciplined "seeking" or *sadhana* and realized through them. The Sukta 10.191, the last *Sukta* of the *Rigveda*, suggests that this is not, and cannot be, something on the part of an individual alone, but is rather the "collective" enterprise of all "humankind" and names the "god" of this *Sukta* "Somjnanam" emphasizing the "Togetherness" of all "Being" and spelling it out as *Sam Gachhadhwam, Sam Vadadyam, Sambho Manasi Jayatam, Deva Bhagam Jathapurve Sanjanatam Upasate*.[9]

For upholding our world, we need a new culture, political theology, and spiritual ecology of *sahadharma* that nurtures spaces and times of togetherness. Language and common natural resources constitute arenas of *sahadharma*, which includes both conflict and cooperation, and it calls for a new politics and spirituality of *sadhana* and struggle, compassion, and confrontation.

In the field of languages, today there is a deathlike move toward monolingualism. But our mother language, be it Tamil or Odia, nurtures the soul, imagination, and dignity. Those who speak this language come from different ethnic and religious backgrounds. They are not only Tamil Hindus or Odia Hindus, though these groups may be numerically dominant. Today, as some of these mother languages are being marginalized, all of us have a duty, a *dharma*, to nurture and protect this space of *sahadharma*. Here Hindus, Muslims, and Christians and fellow speakers from all religious and nonreligious backgrounds can strive together. Similarly, as our environment is being destroyed and our natural resources depleted, protecting and cultivating this is a matter of a new *sahadharma*. This act of protection, conservation, and renewal of our living environment is related to protecting and recovering our commons, which also calls for a new mode of being with self, other, and the world.[10] Recovering our commons in turn calls for a new politics, ethics, and epistemology of conviviality and cross-fertilization where we take pleasure in each other's presence rather than withdrawing, feeling threatened, and threatening others.[11]

The practice of, and meditation with, *sahadharma* and the recovery of the commons are linked to processes of regeneration of self, culture and society and create movements for bottom-up processes of self and cultural awakening. They also challenge top-down processes of one-sided modernization and now globalization, which resonates with Dallmayr's deep reflections on grassroots globalization.

Integral Development and a New Spiritual Pragmatism of Language, Self, and Society

Integral *Purusartha* and *Sahadharma* challenge us to realize integral development, which is concerned with both material and spiritual development of self and society. It is engaged simultaneously with the historical and the mystical—historical struggles for overcoming entrenched domination and mystical engagement with the limits of the historical and prophetic for realizing the good life.[12] Integral development resonates with Dallmayr's pathway of integral pluralism as an ongoing process of political and spiritual transformation.[13] Integral development also goes beyond the dualism between the pragmatic and the spiritual and embodies multidimensional movements of spiritual pragmatism in vision, practices, societies, and histories.

Integral development calls for a new mode of practice, language, and realization of the very meaning of language. It is not confined to language as a pragmatics of communication, but strives to realize the *spiritual* dimension of pragmatics, which resonates with Dallmayr's deep journey with language.[14] There is a pragmatic dimension to the perspective on language offered by philosophers such as Wittgenstein, Heidegger, and Sri Aurobindo, but this is not an ordinary pragmatics—it has a spiritual dimension, it is spiritual pragmatics. There is, for example, a spiritual struggle in Wittgenstein's concept of form of life. Wittgenstein writes that "an entire mythology is stored in our language."[15] Veena Das builds on this insight to tell us how the mythological aspect of language can help us cross borders and live our everyday lives with mutuality in the midst of differences of many kinds.

As just indicated, there is a dimension of spiritual pragmatics in both Heidegger and Sri Aurobindo as well. Sri Aurobindo talks about a nobler pragmatism. Similarly, Heidegger's reflection on language as a "way-making movement"[16] has a spiritual dimension. To cultivate and nurture living words and to uphold our world, we need to bring out this dimension of the spiritual pragmatism of language. Integral development calls for a new realization of the meaning of life and language as such "way-making movements," touching both the practical and spiritual dimensions of our lives.

But upholding our world calls for manifold movements of spiritual pragmatism and mystical pragmatism. Spiritual pragmatics is, in turn, linked to a new spiritual erotics. It begins with breathing together and creating a new humanity, as Luce Irigaray would urge us to realize.[17] Spiritual erotics as part of spiritual pragmatics is linked to a new evolutionary journey. Upholding our world calls for new initiatives in love and co-realization, and here the critical and transformational phenomenology of Dallmayr can be linked to the *sadhana* of realizing our serpentine energy of love, communication, and transformation. The latter is practiced in traditions such as Tantra, which also involve a *Kundalini sadhana* of going from the lower part of our self to higher realms of our consciousness without being a slave of any a priori hierarchy of the higher and the lower. Kundalini *sadhana* is a *sadhana* of bringing the horizontal and the vertical dimension of self, society, politics, and democracy together. In fact, the democracy to come, which Dallmayr so creatively cultivates,[18] can be facilitated by the integration of the vertical and horizontal as in the *kundalini sadhana* of Tantra.[19] Dallmayr has walked and meditated with pathways of Buddhism and Vedanta from Indic traditions, and now he also may find inspiring resonances from the springs of Tantra.[20]

Regenerating Our Earth

Upholding our word is accompanied by manifold efforts of regenerating our Earth. Our Earth today has been under stress, and with climate change is now bereft of green cover in many parts, which threatens human life on Earth. Sometimes we look at Earth as only dead matter, but with inspiration from Gaia cosmology, which also touches science as well as religious and spiritual traditions of the world, we can relate to the Earth with sacredness. This is the spirit of Pope Francis's encyclical *Laudato Si* and Dallmayr's meditation in his *Return to Nature?* Regenerating our earth is connected to the climate care movement in which we all can take part.[21] It calls for creative discovery of our roots and also a cross-fertilization between roots and routes in creative and transformative ways. It calls for new ways of Earth work, which also consist of new ways of memory works and memory meditations in which we can hear the groaning of our Mother Earth and contribute to Her healings, especially as ravaged by war and climate change.

In his contribution to the symposium "Cross-Fertilizing Roots and Routes," Dallmayr brings the discussion of Earth and World from Heidegger, which also helps us to understand the relationship between upholding our world and regenerating our earth. As Dallmayr writes,

> In Heidegger's presentation, the terms "world" and "earth" refer basically to the difference between openness and sheltering, between revealment and concealment, between the disclosure of future possibilities of life and the reticence of finite origins. . . . what is important to note, however, is that difference is not equivalent to dualism or antithesis, but rather serves as a synonym for counterpoint or differential entwinement. In Heidegger's words, difference here establishes a counterpoint which is a kind of "midpoint" between world and earth, but not in the sense of a stark antagonism. Hence, world is not simply openness and earth not simply closure; rather, there is mutual conditioning and interpenetration. . . .[22]

Dallmayr's call for understanding the entwinement between Earth and World urges us to realize Earth as an open journey of evolution and realization. Upholding our world and regenerating our earth calls for seed works, seed meditations, and a *sadhana* of gardening. It also calls for creative and critical works such as walking and meditating with the vision, discourse, and realization of the Kingdom of God.

The first challenge is to realize that visions like the "Kingdom of God is within you" need deeper quest and realization. As Harvey Cox tells us, the real impulse of this vision in Aramaic is to realize that the Kingdom of God is across you.[23] This brings the *sadhana* of the realization of the Kingdom of God resonating with the spirit of *Sahadharma* and God of togetherness discussed above. We are also invited to transform the language and discourse of the Kingdom of God into a Garden of God. The vision and discourse of the Kingdom of God has many a time been imprisoned within a logic of power where we are prone to valorize God's power in order to valorize our own, especially the logic of sovereignty at the level of self and society, rather than realize God's mercy. We are entrapped in a literal understanding of the Garden of Eden and fall from it by the deviation of the snake, Adam, and

Eve. But we can now transform the vision and discourse into the Garden of God and see the snake, Adam, and Eve as children of both God and Mother Earth. This is an aspect of *Kundalini sadhana* discussed above. We can realize God as a creative Gardener, dancing the cosmic dance of what Dallmayr calls "sacred non-sovereignty and shared sovereignty."[24] With a cross-cultural realization, we can realize that it is possibly the Divine in the Snake that inspired Eve to whisper to Adam to eat the forbidden Apple so that the dance of creation and the Divine play on earth could unfold. We can here draw upon traditions such as *Kundalini* and Tantra from Indic traditions that challenge us to realize the significance of serpentine energy and *Kundalini* in life. Rethinking and transforming the Kingdom of God into the Garden of God opens up new ways of looking at the traditions of political theology and links it to the vision and practice of deeper cross-cultural spiritual realizations. Dallmayr's critique and reconstitution of the cult of sovereignty in political theology is an important tool here that also can be cultivated in the direction of practical spirituality.[25] Dallmayr has invited us to walk and meditate with such new pathways of movement from political theology to practical spirituality.[26]

Lokasamgraha

Lokasamgraha is an important invitation for self, social, and cosmic transformation from the Indic tradition, and it appears briefly in Srimad Bhagbad Gita twice. It is usually translated as the well-being of all, but it also refers to the process of gathering or collecting *loka*—people.[27] It is a creative and critical gathering of people and the accompanying process of mutual care that leads to well-being. As a process of gathering, it is not just confined to the public sphere or public political processes. It also involves in an integrally interlinked manner a gathering of the soul—*atmasamgraha*. *Lokasamgraha* and *atmasamgraha*—gathering of soul and people—lead to a creative gathering of society not just as a mechanical entity but also as a living process of critique, creativity, and transformation. It also leads to regeneration of the commons and a cosmic mobilization of energy. As K. B. Rao writes:

> If the term *Samgraha* is taken as a verb, it stands for the act or process. But taken as a noun it stands for Reality in its dynamic Being." *Lokasamgraha* challenges us to realize that our life, self, society and the world have a cosmic dimension and our cosmos is

not just a dead entity but a living evolving process. *Lokasamgraha* challenges us to a transformation of our cosmology from a mechanical one to a living and a spiritual one. *Lokasamgraha* is not confined to human beings, it includes all beings and therefore challenges us to go beyond an anthropocentric concept of welfare and to "widen the implications of *loka-samgraha* to cover the universal order of Being."[28]

In our earlier discussion, we saw the significance of dharma as *sahadharma* and integral *purusartha* for upholding our world and regenerating our Earth. But there is a link between *Purusartha* and *Lokasamgraha*. As Rao tells us: ". . . the completeness of the *Purusarthas* is possible only when they include Lokartha, that is Lokasamgraha, as an integral part thereof."[29] *Lokasamgraha* challenges us to realize well-being and happiness for all, but for this we are all invited to be creative in our strivings and struggles: it cannot be left to the others, society, and state. At the heart of *Lokasamgraha* is care and responsibility, which connect the vision and practice of *Lokasamgraha* in the Western political tradition, such as in the works of Hannah Arendt and in the Chinese philosophy of Tian-Xia—All Under Heaven.[30] Lokasamgraha challenges us not only to maintain the world but also to uphold it. This upholding is crucially dependent on right living in self and society, which is facilitated by appropriate social policy and public actions as well as by the strivings and preparation of the soul. It also challenges us to regenerate our earth by planting new seeds and trees of life in the landscape of despair and destruction, especially of climate change.

Lokasamgraha: With and Beyond Cosmopolitanism

Dharma in the Indic scheme of *Purusartha* ought to be brought together with similar visions and practices, such as *Dhamma* in Buddhism and rites in Confucian traditions. Here we also are challenged to rethink the vision and practices of human development that can learn from visions of *Purusartha* in creative ways in the process both of opening *Purusartha* and human development to cross-cultural, cross-religious, and cross-civilizational dialogues. For instance, it is helpful to explore the parallels of *purusartha* in other religious and civilizational streams such as Christianity, Islam, Buddhism, and Chinese civilizations. In this we can build on the deep quest of Dallmayr over the years in intercultural dialogue and dialogue among civilizations.

Cosmopolitanism has been a discourse that seems to help us understand our belonging to our world. It helps us realize that we are all citizens of the world. But this itself suffers from Eurocentric and ethnocentric limitations, and now we need to go beyond cosmopolitanism and realize that we are simultaneously citizens of the world and children of our Mother Earth. This is the spirit of planetary *Loksasamgraha*, which resonates with Dallmayr's important reconstructive works on cosmopolitanism.[31] In his creative oeuvre, Dallmayr has walked and meditated with multiple pathways and movements of co-creativity, and taking inspiration from him we can offer ourselves to further movements of critical and transformative creativity and co-creativity in our lives and the world.

Notes

1. Ananta Kumar Giri, *Sociology and Beyond: Windows and Horizons* (Jaipur: Rawat Publications, 2012).

2. Ananta Kumar Giri, *Knowledge and Human Liberation: Towards Planetary Realizations* (London: Anthem Press, 2013); Fred Dallmayr, "Love and Justice: A Memorial Tribute to Paul Ricouer," in *Paul Ricouer: Honoring and Continuing the Work*, ed. Farhang Erfani (Lanham, MD: Lexington Books, 2011).

3. Gurucharan Das describes the need to cultivate dharma vis-à-vis our relationship to non-humans in his interpretation of Mahabharata (see his *The Difficulty of Being Good* [New Delhi: Penguin, 2009]).

4. Irawati Karve, *Yuganta: The End of An Epoch*, https://archive.org/stream/Yuganta-TheEndOfAnEpoch-IrawatiKarve/yuganta_djvu.txt.

5. Jeremy Rifkin, *Empathic Civilization: The Race to Global Consciousness in a World in Crisis* (New York: Jeremy P. Tarcherer, 2009).

6. Fred Dallmayr, *Alternative Visions: Paths in the Global Village* (Lanham, MD: Rowman and Littlefield, 1998).

7. Daya Krishna, "Time, Truth and Transcendence," in *History, Culture and Truth: Essays Presented to DP Chattopadhyaya*, ed. Daya Krishna and K. Satchidananda Murty (Delhi: Kalki Prakashan, 1991), 323–26.

8. Fred Dallmayr, *The Other Heidegger* (Ithaca: Cornell University Press, 1993).

9. "Rg Veda: The Mantra, the Sukta and the Mandala or the Rsi, the Devata, the Chanda: The Structure of the Text and Problems Regarding It," *Journal of Indian Council of Philosophical Research* 23, no. 2 (April–June 2006): 1–13.

10. Herbert Reid and Betsy Taylor, *Recovering the Commons: Democracy, Place, and Global Justice* (Urbana-Champagne: University of Illinois Press, 2010).

11. Arjun Appadurai, *Fear of Small Numbers: An Essay on the Geography of Anger* (Durham: Duke University Press, 2006).

12. Sebastian Painadath, *We Are Co-Pilgrims* (Delhi: ISCPK, 2007).

13. Fred Dallmayr, *Integral Pluralism: Beyond Culture Wars* (Lexington: University of Kentucky Press, 2010).

14. Fred Dallmayr, *On the Boundary: A Life Remembered* (Lanham, MD: Hamilton Books, 2017).

15. Quoted in Veena Das, "Moral and Spiritual Striving in the Everyday: To Be a Muslim in Contemporary India," in *Ethical Life in South Asia*, ed. Anand Pandian and Daud Ali (Delhi: Oxford University Press, 2011), 240.

16. Martin Heidegger, "On the Way to Language," in *Basic Writings of Martin Heidegger* (New York: Basic Books, 2004).

17. Luce Irigary, *Between East and West: From Singularity to Community* (New York: Columbia University Press, 2002).

18. See Fred Dallmayr, *The Promise of Democracy: Political Agency and Transformation* (Albany: State University of New York Press, 2009); Dallmayr, "Democracy to Come," in *Theory After Derrida: Essays in Critical Praxis*, ed. Kailash Baral and R. Radhakrishna (Delhi: Routledge); and Dallmayr, *Democracy to Come: Politics as Relational Praxis* (New York: Oxford University Press, 2017).

19. There is a *sadhana* of Tantra in many seekers of transformation such as Sri Aurobindo and Gandhi. Dallmayr has been deeply engaged with Gandhi, and this engagement can be further illumined if we bring a Tantric perspective to understand Gandhi's vision and practice. As Ramachandra Gandhi, the Mahatma's philosophical grandson, tells in a conversation with U. R. Ananthamurthy: "Perhaps the world has never seen a bigger *tantrik* than Gandhiji." See U. R. Ananthamurthy, *Suragi* (Delhi: Oxford University Press, 2018), 324. Ananthamruthy then writes: "He [Ramachandra Gandhi] believed Gandhi's acts—from spinning the charkha, through the salt satyagraha, to the march in cleaning the latrines, and streets lined with stones and thorns—were like the rituals the *tantriks* deployed to achieve their heart's desire" (ibid.).

20. See Marcus Bussey, "Tantra as Episteme," *Futures* 30, no. 7 (September 1998): 705–16.

21. M. S. Swaminathan, *In Search of Biohappiness: Biodiversity and Food, Health and Livelihood Security* (Singapore: World Scientific, 2011).

22. Fred Dallmayr, "Earth and World: Roots and Routes," *Social Alternatives* 36, no. 1 (2017): 12.

23. Harvey Cox, *How to Read the Bible* (New York: HarperCollins, 2016).

24. Fred Dallmayr, *Small Wonder: Global Power and Its Discontents* (Lanham, MD: Rowman and Littlefield, 2005).

25. Ibid.

26. In his insightful foreword to our edited book *Practical Spirituality and Human Development* (Dallmayr 2018a), Dallmayr suggests this. See Ananta Kumar Giri, ed., *Practical Spirituality and Human Development*, vol 1: Transformation of Religions and Societies (Singapore: Palgrave Macmillan, 2018).

27. K. B. Rao, *The Bhagavad Gita as the Philosophy of Loka-Samgraha or Cosmic Consolidation* (Bengaluru: Darpan Books, 2016).

28. Ibid.
29. Ibid., 167.
30. Fred Dallmayr, *Against Apocalypse: Recovering Humanity's Wholeness* (Lanham, MD: Lexington Books, 2015).
31. As in his foreword to the book on cosmopolitanism I have edited, *Beyond Cosmopolitanism: Towards Planetary Transformations* (Singapore, Palgrave Macmillan, 2018).

Chapter 12

Philosophy and the Colonial Difference Revisited

WALTER D. MIGNOLO

I got to know Fred Dallmayr through reading *Beyond Orientalism: Essays on Cross-Cultural Encounter* (1996). I had recently published *The Darker Side of the Renaissance: Literacy, Territoriality and Colonization* (1995). Just looking at *Beyond Orientalism*'s table of contents and seeing Heidegger next to Bhakti and Vedanta resonated strongly with my argument in *The Darker Side*, although the scenario was at the other end of the East-West division and three centuries later. At that moment, I thought that I could have very well subtitled my book *Beyond Occidentalism*.

The conversation in South and North America in the mid-1980s and early 1990s was on "Occidentalism." Those of us in that conversation were looking East toward Europe, and Europe was looking East toward the "Orient." From the Americas (including the United States), South and North, Asia is to the "West." However, the rules of the game have been settled since the sixteenth century, when Pope Alexander VI and the Spanish monarchy decided to label "Indias Occidentales" what would become "America" and "Indias Orientales" the land that was already named "Asia" in the Christian medieval T/O maps. During those conversations, it was clear that it was the necessary condition for "Orientalism." In retrospect, "Orientalism" was paradoxically one specific chapter in the history of "Westernization or Occidentalization" of the planet (to say it in Serge Latouche's vocabulary)[1] since the sixteenth century.

It was in 1984, when invited to a conference in Baroda, India, that Dallmayr had the epiphany he narrates in *On The Boundary*.[2] He realized that while his Indian philosophy colleagues, seniors, and juniors could discuss Plato and Heidegger, Gadamer, and Foucault with him, he was unable to engage in a conversation with them about Indian systems of thought. What Dallmayr felt—in my interpretation—was the colonial difference, its floating presence all over the planet. The philosophical colonial difference is one dimension of the epistemic and ontological colonial differences. The epistemic colonial difference was silencing, operating in the belief since the sixteenth century, that non-Europeans were epistemically deficient and therefore ontologically as well: inferior beings equated with inferior minds. Western philosophy (whether theological or secular) was the terrain where colonial differences operated.

Philosophy is a language enterprise or, more specifically, is engaging in languaging around assumptions, frames, and concepts to which the practitioners of a given discipline (in this case philosophy) agree and within which they debate; and it is in languaging that the epistemic colonial differences could be more clearly detected. "Philosophy" is not only the word that Ancient Greek thinkers used to name what they were doing in their thinking, but it also became the name of a Western discipline. As such, it is grounded in the two Western classic languages (Greek and Latin) and the six European imperial languages: Italian, Spanish, Portuguese, French, German, and English). Philosophy in the colonies (since the inauguration of European expansion in the Renaissance) was exported and practiced by European settlers. For Indigenous people to do philosophy, it was and still is necessary to learn the ethno "languages" of philosophy because non-European ethno languages were not deemed suitable for such privileged enterprise. There you see the colonial difference at work: non-European were not suited to do philosophy and were questionable in their thinking.[3]

"Occidentalism" and "Orientalism" are two signposts of the colonial difference. But that is not all, for the colonial difference became a springboard to put to work another dimension, the imperial difference. While colonial differences were necessary to classify and rank the places and population going through early settler colonialism (in the Americas, Asia, Africa, Oceania, and the Caribbean), the imperial difference was necessary to rank people and regions that have not been colonized. This was so much so that toward the end of the eighteenth century, when "Orientalism" began to emerge, the idea of "the South of Europe" complemented it.

The South of Europe was not colonized; on the contrary, it was the location of former global empires that became displaced by the North. This means that the North (France, Germany, and the UK) were displacing the South not only in controlling money but also, and mainly, in controlling meaning. Colonial and imperial differences are not ontological (there are no ontologically inferior people or inferior regions of the planet that are "represented" in some neutral language) but instituted by actors and institutions controlling money and meaning.

Spanish philosopher José Ortega y Gasset, returning to Spain after studying in Germany alongside Husserl and Heidegger, felt that by doing philosophy in Spain and in Castilian, he was a philosopher "in partibus infidelium." He said it because he was sensing the imperial difference. The imperial difference is still at work today, and we can see it in the very hierarchical structure of the European Union and the attitudes the managers have toward the managed (e.g., the Greece Referendum and the attitude of the European Troika). Let's then concentrate on philosophy and the colonial difference. My "Philosophy and the Colonial Difference" was published in 1999.[4] Because its main thesis has not lost its relevance almost twenty years later, I take this opportunity to revisit it in connection with Dallmayr's interest in "cross-cultural encounters."

In the 1950s, the distinguished ethno-historian of Ancient Mexico, Miguel León-Portilla, published his classical book *La filosofía Nahuatl*.[5] The eleventh edition was published in 2017. When the book was first published in 1956, one of the major attacks against it was his "imprudent" use of the term "philosophy" to designate something that the Aztecs or Nahuatl-speaking people could have been doing. But criticisms were in the first place ambiguous. The "lack" of philosophical discourse among the Aztecs could have meant that they were "barbarians," uncivilized, or not sufficiently "developed" (the word has become popular recently in Latin America). On the other hand, it could have meant just that they were "different." In that case, Nahuatl-speaking people may not have had "philosophy," but the "difference" need not be considered as a lack but an assertion that they had or did something else. Europeans, in their turn, did not have whatever that "something" else could have been.

When dealing with the social role of the tlamatini, León-Portilla did not translate the word into "philosopher" but instead described his role, what the tlamatini was and did: the tlamatinime (plural) were "those who have the power of the word."[6] León-Portilla, as anybody would, had difficulties in defining, first, what philosophy is in order to show, second, that the Aztec or Nahuatl-speaking people indeed had philosophy. He managed, however, to give an acceptable picture of what philosophy was for the Greeks and then matched it with the remains of Aztec documentation from the beginning of the sixteenth century, before Hernán Cortés's arrival in Mexico-Tenochtitlan.

León-Portilla overlooked the fact that philosophy, in Greece, went hand in hand with the emergence of what are today considered the Western alphabet and Western literacy. Indeed, if I had to define what philosophy is (following the Greek legacy), I would begin by saying that it is associated with writing and, more specifically, with alphabetic writing. I would add that alphabetic writing, linked to the concept of philosophy, allowed Western people of letters, since the sixteenth century, to establish the difference between philosophy and other forms of knowledge. There is a caveat in this argument, however: the Arabic language and the Arabic early contact and translation of philosophical texts from Greek to Arabic. I do not pursue this point, because I have to concentrate on Latin America, but it is indeed an issue to keep in mind to understand the emergence of the colonial difference.

Beyond overlooking alphabetic writing in its complicity with the Western self-description of philosophy, León-Portilla accepted without further question (and here he is not alone) that philosophy is a Greek invention and provides a natural point of reference to decide whether something else is or is not philosophy. We can extend the same argument to other practices, to be sure. But let us stay with philosophy. So, the argument goes, philosophy did not exist before the Greeks invented it. Therefore, communities or civilizations before the Greeks, or even those contemporaneous with Greek society but having their own vocabulary, memory, praxis of living, believing, and doing, were guided by thinking people, and of course they did not need to call "philosophy" the thinking that they were doing.

Even after the Greeks came up with the word "philosophy" to name their own praxis of thinking, civilizations like the Aztecs, without any knowledge of Greek existence (and the inverse was true too), did not care about "philosophy" because they had their wise men, the tlamatinime, who were doing exactly what Greek philosophers were doing: thinking the universe, life, living together, the fluidity and interconnectedness of Energy with the living, Téotl, while the Greeks were thinking Kosmos. Spaniards, who had difficulty understanding a cosmology that was not theirs—Greek and Roman legacies—translated Téotl as God. They missed the point: Téotl was not an entity but the Energy from where what exists has been created.

A one-to-one correspondence doesn't obtain, but the legitimacy of both cosmologies is out of the question.

The question is the power differential that was instituted in the sixteenth century to impose Kosmos and Universum over Téotl. That is the colonial difference at its best. And it is still with us. Similar arguments could be made regarding thinking in Mandarin in Ancient China (Confucius, Mencius). There is something odd in this historiographical picture, particularly because it is the result of an argument that places "philosophy" as a good thing to have or to regret if you don't and would like to have it. The oddity vanishes once we realize that it is how the colonial difference works: making you believe that the "difference is ontological or cultural" and not colonial. While Greek thinkers were naming their doing as they saw fit, the problem is that starting in the European Renaissance, "philosophy" became one of the dimensions of the coloniality of knowledge. Decolonially speaking it is of the essence to unravel the colonial difference and to reduce "philosophy" to its own size.

Because I am expounding on the colonial difference, and the colonial difference came into being during the so-called "conquest of America," which in a different macro-narrative corresponds to the emergence of the Atlantic commercial circuit and of the modern/colonial world, I need to move further into this historical foundational moment of the rhetoric of modernity and the logic of coloniality (modernity/coloniality). But to do so, I have to stay a little longer with the famous Greek philosophers. Why, indeed, did León-Portilla have to title his book "Nahuatl Philosophy," and why did people react against this title, asking whether Nahuatl people had, could have had, or had no philosophy? Why shall Greek and later on Western conceptions and disciplinary regulations under the name of "philosophy" be the reference point and the measuring stick? Greek civilization is quite young in the anthropos era (e.g., the anthropocene). And if Greek philosophy is not the reference point, then what are we talking about?

Perhaps we should modify the perspective from which we think about this issue. Instead of assuming that there is something like "philosophy," which the Greeks invented, we should ask what kind of activities the anthropos have been engaging in since time immemorial and what the Greeks, when was their turn to do it, named "philosophy." Let's say that what our ancestors the anthropos were doing since time immemorial was thinking and languaging, languaging in thinking, and thinking in languaging.[7] If we change the question, we change the terms of the conversation. If we keep asking questions within the frame of existing conversations, we may change the content but not the terms of the conversation. We would engage postmodernity but not decoloniality, which is what I am trying to do here. This would be the first question/issue to take seriously.

The second one would be to ask why, once the Greeks invented the name "philosophy" for the kind of thinking they were doing, this was appropriated by the West and projected universally. Why did the Greeks' form of thinking become the point of reference to establish borders and between philosophy and its difference? If we look at what Arabs thinkers did with the Greek concept of philosophy, we find a different scenario. Translated into Arabic, philosophy became *falsafa*, which introduces another dimension of the geopolitics and body (sensing, emotioning) politics of knowledge. I am arguing that "philosophy and its difference" became an issue beginning in the sixteenth century and that the issue was the making of the colonial difference. It is not enough to say that word X is equivalent to word Z: on the one hand because X and Z belong to different local histories, memories, sensibilities, and emotioning; and on the other hand because—in the imaginary of the modern/colonial world order—there is a power differential (the colonial difference) between X and Z.

I do not know whether before the sixteenth century the problem encountered by León-Portilla was a common one. Certainly, communities have had their self-descriptions and many ways of distinguishing themselves from different communities. But never before the sixteenth century did differentiations acquire the dimension that the colonial difference had and still has in the modem/colonial world—a world that was made, shaped, and controlled by European languages, actors, and institutions, from the Spanish to the British Empires going through Dutch, French, and German colonialisms. The European Renaissance (in the south of Europe) and then the European Enlightenment (in the north of Europe) registered two simultaneous achievements. First, the self-image of the West was built in macro-narratives of Western civilization, which means that Western civilization is a concept sustained by innumerable storytellings by actors who conceived of themselves as members of Western civilization. Second, the colonial difference was built into the very process of creating Western identity by defining its interiority and its exteriority: the colonial difference was grounded on the doubtful humanity of the inhabitants of the great civilizations they destroyed. Certainly Vitoria, Sepulveda, and Las Casas did not ask themselves whether the tlamatinimi were equivalent to philosophers. They preempted the question, and it is precisely in their preempting that the colonial difference came into being and established itself as a matter of fact.

In this respect, León-Portilla's was a brave and important move to assume that there was a Nahuatl philosophy even if, in his time, he was too much caught in the spider web of Western categories of thought. What I am attempting is to revalue and rework his valiant efforts from the 1950s into the frame of decolonial thinking. León-Portilla couldn't solve the problem because the concept of "colonial difference" was not available to him. However, his contribution brought to the foreground what today is understood as the work of the colonial difference not only in what he said, but also in his own saying. At the time he published the book (1957), the philosophical debates around decolonization were just at their inception. The decolonization of India took place in 1947, and in 1948 Mahatma Gandhi was assassinated. His writings were not yet in wide circulation. Frantz Fanon's *The Wretched of the Earth* was published in 1961, and he died the same year. What for León-Portilla was a dilemma (to justify Nahuatl philosophy) for sixteenth-century Spanish theologian-philosophers was not a dilemma at all. They could never have ever thought of asking themselves whether the tlamatinimi were philosophers. Even less could this have been a question for the French "philosophes" in the eighteenth century, for at that time "barbarians" mutated into "primitives," and no one in their right mind would think that "primitives" could think and do philosophy.

On this theme of how the colonial difference works (and works us) in the discipline called "philosophy," it is instructive to quote continental philosopher Robert Bernasconi, a specialist in continental philosophy well versed in Heidegger, Levinas, and Derrida who ventured to take African philosophy seriously. He says, "Western philosophy traps African philosophy in a double bind: either African philosophy is so similar to Western philosophy that it makes no distinctive contribution and effectively disappears; or it is so different that its credentials to be genuine philosophy will always be in doubt."[8] I do not quote Bernasconi as an authority, stamping with his quotation what I have been arguing so far. To do so would be falling into the colonial difference that I am both trying to avoid and to make visible. I quote Bernasconi instead as an ethnographic informant in the field of philosophy. The persuasive strength of his argument resides not only in what he says but in the very act of saying it as a continental philosopher. Had the matter been what he said, Bernasconi would have maintained the philosophical authority of one who reports the difference between continental and African philosophy without putting himself at risk in the act of reporting. Bernasconi's observation brings to the foreground the philosophical colonial difference.

It is worth quoting Bernasconi again, this time on decolonization. What is new here is that he, as a continental philosopher and scholar of continental philosophy, has listened to the claim that philosophers, social scientists, and humanists in the Third World have been making for at least thirty years, saying that

> The existential dimension of African philosophy's challenge to Western philosophy in general and Continental philosophy in particular is located in the need to decolonize the mind. This task is at least as important for the colonizer as it is for the colonized. For Africans, decolonizing the mind takes place not only in facing the experience of colonialism, but also in recognizing the precolonial, which establishes the destructive importance of so-called ethno-philosophy and sage philosophy as well as nationalist-ideological philosophy.[9]

León-Portilla confronted the same problem—the colonial difference—but articulated it differently. He argued for the existence of Nahuatl philosophy because the Aztecs' intellectual competence has been questioned when not denied since the very inception of conquest and colonization. Decolonization of philosophy and, more generally, of cultures of scholarship seems to be still a viable project. It is necessary to accept that philosophy is a discipline at once modern and colonial. Philosophical coloniality is unmasked once we bring to light the philosophical and epistemic colonial difference.

For Moroccan philosopher Abdelkhebir Khatibi, dwelling in the borders between Islam and Western modernity, decolonization implied a double critique: neither Islamic fundamentalism nor Western modernity fundamentalism, but decolonization.[10] Khatabi was writing during the trying years of the Cold War when decolonization was geared toward ejecting the settlers and building nation-states. Morocco (Kingdom of he West) gained independence from the French protectorate in 1956 and from the Spanish protectorate in 1957. At the time Khatibi was writing, Morocco was already a constitutional monarchy. Hence the focus of decolonization as decoloniality was the domain of knowledge and subjectivity. And in his case, as a French-trained philosopher with a Muslim upbringing, coloniality was felt in the persistence of Islamic and Western fundamentalism. However, at the time of his writing, Western fundamentalism was in the privileged position within the power differential: the philosophical and epistemic colonial difference was at work then and there too.

Hence decolonization as decoloniality in Khatibi is simultaneously an undoing and a redoing. It is an undoing (double critique) of the colonial difference and a redoing in terms of what I have called elsewhere "border thinking." I would add now that border thinking presupposes dwelling on the border, and consequently it emerges from the praxis of living rather than as an abstract conceptual construction, whereas the thinker and doer dwells in the territory. Border thinking, in other words, is the privilege of border dwellers just as territorial thinking is the privilege of those who dwell in the territory. It is not a question of either/or but of and/and. It is a question of coexistence regulated by the power differentials that have been structured around the persistence of colonial differences. Needless to say, border thinking cannot be an abstract universal because border dwellers bring to the foreground and to the public sphere the singularity (diverse of course in their singularity) of local histories entangled with the plurality of spatial and temporal intrusion of Western civilization in the singular diversity of local histories.

Confronting the "either/or" logic of exclusion, Khatibi finds out that decoloniality demands "une pensée autre" ("an other thinking"), which is the logical consequence of the double critique. "An other thinking" takes us to the logic of "and/and" confronted and coexisting with the logic of either/or. Confronting and coexisting means that decoloniality is not a mission to convert and supplant the logic of either/or imposing a decolonial universalism, but an option that affirms itself in confrontation with other options (epistemic, economic, political, ethical, religious, esthetical) instituted by Western modernity. By so doing, decoloniality reveals that we live among options not with any universal truth that has to be defended. Universal truths (religious, scientific, philosophical) are options that are not seen by the actors who postulate them as an option but as reality. Today, the truth of that reality is supported and defended by governments, banks, corporations, armies, and the mainstream mass media.

Yet the confrontation that decoloniality opens up cannot be in the sphere of the state, the banks, the corporations, the armies, and the media, but in the sphere of knowledge without which the complicity between those other institutions cannot be sustained. The target of decolonial pursuits resides in the sphere of knowledge because subjectivities are formed, transformed, and manipulated by force no doubt but by knowledge mainly.

There is a limit to the number of people who could be manipulated by force, while the number of people who can be manipulated by knowledge, trickling down from the institutions (schools, universities, museums, media, religious institutions, the state, the corporations) that generate, transform, and transmit it, is unbounded.

This question of philosophy, the colonial difference, and decoloniality can be tackled from another geopolitical angle. The philosophy of liberation was the philosophical version of what became merged with decoloniality.[11] Decolonization as decoloniality also invaded the social sciences. Whereas the struggles for decolonization in Asia and Africa took place during the Cold War, in South America they were fought during the nineteenth century. In the second half of the twentieth century, when the Colombian sociologist Orlando Fals-Borda was thinking, doing, and writing, his call for the decolonization of sociology,[12] similar to Khatibi's during the same period, was a call for epistemic decolonization as decoloniality. Enrique Dussel had also perceived something similar during those years since the early 1970s and raised questions about the significant contribution made by Emmanuel Levinas to underlining the Eurocentric bent of his philosophy. Let me quote an observation made by Dussel in 1975:

> Hablando personalmente con Levinas en Paris, en 1971, pude comprobar el grado de similitud de nuestro pensar . . . pero al mismo tiempo la radical ruptura que ya en ese entonces se habia producido. Me conto como las grandes experiencias politicas de su generacion habian sido la presencia de Stalin e Hitler (dos totalizaciones deshumanizantes y fruto de la modernidad europeo-hegeliana). Pero al indicarle que no solo la gran experiencia de mi generacion sino de!ultimo medio milenio habia sido el ego de la modernidad europea, ego conquistador, colonialista, imperial en su cultura y opresor de los pueblos de la periferio, no pudo menos que aceptar que nunca habia pensado que "el Otro" pudiera ser "un indio, un africano o un asiatico." "El otro" de la totalidad de] mundo Europeo eran todas las culturas y hombres que habian sido constituidos como cosas a la mano, instrumentos, ideas conocidas, entes a disposicion de la "Voluntad de poder europea" (y despues ruso-norteamericana).[13]

> Speaking with Levinas in Paris, in 1971, I could verify the degree of similarity of our thinking . . . but at the same time the radical rupture that had already occurred at that time. He

told me how the great political experiences of his generation had been the presence of Stalin and Hitler (two dehumanizing totalitarian outcomes of European-Hegelian modernity). But by pointing out that not only the great experience of my generation but also that of the last half-millennium had been the Ego of European modernity, a conquering Ego, colonialist and imperial in its culture and oppressive of the peoples of the periphery, it could not help but to accept that he had never thought that "the Other" could be "an Indian, an African or an Asian." "The other" of the whole of the European world were all cultures and people who had been constituted as things at hand, instruments, known ideas, entities at the disposal of the "Will of European power" (and later Russian-American).

Here we face another scenario where the philosophical colonial difference drives. No longer the scenario between Christian theology and Nahuatl thoughts, no longer between continental philosophy and African thinking, but between continental philosophy in Paris and the colonial version of continental philosophy in Argentina and South America, learned and debated by people of European descent (like Dussel and me). There is another story when we look at the legacies of Indigenous thinking today and also Afro-Caribbean thinking and the confrontation with continental philosophy.[14] At the time Dussel was saying this, the philosophy of liberation was entangled in its most enduring guilt, justly criticized by Horacio Cerutti-Guldberg.[15] Its complicity with political populism left a bad taste in the memory of Argentina in particular. The question is, however, why even the most enlightened new left was not safe from such dangers.

Another aspect of the philosophy of liberation, particularly in Dussel's version, should not to be forgotten. Dussel's observations in 1975 coincide with Bernasconi's judgement of Levinas's philosophy in 1997:

> The Eurocentric view of philosophy is still largely intact, both in the institutional presentation of philosophy and in the declarations of some of Western philosophy's finest minds. Take Levinas, for example. In spite of the pluralism that his thought celebrates, Emmanuel Levinas was quite explicit that he was not willing to look beyond the Bible and the Greeks as models of excellence. "I always say—but in private—that the Greeks and the Bible are all that is serious in humanity. Everything else is dancing." Derrida does not exhibit the same prejudice, but insofar as

Western metaphysics has from the outset been deconstruction's primary object, deconstruction has had little use for what falls outside Western metaphysics.[16]

If we think back to León-Portilla's argument in 1957, we may see that it opened up a can of worms that unfortunately went unnoticed in Latin American philosophical circles, even though the question "Is there a Latin American philosophy?" occupied the minds of philosophers beginning in the late 1960s.[17] There was a parallel at that time between sub-Saharan Africa and Latin American philosophers who were becoming aware of the colonial difference. For to ask "Is there an African or a Latin American philosophy?" is to respond to the demands of the colonial difference. León-Portilla did it in this way, as an ethno-cultural historian and not as a philosopher. He did not ask whether the Nahuatl had philosophy. He assumed they did, but in doing so, he had to make an enormous effort to put the Nahuatls next to the Greeks and then to defend his move in front of his ferocious critics. That is, against the "malaise and the discomfort" provoked by the hidden colonial difference. Needless to say, the colonial difference is a decolonial concept, and therefore it became visible because of decolonial thinking. This is similar to the unconscious: the visibility of the unconscious presupposes psychoanalytic thinking.

Philosophy is a regional and historical practice, named such in Ancient Greece and recovered by and in the making of Europe, from the Renaissance to the Enlightenment. Coupled with religious and economic expansion, philosophy became the yardstick to measure other ways of thinking. But perspectives have been changing, and now "philosophy" is located on the edge of the colonial difference—recognized because Western expansion touched every corner of the planet, displacing and disavowing any praxis of living and thinking that did not correspond with Europeans' praxis of living and thinking: the philosophical (epistemic and ontological) colonial difference did the work. To start from the colonial difference instead of starting from Ancient Greece means assuming philosophy as a regional practice and simultaneously thinking against and beyond its normative and disciplinary regulations.[18] After all, it was a certain way (their way) of "thinking" that the Greeks called philosophy. Going back to the beginning of my argument based on Aztec *tlamatinimi* thinking and expressing themselves in Nahuatl, their concern was not the search for "truth" but the principles of balance and equilibrium of the living (I mean those living on the planet, not just human life). Not the "truth" but the "way" to maintain the balance and equilibrium in the "slippery earth": "Nahua philosophy is better understood as a 'way-seeking' rather than as a 'truth-seeking' philosophy."

> Way-seeking" philosophies such as classical Taoism, classical Confucianism, and contemporary North American pragmatism adopt as their defining question, "What is the way?" or "What is the path?" In contrast, "truth-seeking" philosophies such as most European philosophies adopt as their defining question, "What is the truth?"[19]

The future demands thinking beyond the Greeks and Eurocentric epistemic and hermeneutical assumptions. Raul Fornet-Betancourt, a Cuban philosopher residing in Germany, has proposed "intercultural philosophy" to solve some of the puzzles presented by the colonial difference.[20] It is certainly a way of dealing with thinking beyond Eurocentrism. However, one of the issues that should be confronted is the translation of "intercultural" into colonial differences. Such translation would show that the very concept of "culture" is a colonial construction and that, indeed, "cultural difference" and "intercultural relations" are the effect and the work of the coloniality of power. The idea of "cultural differences" highlights basically a semantic question, while "colonial difference" underlines power differentials, the coloniality of power masking colonial into cultural differences. Colonial difference is indeed the underlying logic, and power relations holding together cultural differences that have been articulated by the coloniality of power, from early Christian global designs to current global coloniality driven by the metaphysics of the market. Intellectual decolonization, and in the case at hand the decolonization of the assumed universality of philosophy, shall open up the "ways" toward the marvelous pluriversality of languaging and thinking rather than defending the universality of "truth."

Notes

1. Serge Latouche, *L'occidentalization du monde* (Paris: La Découverte, 1989).

2. Dallmayr, *On the Boundary: A Life Remembered* (New York: Hamilton Books, 2017), 56ff.

3. Hamid Dabashi, *Can Non-Europeans Think?* (London: Zed Books, 2015). See also my preface to this work, Walter D. Mignolo, "Yes, We Can," viii–xli.

4. Walter D. Mignolo, "Philosophy and the Colonial Difference," *Philosophy Today* 43 (4): 36–41.

5. Miguel León-Portilla, *La filosofía Náhuatl estudiada en sus fuentes* (Mexico: Universidad Autónoma de México, 1956).

6. Miguel León-Portilla, *Aztec Thoughts and Culture: A Study of the Nahuatl Mind*, rev. ed. (1976; repr., Norman: University of Oklahoma Press, 1990). For the case of "philosophy" in the Andes, see also Walter D. Mignolo, "Decires fuera de lugar sujetos dicentes, roles sociales y formas de inscripción," *Revista de critica literaria latinoamericana* 41 (1995): 9–32.

7. Humberto Maturana and Francisco Varela, *The Three of Knowledge: The Biological Roots of Human Understanding* (Boston: New Science Library, 1987), 234–48.

8. Robert. Bernasconi, "African Philosophy's Challenge to Continental Philosophy," in *Postcolonial African Philosophy: A Critical Reader*, ed. Emmanuel Chukwudi Eze (Oxford: Blackwell, 1997), 183–96, 188.

9. Ibid., 191.

10. Abdelkebir Khatibi, "Double Critique. Decolonization de la sociologie," in *Maghreh Pluriel* (Paris: Denoel, 1982).

11. Enrique Dussel, "Without Epistemic Decolonization There Is No Revolution," October 21, 2016, https://venezuelanalysis.com/analysis/12734.

12. Orlando Fals-Borda, *Ciencia propia y colonialismo intelectual* (Bogota: Carlos Valencia, editores, 1970, 1987).

13. Enrique Dussel, *Para una fundarnentación filosojica de la liberación Latinoamericana* (Buenos Aires: Editorial Bonum, 1975), 8.

14. Fausto Reinaga, *La revolución India*, Edición Homenaje, 1970; Paget Henry, *Caliban's Reason: Introducing Afro-Caribbean Philosophy* (London: Routledge, 2003).

15. Horacio Cerutti Guldberg, *Filosofia de la liberación Latino-Americana* (Mexico: Fondo de Culturas Economica, 1983).

16. Bernasconi, "African Philosophy's Challenge to Continental Philosophy," op. cit., 185.

17. Augusto Salazar Bondy, *¿Existe una filosofia en Nuestra America?* (Mexico: Siglo 2 l, 1968, 1996).

18. Eze, *Postcolonial African Philosophy: A Critical Reader*, op. cit., Dussel, 1995, 1998.

19. James Maffie, "Aztec Philosophy," *Internet Encyclopedia of Philosophy*, https://www.iep.utm.edu/aztec/.

20. Paul Fomet-Betancourt, *Filosofia Intercultural* (Mexico: Universidad Pontifica de Mexico, 1994).

Chapter 13

Dallmayr's Reply to Contributors

FRED DALLMAYR

This book is a gathering and a *vademecum*. It gathers the voices of a number of friends and colleagues who have accompanied me on my journey, sometimes journeys along dark alleys where, without them, I might have lost my way. Whether supportive or critical, these voices have kept me on a certain path that I discovered to be my own. As it happens, apart from reminding me of their views, this book also reminds me of this path, thus aiding in a kind of self-discovery. As I find, my path has never been a linear development from one point to another, say: from agnosticism to faith or from faith to agnosticism, or from Aristotle to Hobbes or vice versa. It is more like, in my early life, my path was hidden in a tightly folded map, while in the ensuing decades, the map was slowly but steadily unfolded, giving me a better view of the geography of my world. It is not for me to say whether the path I followed was my own choice or whether it was just waiting for me all along.

I say this because, in reading the chapters in this book, I was reminded of the first book I published in 1981, titled *Beyond Dogma and Despair*.[1] What this title gestured toward was my (still inchoate) sense of being located between two polar opposites: on the one hand, the claim to possess absolute knowledge of the ultimate meaning of social and personal life; and on the other hand, the claim of the total absence or unavailability of any such knowledge. The first claim I associated with dogmatism (which comes in many forms); the second with a narrow positivism and radical skepticism. As it happens and as I noticed, this in-between position had been strongly endorsed by Socrates and his seemingly paradoxical "knowing ignorance" ("I know that I do not know"). As Socrates made clear in the *Meno*, his combination of knowing and not-knowing is the required stimulus for serious inquiry—an inquiring that is stymied by the claimed possession of knowledge and truth and equally stymied by the belief that there is nothing to be known (or that there is not truth).[2] By contrast, knowing ignorance keeps us searching or on the way because, as we grasp one aspect of truth, we discover that truth or true knowledge is really infinite. I have always been fond of a saying ascribed to Edmund Husserl, the founder of phenomenology, in his advanced age (perhaps my age): "Now I am finally a true beginner."

Given this background, I was delighted by Michiko Yusa's paper and her reference to Nicolaus of Cusa, known for his ideas of "*docta ignorantia*" (learned or wise ignorance) and *coincidentia oppositorum* (coincidence of opposites). In 2007 I published the book *In Search of the Good Life: A Pedagogy for Troubled Times*. It contains a chapter titled "Wise Ignorance: Nicolaus of Cusa's Search for Truth," where I discuss several writings by Cusanus, including his *Idiota de Sapientia* (The Layman on Wisdom).[3] There, a poor layman (*pauper quidam idiota*) reprimands a learned scholastic philosopher, saying: "You trust in authority and in this way you are deceived; because someone has written a text, you are ready to believe. But"—and here comes Nicolaus of Cusa's (and my own) cri de coeur—"I want to tell you that wisdom cries out in the streets, and her very cry indicates how she dwells in the highest" (*habitat in altissimis*). In a later text, *De Venatione Sapientiae* (On Hunting for Wisdom), Cusanus discusses several topics where learned ignorance can pursue fruitful inquiries. One such topic is the problem of the "not-other" (*non-aliud*). In going beyond oneself, he notes, one encounters others and "otherness" itself. But how can one come to "know" the other as "not-other" without relinquishing his otherness? "The not-other does not simply mean identical or the same. For whereas the same is none other than the same, the not-other precedes the same and everything that can be so designated." Surely a delightful hunting ground for learned ignorance.

In his later years, Cusanus penned a number of practical-ecumenical writings or reflections, texts that established his reputation as an interfaith and intercultural thinker. Most prominent among them is his book *De Pace Fidei* (On Interreligious Peace), published in 1453 in the immediate aftermath of the Turkish conquest of Constantinople—a time when interreligious hatred and Islamophobia were at a fever pitch throughout Europe. Far from being a doctrinal tract or the rehearsal of dogmas, the book takes the form of a wide-ranging dialogue or conversation among representatives of no fewer than seventeen major religious and cultural traditions around the world. The goal is not the imposition of dogmatic unity but the fostering of mutual understanding and concord among religions and cultures despite acknowledged differences. As can be seen, the text is quite in accord with *docta ignorantia* and the hunting grounds mentioned before. As finite beings, individuals or groups can never have an absolute grasp of the infinite or a monopoly of the divine. At the same time, they are not completely ignorant or left stranded but inhabited by a yearning for truth and the divine. Thus, *De Pace Fidei* does not just carry peace into faith, but seeks to kindle peace "from faith"—by invoking the divine "prince of peace." As the book's introduction states: "Lord, come to our aid. For this rivalry (among religions) exists for the sake of *you* whom all revere in everything they claim to worship. If you would deign to do this, the sword and the bilious spite of hatred and all sufferings would cease."[4]

No doubt, the writings of Cusanus have greatly influenced me (as did the words of Socrates before). Broadly speaking, their teachings pointed me in the direction of an ecumenical "civility" in both a religious-spiritual and a secular-political sense. My friend Richard Falk ascribes to me generously an outlook of "spiritual cosmopolitanism," which, in his view, should not be confused with a "theological metaphysics" insisting on a "top-down" hierarchy or doctrine. I feel honored by this ascription. I have written much (perhaps too much) on cross-cultural and interfaith relations, have edited a book series called "Global Encounters," and have sponsored an inquiry that has come to be known as "comparative political theory." Here, I should insert a reminder. In spreading my concern out to many topics, people, and cultures, I may sometimes have given the impression of being "eclectic" in making random selections. But I am not just a tourist or a neutral anthropologist offering a scientific overview. My intent in all I have done has always been practical-ethical (and spiritual), in line with the adage *opus iustitiae pax*. For this reason, I am grateful to Richard for mentioning the name of Mahatma Gandhi, who—together with Nelson Mandela, the Dalai Lama, and some others—has been an enduring beacon of light in my life.[5]

As Gandhi has shown, engagement for freedom and democracy is always an uphill struggle because of the tight grip on power by domestic and global (military and economic) elites. To make a dent in this situation and avoid being drawn into the brute power game, his example counseled nonviolent resistance (*ahimsa*) and reliance on (mostly) indigenous ethical resources. Thus, to achieve "self-rule" (*swaraj*) in the proper sense, Indians in his view had to be able to "rule themselves" by curbing selfish desires (as taught in the *Bhagavad Gita*). As it happens, most countries and cultures in the world have similar indigenous resources (although often untapped). In her chapter, Marietta Stepanyants presents an enticing panorama of "normative moral systems" in three Eastern cultures: India (Hinduism and Buddhism), China (from Book of Changes to Confucianism), and the Islamic world. The panorama discloses stark differences between ethical paradigms, especially between "cosmocentric" and "theocentric" models—which in turn are profiled against the anthropocentrism of the modern West. The basic question raised by Marietta is this: In view of the worldwide arsenal of ethical resources, is it possible and legitimate to speak of a "global" or "world ethic"—an idea forcefully sponsored by Hans Küng and the Parliament of the World's Religions? She also mentions some opposing voices, such as that of philosopher Richard Rorty, who denounced "universal truths" as shallow "platitudes" often invoked for power-political aims. This confrontation conjures up a basic conundrum with which I have wrestled for most of my life: that between universalism and particularism, between absolutism and relativism, or (again) between "dogma and despair." Together with Marietta, I endorse the *via media* of dialogue and mutual learning, where questioning is linked with being called into question. Basically, I associate ethics more with praxis and experiential conduct than with doctrinal systems. I ask: Even in the absence of universal doctrines, how does it happen that injustices in distant countries disturb or upset my "moral universe"? How is it that the sufferings and torments inflicted on people around the globe today—and they are legion—manage to deeply unhinge my world and my life?

As it appears to me, ethics in large part involves a transformative seasoning of our sensibilities, a seasoning opening up our "buffered" self to others and otherness. Asma Afsaruddin introduces us to the tradition of ethical seasoning through education in the Islamic world. She reminds us of the Prophet's counsel: "Seek knowledge even unto China," a counsel that has led to the equation of genuine education (*adab*) with a "*journey in search for knowledge*," rather than the possessive hoarding of doctrines. In my view, Asma's chapter—widely disseminated—can serve as powerful antidote to twin evils troubling our time: jihadism and Islamophobia. For how could these twin evils survive if genuine education were practiced widely both in Islamic countries and the West? She acquaints us with traditional institutions of learning in the Muslim world—such as the *madrasa*, al-Azhar (as *mosque-madrasa*), libraries, and "houses of wisdom" (*beyt al-hikma*)—in addition to telling us about curricula and types of studies, with special attention to the "humanities." One issue that had to be negotiated in all traditional studies was the relation between Islamic religious texts and Greek philosophical teachings, that is, the relation between faith and reason (a major issue also in medieval Christianity). What Asma stresses in her chapter is the tradition—largely ignored today—of an Islamic "humanism" nourished by numerous sources. If properly cultivated, she suggests, this tradition might also support an "ethos of cosmopolitanism" (or a cosmopolitan civility) in our time.

One feature of genuine Islamic education is the legacy of political thought or philosophy, a legacy represented especially by the towering figures of Al-Farabi, Ibn Sina (Avicenna), and Ibn Rushd (Averroes). Ahmet Okumuş focuses mostly on the work of Farabi, a work shaped both by Islamic faith and the teachings of Plato and Aristotle. Reflecting the influence of classical Greece, one of his political texts was titled "The Just City" (*al-madina al-fadila*), where "just" refers to the aim of a virtuous public life. In his account, Okumuş concentrates mainly on the notion of "regime" or *politeia*. Although acknowledging that, on the surface, the term designates a constitutional code, he maintains that there is also a "depth meaning" where it refers to the "common ethos of a people" nourished by moral and spiritual sources. Like all "classical" Muslim thinkers, Farabi had to wrestle with the confluence and possible conflicts between religious and secular-philosophical arguments (the former exacerbated by the role of Islamic law or *fiqh*). In my view, this confluence of sources—apart from its historical interest—has also a continuing relevance by prodding ever-renewed reflection. Clearly, if religious literalism-cum-legalism is given the upper hand, the kind of "humanism" extolled by Afsaruddin has little or no chance. On my own part, I have explored this juncture of influences in the case of Ibn Rushd (Averroes), that eminently humanist Aristotelian and Muslim thinker of Cordoba.[6]

Following the sequence of ethical "paradigms" mentioned by Stepanyants, my comments proceed to India, native home of both Hinduism and Buddhism. Here we have the benefit of the valuable insights of Ananta Giri's chapter on "Planetary *Lokasamgraha*." In his text, Giri introduces us to the classical teaching of the fourfold goals of human life, the so-called "*purusarthas*," combining the aims of pleasure (*karma*), wealth or worldly achievement (*artha*), right conduct (*dharma*), and salvation (*moksha*). As he points out, these aims are sometimes pitted against each other, but this treatment falls short of the prospect of an integrated humanism. "We need to overcome," he says, "any isolated treatment of the *purusartha* elements and look at them instead in a creative spirit of both autonomy and interpenetration." Such an integral ethical view promotes the "flourishing" of human life and, at the same time, the maintenance of a proper world order (*lokasamgraha*). Very important are Giri's observations on *dharma*. As he notes, the term refers indeed to the practice of right conduct and right thinking, but this differs from "righteousness seen as a fixed system of classification between right and wrong," especially when that system is "imprisoned" in a web of ideological or theological dogmas. Taken in the proper sense, *dharma* is neither purely anthropocentric nor theocentric, but involves a broad responsibility extending to the "non-human" and to nature. As Giri adds, *dharma* opens the door to global cross-cultural and interreligious explorations. In this sense, *dharma* and *purusarthas* are building blocks for the enterprise of "world-maintenance" (*lokasamgraha*) and thus for the cultivation of cosmopolitan civility.

As Giri indicates, there are significant parallels between classical Indian ethics and East Asian, particularly Confucian teachings. Two chapters in this volume deal with Confucianism, one on a theoretical level, the other from a more practical-political vantage. The first, penned by Chenyang Li, focuses on the Confucian notion of the "triadic harmony" of heaven, earth (nature), and humanity. In the classical view, he writes, harmony is "not a mere agreement or superficial stability," but rather a "dynamic generative process in which the prospect of every party getting its due is optimized." The mission of humanity in this triad is "to work with heaven and earth" to promote a judicious balance of elements. Despite this emphasis on equilibrium, Chenyang proceeds to accord special preeminence and even centrality to the human factor in our age, termed "the epoch of the Anthropocene." As he states, because of a battery of challenges—ecological, technological, biochemical—the contemporary epoch calls for a "new humanism," in fact a "mega-humanism," where the human species acts as "the dominant force in shaping the world." This account clearly puts pressure on Confucianism and, in fact, on any genuine conception of ethics (which always implies an effort of self-limiting or self-overcoming). The danger of "mega-humanism" is clearly recognized by Chenyang when he states that "humanity possesses overwhelming power over nature to either destroy or perfect it" and warns against an "intoxicated obsession with human narcissism." What one can agree to—and what I would agree to—is that our time places a "mega-responsibility" on humanity, but the chances of this responsibility being fulfilled are slim in the absence of a robust ethical (and political) renewal.[7]

From a practical-ethical perspective, Sungmoon Kim explores the relevance of Confucianism for the promotion of democracy in East Asia. As Sungmoon correctly notes, my endeavors in the field of democratic theory have sought to overcome entrenched binaries: between liberal individualism and communitarianism, between elitism and populism, and also between laïcism and religious dogmatism. More concretely, my work in this area has tried to steer a path beyond "minimalist democracy" (anchored in pure self-interest) and "agonistics (rooted in brute struggle for power). This path has led me in the direction of a "deliberative" perspective, where deliberation does not just mean a cognitive-rational discourse, but also an interactive sharing of life experiences, a mutual search for or "inquiry" into the prospect of an ethical democracy (in John Dewey's sense). For me, Confucianism is precisely such a deliberative framework, an inquiry rather than a doctrine—which makes it a potential ally for democracy (even if this alliance is only "*à venir*"). For this reason, together with Sungmoon, I have opposed the elevation of Confucianism into a "comprehensive worldview" and especially a "state religion" in East Asian societies. This opposition to "maximalism" still leaves intact the genuine role of Confucian teachings in everyday life, as a valuable antidote to capitalist materialism, consumerism, chauvinism, and ecological devastation.

After this excursion into "non-Western" paradigms, my comments return to the Western context and the connection between ethics and democracy. In her contribution, Herta Nagl-Docekal draws attention to an important ethical legacy: that of the great philosopher of Königsberg and his insistence on the "categorical" character of ethical obligation. As she reminds us, the categorical imperative was not derived from the edicts of worldly potentates but from our own reason and conscience through an act of self-legislation. In our age, dominated by utilitarianism (good is what is useful) and hedonism (good is what is pleasurable), this Kantian teaching has little appeal. Its appeal is muted even in the case of thinkers otherwise attracted to Kantianism, such as (second generation) Frankfurt theorists. In the latter case, Herta argues, Kant's imperatives have been reduced to contractual agreements or "the logic of the contract" (where contract is only subjectively binding). To be sure, in their approach, Frankfurt theorists were motivated mainly by the desire to move from the *cogito* to intersubjectivity (and language) and thus to avoid Kantian "monologue." Herta is quite willing to accept a certain logo-centrism, as when she writes that Kant locates the source of morality "primarily in the acting subject" or the "original moral disposition in us."

However, as her chapter shows, this "subjectivism" is amply balanced or compensated by Kant's stress on social solidarity and the commitment "to provide unconditional help and support to others." To this extent, Herta finds in Kant's work a plea in favor of an "ethical community" of peoples or a cosmopolitan civility. To me, her reading renders the Königsberg philosopher eminently attractive. Where I still have reservations is Kant's separation of "is" and "ought" and his (seeming) prioritizing of cognition over practical conduct.

Another type of muted Kantianism is the work of John Rawls, a philosopher known mainly for his rejection of "comprehensive doctrines" (when used as props of political regimes) and his advocacy of a "neutral" liberal state. In his chapter, Ronald Beiner explores the repercussions of Rawls's work in the United States and elsewhere; while being ambivalent on "comprehensive doctrines" (rejecting mainly religious ones), he is critical or non-neutral on the "neutrality" of the state. He cites alarming examples of autocratic and even "theocratic" leanings among right-wing evangelicals in the United States—as when a religious advisor ascribes to the U.S. president a "divine sanction" to lead the country into World War III.[8] For me, the banning of religious autocracy or theocracy is not so much a "liberal compromise" (Rawls's view) as a *democratic* imperative (inscribed in the constitutional prohibition of religious "establishment"). Because contemporary democracy has citizens of many faiths as well as citizens of no faith, no creed can have privileged sway. This means there cannot be a Christian, an Islamic, or a Jewish state—at least not as a *democracy*. I stress here the democratic over the liberal aspect—because some liberals may be confused enough to think that theocracy is a liberal choice. Ronald seems to agree with me when he writes that "the illegitimacy of theocratic politics is an entailment of a strong doctrine of [democratic] citizenship." To be sure, as a pluralist (though not a relativist), I acknowledge that there can be many different varieties of the "separation" of church and state. The same constitution that prohibits "establishment" also upholds the "free exercise of religion" in many forms. Thus, negation and affirmation are closely linked. (This, by the way, was also Gandhi's understanding of "secularism.")

A more difficult issue is raised by the notion of the "neutral" state. In my view, disestablishment does not entail or equal neutrality. As I see it, no political regime—and no individual—can be neutral with regard to justice and injustice, well-being and domination, "good life" and violent death. To claim neutrality here is to escape from humanity into the realm of automata. Again, Ronald seems to agree with me, saying: "If our state is founded on notions of liberty, equality, and upholding the common dignity of all citizens, then there are definite conceptions of the good instantiated in that state." (Curiously, he is ready to call this view a "civic comprehensive doctrine"). The question, for me, is how one fosters this kind of "civic or public ethos" or (what Montesquieu called) the "spirit" of a regime: through domineering doctrines in a top-down fashion or through inquiry, learning, and shared practices?[9] I am afraid that political liberalism today has outlawed not only theocracy and autocracy, but also learning, Deweyan inquiry, and the "uplifting to humanity" (as Herder called it). This means that anything pointing beyond the self-interest of "buffered" liberals appears already suspect. In his "What is Metaphysics?," Heidegger once made the startling claim that positivist science "wants to know nothing about nothing" (where nothing means "no-thing" or "no-being"). Has liberalism in our time become a form of "knownothingism"? In the concluding pages of his chapter, Ronald returns to the issue of "comprehensive doctrines." Although having himself endorsed a secular variety, he seems troubled (in a Rawlsian vein) by other such doctrines. Turning to some of my own writings, he finds troublesome my endorsement of Raimon Panikkar's "cosmotheandric" vision. To me, this is puzzling. How can Panikkar's expression be a comprehensive "doctrine"—when it actually is nothing but a string of riddles? Panikkar simply raises the questions: How is God (or the divine) related to humans and to nature, and how are humans related to the divine and the cosmos? Surely these are questions that any thinking human being is bound to raise at some point. Ronald is certainly wrong when he calls the expression "a specific doctrine of the unity of God, nature and humanity" (completely bypassing both its nonpolitical and its "*Advaita*" character).

Perhaps I should add a few more words about the liberal "neutral" state. Although it may have promoted a multitude of life options in the West, the same liberal state has not acted in the same way in the rest of the world. Even when secular and civic-republican in character, Western states have not been reluctant to embark on missionary or millenarian projects abroad. Thus, at the time when Rawls and his followers were celebrating public neutrality, powerful Western armies were waging semi-colonial wars in Southeast Asia, West Asia, and elsewhere. As a Latin American, Walter Mignolo is well aware of the "floating presence" of colonialism and imperialism hovering over the world; he has paid close attention to the "dark side" or underbelly of Western "civilization." His chapter introduces us to the work of Miguel León-Portilla, the ethno-historian of Ancient Mexico who explored the thinking of the Aztecs or Nahuatl-speaking people. For Westerners, this thinking did not qualify properly as "philosophy," and the people were seen as underdeveloped. But for Leon-Portilla, Nahuatl thinking was inhabited by a "difference" that remains a challenge for Western academic philosophers. Mignolo also alerts us to the Moroccan Abdelkarib Khatibi, a thinker dwelling "on the borders of Islam and Western modernity" and thus a witness of the evolving "decolonization as decoloniality." For Khatibi, decolonization was both an undoing of the colonial "difference" and a creative redoing of what can be called a "border thinking" located beyond binary opposites. In the end, Mignole suggests that Nahuatl thinking may be better described as a "way-seeking" than an apodictic "truth-seeking" philosophy—a character it shares with Daoism, Confucianism, and (perhaps) Deweyan inquiry.

Before bringing this discussion to a close, I want to say a word about the fine chapter by Edward Demenchonok titled "Philosophy of Hope." The chapter offers a very competent and sensitive exposition of my writings and way of thinking. As he knows, my life has not been immune from despair, but it also has not been a stranger to hope (as long as hope is not stylized as a doctrine). Demenchonok offers an entry to my "dialogue with Heidegger's legacy," pointing out some important topics of this dialogue. Appropriately, he pays attention to the notion of "*Ereignis*" (often translated as "event"), a happening located on the cusp between doing and not-doing or suffering. He also discusses my extensive endeavors in the field of "intercultural dialogue," noting correctly that my motivation in this field was never a mere delight in diversity but an attempt to "recover humanity's wholeness." Beyond conflict-ridden interstate relations and hegemonic-imperial derailments, he writes, the loadstar has always been a "domination-free, cross-cultural, dialogical world order of peace and justice." There is nothing I could add. So, let me end this symposium by thanking wholeheartedly all the participants. For me, it has been another rich learning experience. Together, we have explored those delightful "hunting grounds" of the spirit of which Cusanus speaks. In our exchanges, we have been "other" to each other without ever being completely other or alien (*non-aliud*).

Notes

1. Fred Dallmayr, *Beyond Dogma and Despair: Toward a Critical Phenomenology of Politics* (Notre Dame, IN: University of Notre Dame Press, 1981).

2. As Socrates says in the *Meno*: "You look on this as a piece of chop-logic, don't you see, as if a man cannot try to find either what he knows or what he

does not know. Of course, he would never try to find what he knows, because he knows it and in that case he needs no trying to find; or what he does not know, because he does not know what he will try to find." See *Great Dialogues of Plato*, trans. W. H. D. Rouse, ed. Eric H. Warmington and Philip G. Rouse (New York: Mentor Books, 1956), 41.

3. Fred Dallmayr, *In Search of the Good Life: A Pedagogy for Troubled Times* (Lexington, KY: University Press of Kentucky, 2007), 58–79.

4. Nikolaus von Cusa, *On Interreligious Harmony*, ed. James E. Biechler and H. Lawrence Bond (Lewiston, NY: Edwin Mellan Press 1990), 5–7.

5. I have written extensively on Gandhi, especially on his notions of self-rule (*swaraj*), nonviolent resistance (*ahimsa*), and justice-doing (*satyagraha*). Given contemporary interreligious and interethnic conflicts, this piece seems particularly revealing: "Gandhi and Islam: A Heart- and Mind-Unity?," in my *Peace Talks—Who Will Listen?* (Notre Dame, IN: University of Notre Dame Press, 2004), 132–51.

6. In his *Fasl al-maqal*, Ibn Rushd explored the compatible difference between reason and faith, philosophy and religion. See my "Reason, Faith, and Politics: A Journey to Muslim Andalusia," in my *Dialogue among Civilizations: Some Exemplary Voices* (New York: Palgrave Macmillan, 2007), 121–46.

7. My worry about "mega-humanism" is its closeness to a Nietzschean "will to power." I am more in agreement with Chenyang's statement: "Nor is humanity the center of the cosmos. . . . Humanity is not part of heaven or earth; it is their guardian and partner." This is close to Heidegger's view in "Letter on Humanism" that we are more like shepherds or caretakers. See "Letter on Humanism," in *Martin Heidegger: Basic Writings*, ed. David F. Krell (New York: Harper & Row, 1977), 193–242.

8. In this genre, one may consult with benefit Bill Beckow, "Christian Dominationists Meet at Trump's Washington Hotel to Answer the 'Divine Call to War,'" *Truth-Out*, March 9, 2018; http://www.truth-out.org/news/item/43799-christian-dominationists.

9. As I see it (I may be mistaken), Beiner erects a sharp division between "pure" philosophy and political theory concerned with civic life. As he writes, "the task of philosophy is the pursuit of truth . . . uncompromisingly," while liberal political theory (as practiced, e.g., by Charles Taylor) subordinates this pursuit to the promotion of better citizenship. I do not accept this division. Philosophizing means to raise basic questions. In this quest, we may find some answers. But we also find that every answer raises many new questions, and ultimately infinite questions. Not being able to know infinitely, we come to realize our partial ignorance (*docta ignorantia*), and this realization makes us humble and induces us to respect the views and opinions of others—which leads us to tolerant citizenship. This is the wisdom contained in Ovid's adage "*abeunt studia in mores*" (learning conduces to ethical-civic praxis). Regarding my opposition to "politicized" religion, see my "Religious Freedom: Preserving the Salt of the Earth," in my *In Search of the Good*

Life: A Pedagogy for Troubled Times, 205–219; "Postsecular Faith: Toward a Religion of Service" and "Religion and the World: The Quest for Justice and Peace," in my *Integral Pluralism: Beyond Culture Wars* (Lexington, KY: University of Kentucky Press, 2010), 67–83, 85–101; regarding theocracy, see my "Theocracy as Temptation: Empire and Mindfulness," in my *Mindfulness and Letting Be: On Engaged Thinking and Acting* (Lanham, MD: Lexington Books, 2014), 127–30.

Contributors

Ruth Abbey

Ruth Abbey is Professor and Chair of the Department of Social Sciences at Swinburne University, Australia. A political theorist, she has research interests in the work of Friedrich Nietzsche, Charles Taylor, feminist thought, liberal thought, friendship, and animal ethics.

Asma Afsaruddin

Asma Afsaruddin is a professor of Near Eastern Languages and Cultures in the Hamilton Lugar School of Global and International Studies at Indiana University, Bloomington.

Her research interests include Islamic religious and political thought (modern and premodern), Islamic intellectual history, Qur'an and hadith, and gender in Islam. She is the author and editor of seven books, including *Contemporary Issues in Islam* (Edinburgh University Press, 2015); the award-winning *Striving in the Path of God: Jihad and Martyrdom in Islamic Thought* (Oxford University Press, 2013), which is currently being translated into Bahasa Indonesian; and *The First Muslims: History and Memory* (OneWorld Publications, 2008), which was translated into Turkish in 2014 and Bahasa Malay in 2018. She has published more than sixty research articles and book chapters on various aspects of Islamic thought. Afsaruddin's research has been funded by grants from, among others, the Harry Frank Guggenheim Foundation and the Carnegie Corporation of New York, which named her a Carnegie Scholar in 2005.

Ronald Beiner

Ronald Beiner is a professor of political science at the University of Toronto and a Fellow of the Royal Society of Canada. His research interests span the Western tradition of political thought.

Beiner is author of *Political Judgment* (1983), *What's the Matter with Liberalism?* (1992), *Philosophy in a Time of Lost Spirit* (1997), *Liberalism, Nationalism, Citizenship* (2003), *Civil Religion* (2011), *Political Philosophy: What It Is and Why It Matters* (2014), and *Dangerous Minds* (2018). His edited or coedited books include *Democratic Theory and Technological Society* (1988), *Kant and Political Philosophy* (1993), *Theorizing Citizenship* (1995), *Theorizing Nationalism* (1999), *Canadian Political Philosophy* (2001), and *Judgment, Imagination, and Politics* (2001).

Edward V. Demenchonok

Edward V. Demenchonok is a professor of foreign languages and philosophy at Fort Valley State University, Georgia, US. His research interests include the philosophy of culture, political philosophy, and ethics.

Demenchonok's publications include "Intercultural Philosophy and the Quest for Spirituality," in *Bildung, Spiritualität und Universität* (Aachen: Wissenschaftsverlag Mainz, 2018); "Michel Foucault's Theory of Practices of the Self and the Quest for a New Philosophical Anthropology," in *Peace, Culture, and Violence* (Brill Rodopi, 2018); "The Quest for Change: From Domination to Dialogue" (Berlin: Dialogue of Civilizations Research Institute, 2016); "Zur Debatte über kulturelle Diversität und Interkulturalität in den USA und Kanada," in *Zur Geschichte und Entwicklung der Interkulturellen Philosophie* (Aachen: Wissenshaftsverlag Mainz, 2015); "Intercultural Transformation of Philosophy and Society as an Alternative to Crisis," *Topologik* 19 (2016); "Демократия в рецессии?" [Is Democracy in Recession?], *Public Policy Journal* 2 (2017); "La filosofía latinoamericana de la liberación y su recepción en Rusia," *Cuadernos Americanos*, México 2017/2. He has edited and contributed to *Between Global Violence and Ethics of Peace: Philosophical Perspectives* (Wiley-Blackwell, 2009); *Philosophy after Hiroshima* (Cambridge Scholars Publishing, 2010); *Intercultural Dialogue: In Search of Harmony in Diversity* (Cambridge Scholars Publishing, 2016), and *A World Beyond Global Disorder: The Courage to Hope* (with

Fred Dallmayr, Cambridge Scholars Publishing, 2017). He has worked as a senior researcher at the Institute of Philosophy of the Russian Academy of Sciences, Moscow.

Richard Falk

Richard Falk is a professor of international law and international relations, Emeritus, Princeton University; and research fellow, Orfalea Center of Global Studies, University of California, Santa Barbara. His research interests include international relations, international law, international institutions, political theory, and world order studies.

Falk's works within the last decade alone include *Achieving Human Rights* (2008); *International Law and the Third World: Reshaping Justice (Routledge-Cavendish Research in International Law)*; editor, *The Path to Zero: Dialogues on Nuclear Dangers* with David A. Krieger; *Palestine: The Legitimacy of Hope* (2014); *(Re)imagining Humane Global Governance* (2014); *Chaos and Counterrevolution: After the Arab Spring* (2015); *Humanitarian Intervention and Legitimacy Wars: Seeking Peace and Justice in the 21st Century* (2015); *Power Shift: On the New Global Order* (2016); and *Revisiting the Vietnam War* (coedited with Stefan Andersson, 2017).

Ananta Kumar Giri

Ananta Kumar Giri is a professor at Madras Institute of Development Studies, Chennai, India. His research interests include social movements and cultural change, criticism, creativity and contemporary dialectics of transformation, theories of self, culture and society, and creative streams in education, philosophy, and literature.

Giri's books include *Global Transformations: Postmodernity and Beyond* (1998); *Sameekhya o Purodrusti* (Criticism and Vision of the Future, 1999); *Patha Prantara Nrutattwa* (Anthropology of the Street Corner, 2000); *Mochi o Darshanika* (The Cobbler and the Philosopher, 2009); *Sri Jagannathanka Saha: Khyaya, Khata o Kehetra* (with Sri Jagannatha: Loss, Wound and the Field, 2018); *Conversations and Transformations: Toward a New Ethics of Self and Society* (2002); *Self-Development and Social Transformations? The Vision and Practice of Self-Study Mobilization of Swadhyaya* (2008); *Mochi o*

Darshanika (The Cobbler and the Philosopher, 2009); *Sociology and Beyond: Windows and Horizons* (2012), *Knowledge and Human Liberation: Towards Planetary Realizations* (2013); *Philosophy and Anthropology: Border-Crossing and Transformations* (coedited with John Clammer, 2013); *New Horizons of Human Development* (editor, 2015); *Pathways of Creative Research: Towards a Festival of Dialogues* (editor, 2017); *Cultivating Pathways of Creative Research: New Horizons of Transformative Practice and Collaborative Imagination* (editor, 2017); *Research as Realization: Science, Spirituality and Harmony* (editor, 2017); *Beyond Sociology* (editor, 2018); *Social Theory and Asian Dialogues: Cultivating Planetary Conversations* (editor, 2018); *Practical Spirituality and Human Development: Transformations in Religions and Societies* (editor, 2018); *Weaving New Hats: Our Half Birthdays* (2018); and *Beyond Cosmopolitanism: Towards Planetary Transformations* (editor, 2018).

Sungmoon Kim

Sungmoon Kim is a professor in the Department of Public Policy, City University of Hong Kong. His research interests include comparative political theory, democratic theory, and history of East Asian political thought.

Kim is the author of *Confucian Democracy in East Asia: Theory and Practice* (2014) and *Public Reason Confucianism: Democratic Perfectionism and Constitutionalism in East Asia* 2016), editor of *Confucianism, Law, and Democracy in Contemporary Korea* (2015), and coeditor of *Confucianism, a Habit of the Heart: Bellah, Civil Religion, and East Asia* (2016). He is working on a book project titled *Democracy after Virtue: The Philosophical Challenges for Confucian Democratic Theory*. His essays have appeared or will appear in the journals including *American Political Science Review*, *British Journal of Political Science*, *Constellations*, *Contemporary Political Theory*, *Critical Review of International Social and Political Philosophy*, *History of Political Thought*, *Journal of the History of Ideas*, *Journal of Politics*, *Philosophy East and West*, *Philosophy & Social Criticism*, and *The Review of Politics*, among others.

Chenyang Li

Chenyang Li is a professor of philosophy at Nanyang Technological University. His research interests include Chinese philosophy and comparative philosophy.

Li's publications include *The Confucian Philosophy of Harmony* (2014), *The Tao Encounters the West: Explorations in Comparative Philosophy* (1999); *The Sage and the Second Sex: Confucianism, Ethics, and Gender* (editor, 2000); *The East Asian Challenge for Democracy: Political Meritocracy in Comparative Perspective* (coedited with Daniel A. Bell, 2013); *Moral Cultivation and Confucian Character* (coedited with Peimin Ni); *Chinese Metaphysics and Its Problems* (coedited with Franklin Perkins, 2015); and more than 100 journal articles and book chapters.

Walter Mignolo

Walter Mignolo is William H. Wannamaker Professor of Literature and Romance Studies at Duke University. His research interests include semiotics and literary theory, the formation, transformation and current configuration of the modern/colonial world order. He has elaborated on concepts such as geopolitics of knowing, colonial and imperial differences, global coloniality, border thinking, and pluriversality.

Mignolo's recent publications include *The Darker Side of Western Modernity: Global Futures, Decolonial Options* (2011) and (coauthored with Catherine Walsh) *On Decoloniality: Concepts, Analytics, Praxis* (2018). His previous publications include *The Idea of Latin America* (2005); *Local Histories/Global Designs: Coloniality, Subaltern Knowledges and Border Thinking* (2000); and *The Darker Side of the Renaissance: Literacy, Territoriality and Colonization* (1995). He is editor and coeditor of numerous volumes, among them *Globalization and the Decolonial Option*, coedited with Arturo Escobar; and *Re-reading the Black Legend: the Discourse of Racial and Religious Differences in the Renaissance Empires*, coedited with Margaret R. Green and Maureen Quilligan (2007).

Herta Nagl-Docekal

Herta Nagl-Docekal is University Professor I.R. at the Department of Philosophy, University of Vienna, Austria. Her research interests include gender, Western philosophy, religion, and culture.

Nagl-Docekal's books include *Innere Freiheit. Grenzen der nachmetaphysischen Moralkonzeptionen* (Deutsche Zeitschrift für Philosophie, Sonderband 36, 2014); *Hegels Ästhetik als Theorie der Moderne* (coedited, 2013); *Jenseits der Säkularisierung. Religionsphilosophische Studien* (coedited,

2008); *Viele Religionen—eine Vernunft? Ein Disput zu Hegel* (coedited, 2008); *Glauben und Wissen. Ein Symposium mit Jürgen Habermas* (coedited, 2007); *Geschichtsphilosophie und Kulturkritik* (coedited, 2003); *Feministische Philosophie. Ergebnisse, Probleme, Perspektiven* (2000 u. 2004; American 2004, Japanese 2006, Hungarian 2006, Czech 2007); *Continental Philosophy in Feminist Perspective* (coedited, 2000); *Der Sinn des Historischen* (coedited, 1996); *Politische Theorie. Differenz und Lebensqualität* (coedited, 1996); and *Postkoloniales Philosophieren: Afrika* (coedited, 1992).

Ahmet Okumuş

Ahmet Okumuş is an assistant professor of political science and international relations, Istanbul Sehir University. Okumuş received his PhD in political science from Sabanci University. His dissertation explored the possibility of "Reconciliation of Virtue and Freedom in Contemporary Political Philosophy." He participated in the founding of Istanbul Sehir University, where he has been teaching since 2010.

Okumuş is currently the president of Bilim ve Sanat Vakfi (Foundation for Sciences and Arts) in Istanbul, which is a nonprofit organization (*waqf*) devoted to advanced studies in humanities and social sciences, and which is also the founder of Istanbul Sehir University. His research interests include contemporary political theory, democratic politics, religion, politics and secularism, theories of modernity and comparative political theory.

Marietta Stepanyants

Marietta Stepanyants is Distinguished Scholar of the Russian Federation; Chief Research Fellow at the Department of Oriental Philosophies; and holds the UNESCO chair, "Philosophy in the Dialogue of Cultures," Institute of Philosophy, Russian Academy of Sciences, Moscow.

Her research interests include oriental philosophies and comparative intercultural philosophy. Stepanyants's main works include *Philosophy and Science in Cultures of East and West* (editor, 2014); and *Knowledge and Belief in the Dialogue of Cultures* (editor, 2011); *Восточные философии* (Eastern Philosophies, 2011); *Исламский мистицизм* (Islamic Mysticism, 2009); *Мир Востока. Философия: прошлое, настоящее, будущее* (Eastern World. Philosophy: Past, Present, Future, 2005); and *Introduction to Eastern Thought* (2002).

Michiko Yusa

Michiko Yusa is a professor of Japanese and East Asian Studies in the Modern and Classical Languages Department and the Center for East Asian Studies, Western Washington University.

Her research interests include Japanese religion and philosophy. Yusa is the author of *Zen and Philosophy: An Intellectual Biography of Nishida Kitarō* (2002); *Japanese Religious Traditions* (2002); *Denki: Nishida Kitarō* (1998); *Basic Kanji* (1989); and *Isamu Noguchi & Skyviewing Sculpture* (coedited) (2005). She has also published many articles and book chapters.

For a current and comprehensive list of Fred Dallmayr's writings, see http://freddallmayr.com.

Index

Anthropocene, the, 3, 4, 58–59, 61, 64–66, 177, 190, 192
Apel, Karl Otto, 12, 23
Arendt, Hannah, 88, 169
Aristotle, 7, 31, 103, 112, 114, 115, 116, 117, 155, 187, 191

Bhagavad Gita, the, 20, 21, 150, 163, 190
Buddhism, 1, 8, 133, 136–39, 150, 151, 166, 169, 190, 191

Christianity, 6, 7, 21, 60, 69, 70, 73, 74, 86, 90, 98, 102, 103, 106–107, 108, 129, 130–32, 153, 164, 169, 183, 185, 191, 194
Cold War, the, 13, 19, 36, 180, 182
Confucianism, 3–4, 8, 21, 42, 47–52, 58, 60–66, 146–47, 151, 169, 185, 190, 192–93, 196

Dalai Lama, the, 2, 31, 189
Democracy, 1, 2, 3, 7, 20, 23, 24, 31, 32–34, 36, 42–55, 70, 85, 112, 113, 166, 189, 193, 194
Derrida, Jacques, 1, 12, 33, 42, 46, 47, 179, 183
Dewey, John, 3, 23, 31, 34, 41–47, 51, 155, 193, 195, 196

Dialogue, 2, 3, 12, 18–20, 22–25, 35, 36, 69, 77, 78, 107, 120, 154, 156, 169, 189, 190, 196
Dussel, Enrique, 47, 182, 183

Farabi, Al, 7, 114–19, 191
Forst, Rainer, 5, 87, 88
Foucault, Michel, 1, 12, 174

Gadamer, Hans-Georg, 12, 18, 19, 174
Gandhi, Mahatma, 2, 21, 31, 36, 42, 179, 189, 194

Habermas, Jürgen, 1, 5, 23, 84, 87, 154, 155
Hegel, G. W. F., 1, 5, 14, 31, 44, 45, 83–86, 155, 183
Heidegger, Martin, 1, 2, 3, 12–18, 21, 22, 23, 31, 33–35, 164, 165–67, 173, 174, 175, 179, 195, 196
Hermeneutics, 1, 19, 23, 35, 41
Hinduism, 8, 60, 77, 108, 143–45, 150, 155, 163–64, 190, 191
Hobbes, Thomas, 31, 91, 155, 187
Holism, 22, 23, 33, 44, 45, 61, 63, 66, 105, 129
Honneth, Axel, 5, 84–88
Husserl, Edmund, 175, 188

Islam, 1, 6, 7, 8, 19, 21, 73, 98–108, 112, 114, 117–20, 148–49, 151, 153, 154, 156, 163, 164, 169, 180, 190–91, 194, 196

Jewish tradition, the 21, 102, 106, 107, 108

Kant, Immanuel, 5–6, 21, 31, 84, 87–93, 155, 193–94
King, Martin Luther, 2, 31

Levinas, Emmanuel, 18, 46, 179, 182, 183

Mandela, Nelson, 31, 189
Mencius, 63, 177
Merleau-Ponty, Maurice, 12, 18
Montesquieu, 31, 32, 42, 115, 195

Nationalism, 3, 32, 33, 37
Nietzsche, Friedrich, 16, 17, 155

Panikkar, Raimon, 5, 12, 18, 22, 31, 33, 66, 77–78, 195
Phenomenology, 1, 41, 134, 136, 166, 188

Plato, 7, 16, 18, 31, 103, 112, 115, 155, 174, 191
Pluralism, 23, 44, 46, 48, 72, 76, 156, 165, 183, 194
Pope Francis, 2, 31, 166

Rawls, John, 4, 5, 49, 50, 60, 61, 69–76, 78, 194, 195
Ricoeur, Paul, 1, 22

Socrates, 188, 189
Strauss, Leo, 7, 112–13
Sufism, 8, 21, 101, 151–52

Taoism, 8, 151, 196
Taylor, Charles, 4, 5, 57, 71–78, 197
Tocqueville, Alexis de, 42, 43
Todorov, Tzvetan, 42, 47
Trump, Donald, 32, 33, 69–70
Tutu, Desmond, 2, 31

Weber, Max, 44
Weiming, Tu, 42, 62, 64, 65
Whitehead, Alfred North, 23, 31, 35, 155

www.ingramcontent.com/pod-product-compliance
Lightning Source LLC
Chambersburg PA
CBHW030652230426
43665CB00011B/1065